RUMBLE SEAT

RUMBLE SEAT

HELEN PIDDINGTON

HARBOUR PUBLISHING

Harbour Publishing Co. Ltd.
P.O. Box 219, Madeira Park, BC, V0N 2H0
www.harbourpublishing.com

All photographs from the author's collection. Abbreviations in credits:
A.G.P — Arthur Grosvenor Piddington, H.M.P. — Helen Mary de Tessier Piddington, H.V.P — the author, J.A.P — James Arthur Piddington, T.A.P — Thomas Angelo Piddington
Edited by Audrey McClellan
Cover design by Teresa Karbashewski
Text design by Martin Nichols
Printed and bound in Canada

THE CANADA COUNCIL | LE CONSEIL DES ARTS
FOR THE ARTS | DU CANADA
SINCE 1957 | DEPUIS 1957

BRITISH
COLUMBIA
ARTS COUNCIL
Supported by the Province of British Columbia

Harbour Publishing acknowledges financial support from the Government of Canada through the Canada Book Fund and the Canada Council for the Arts, and from the Province of British Columbia through the BC Arts Council and the Book Publishing Tax Credit.

Library and Archives Canada Cataloguing in Publication

Piddington, Helen, 1931–

    Rumble seat : a Victorian childhood remembered / Helen Piddington.

ISBN 978-1-55017-506-6

    1. Piddington, Helen, 1931- —Childhood and youth. 2. Victoria (B.C.)—Social conditions. 3. Victoria (B.C.) —Biography. I. Title.

FC3846.26.P53A3   2010 971.1'2803092   C2010-903676-X

BIOGRAPH

CONTENTS

to my family:
past, present & future

1. THE FIELD IN SNOW

I am slicing apples, drying them on racks above the wood stove. Bears were in the orchard yesterday so we picked all remaining fruit and removed windfalls. As I work I'm listening to *Writers and Company* on CBC Radio. Doris Lessing has just spoken, as if from my mouth. She tells the host, Eleanor Wachtel, *my* secret: how she has kept certain memories fresh—hugging them to her *to retain the truth.*

And I am there, with the others, in that snowy field—scrunching downhill to the Sismans' place. It is bitter cold and late. We carry lanterns and sing to keep our spirits high.

We had marched through our garden, down past the stables to the golf links, then up under those twisted oaks to the height of land and the rocks with their thickets of broom where we build forts in summer, and on to the flat open area beyond, known to us as the Riding Ring, where the horses are exercised and the family plays polo. Then down and down till we reach the field. There it strikes me: *This is important—as long as we are together all will be well. I must remember this!*

Why didn't we go the usual way: down Lampson Street to Munro, through their front gate to their front door? But we are here in this field—five siblings in descending order: Joan, Mary, Hilly, Michael and me—out in this bitter starlit night while the rest of the family sit at home by the fire. Snow crunches underfoot. We hear muffled foghorns and imagine the snow-covered mountains gleaming across the sea. Soon we'll slip through their long scary orchard to their back door—to be greeted by Major Sisman, with his smiling spaniel face, and his wife, equally kind but puzzled: What are these children doing out so late? Somewhere in the background Francie hovers. Nipper nips and yaps and shudders at our feet. Mrs. Sisman asks, "Dear children, won't you come in and have a hot drink?"

"No, thank you," says Joanie, the eldest. "We must go straight home. It is late for Ba." We give them the message and the package and leave.

But there was no homeward journey. All five of us are scrunching still, down that sloping snowy field. Forever on our way to the Sismans'. I'm bound to this memory. I blow on it. Polish it. Hug it to me.

Here are five of the children, lined up in ascending order for early morning deep breathing at the lake, ca. 1934: me, Michael, Hilly, Mary and Joan.

And the others? They don't remember any of it. Not one of them. Nor do they care.

But I do. And I can't help wondering why in the world we were sent out like that, so late at night, to deliver whatever it was. Why the urgency? Or was a walk in the snow at night considered sufficient unto itself, a rare and wonderful treat? A time to remember!

2. MEMORIES

There are some memories I'd like to forget—especially my earliest conscious one.

I am in a cradle, moved for some reason from the nursery to another quieter room—probably my eldest brother's bedroom, the pink and green one. I guess there is a dance or a dinner party going on and one of the guests has asked to see the baby. All I know is that I wake to a strange face peering down over my crib. Backlit from the hall behind, the face seems huge. It has scarlet ears and nostrils and flesh of purple and orange. I scream and it pulls away.

Eventually, when I had to sleep in this room by myself, I couldn't have managed without the print of my hero, *The Laughing Cavalier*, on the wall beside me.

Then my second memory, at Savira this time, our summer cottage on Shawnigan Lake.

I am sleeping in #8 bedroom in a cot in the corner, under the attic stairs. I wake to find a dog standing on my covers, paws on my shoulder, licking my face! He is a "His Master's Voice" sort of dog, small and white with black spots. I shriek and everyone comes rushing but no one believes me—until someone finds him, down the hall, in one of the other rooms. He's not a dog anyone knows—nor do the neighbours. But he was there all right. I can feel his rough tongue on my cheek to this day.

Years later, and again at the Lake, though it could just as easily have been "Down Below," as we called Esquimalt while at Savira, there's another memory.

After a long and horrendous row with Dad, Mum appears in #3 bedroom, where Hilly, Mike and I are sleeping. She wakes us and says she is leaving Dad. Will we come with her? We say, "Yes! Of course we will!" And go back to sleep, sobbing. But in the morning the two of them are smiling and happy. Whatever the problem, it's been resolved. Yet Mum's question lingers. It sets a crack in what had been the rock-solid foundation of our lives.

Luckily most of my childhood memories are happy, wonderfully happy. But sometimes, even now, I wake in the night and feel my cheek—is it dog wet? Or I'm gasping, "Of course I'll come. Of course I'll come with you, Mum!" Or when the light is just off and I lie there, staring into darkness, sometimes those dancing specks of residual colour start to form *that face*. Then I must get up and read until sleep comes easily.

3. THE ISLAND

I had my nap upstairs today, in what used to be our son's bedroom, built for him when our children grew beyond sharing a room. When I woke, a thin winter sun shone happily on a painting I did years ago of what we knew first as the Netzers' Island, and later, when the Netzers got too old and moved away, as Dr. Hunter's Island. From our summer place on Shawnigan Lake, the late sun cast a plum-coloured glow on this island and on Baldy Mountain behind it. And if the lake was calm, that mountain was reflected as a plum-like shape with the island its stone. Using considerable artistic licence I made that plum a pinkish scarlet with sky and lake pale pink.

Officially for us the term "the island" meant Grandpapa's house, Les Groisardières on l'île d'Orléans in Québec. But at Shawnigan, a place of many islands, "the island" was not our two islands, Bunny or Teeny Wee, nor Long Island (once offered to Dad in its entirety for one thousand dollars) nor Memory Island, given by its owners as a park for lake dwellers and visitors, in memory of their son and all who died during the 1939–45 war. No, at the Lake "the island" meant Netzers' Island, that enchanted place, the plum stone we peered at daily all summer long—but visited perhaps three or four times.

The Netzers were not close friends. We would see them arriving each summer, their motorboat jammed full of supplies, crossing and re-crossing from boathouse to island, ferrying all they needed for the summer. Sometimes we might pass them in the canoe or the skiff and chat a bit. At some point Mum asked them to tea. By chance, on their first visit, she made a cake with pale green icing, inspired per-haps by the green Japanese tea set that came with the house. What-ever Mum's reason, the Netzers made such a fuss over it, she felt obliged to ice all subsequent cakes made in their honour the same way. So they called her *the woman of the green icing*. They were, I believe, German Swiss, appreciative and charming, with delightful manners.

When we rowed across and had tea with them, we children sat squirming on their verandah, trying to be polite but longing to run along all the little paths and trails they had cut through their arbutus woods. Woods so unlike ours. Eventually they'd say: "Now you young things, wouldn't you like to go exploring?" That last word ending on a breath-less *high* note. So we were sad when they grew too old for island life.

Hilly was the only one of us to meet the next owner. He was, by all accounts, kind and gentle too, and he tried to solve her poor circula-tion. "You should," he said, "be wrapped in wool year-round and have a good swig of brandy every day." A lovely idea, I thought. But none of us ever went to that island again.

Because of that curious pink painting I did so long ago, I decided to make that otherwise empty upstairs bedroom my office—a place where I can keep warm and have peace and quiet. And, thanks to the painting, as I sit at my desk I'm transported daily—right back to those long-ago days when we would go exploring on that island. Those wonderful up-and-down days, when we enjoyed both of those worlds, Savira and Esquimalt, and lived in bliss!

4. QUÉBEC

Ours was an ordinary family, forced by circumstance to migrate from Québec to Vancouver Island, yet we remain, all of us, part of that place. For the first seven, born there, or the last three, born

Québec was in our mother's milk, our father's songs and stories: Mum and Aunt Ara sit on the ice bridge between l'île d'Orléans and Québec City.
A.G.P. photo

on the West Coast, Québec was in our mother's milk, our father's songs and stories—we are connected by the heart. There is no escaping it. That province looms—a shape one can walk around, just as the topmost ridges of mountains seem manageable while travelling by sea; its air luminous, almost incandescent, shimmers like a mirage, an oasis, glimpsed by the weary, lost in distant lands.

My favourite of Dad's tales has him lost—not in the desert, but in Québec's Eastern Townships, in snow. He had business to do a long but easy ride from home. On his return, a blizzard forced him to shelter at a habitant's farm. The family was welcoming: stabled his horse and fed them both. But they were fussed. Their baby had a raging fever and lay swaddled in a cradle beside a roaring stove. They could not afford a doctor so resigned themselves to its imminent death. Dad asked if he might help. He unwrapped the child and cooled its tiny body with damp compresses. Then he walked back and forth across the kitchen all night long, carrying the baby and singing to it, as he did to us when we weren't well. By morning it was cooing happily.

Dad was exuberant, passionate, kind and gentle—concerned with the *here and now:* world affairs, politics, the well-being of his family, his garden and horses. Over his desk in the library hung mysterious lithographs of a man and a woman who I've only just discovered were his paternal grandparents. Thomas looks kind and gentle. Eliza, née Mitchell, rather pretty. She had married him with a son, Willy Lerandu, who was never spoken of. The Piddingtons were English but might as well have been Irish—they were so volatile. A large and well-to-do family, they lived for generations in and around Grosvenor Square, in London, until a quarrel over a will turned brother against brother to such an extent it became a feud. Like a ripe seedpod they burst in all directions—one brother going as far as Australia. Was the mysterious Willy the cause of all this? Thomas and Eliza moved to Jersey with Willy and then had six children. Their eldest, our grandfather Thomas Angelo Piddington, was born in 1844.

An uncle by marriage, William John Withall, had sailed from Jersey in 1840, left his ship in the Gaspé and walked barefoot to

Québec City. (Had someone stolen his boots, his belongings?) No matter, he did extremely well and became prosperous. With no heir, he sent for his nephew Thomas, my grandfather, who was still in his teens. Whether his family came with him then or later is unclear, but at some point they arrived in a body, including Willy Lerandu.

On his arrival in Québec City my grandfather was sent to Thom's Private Business Academy to learn "the rudiments of business." Then he worked with his uncle in various successful ventures. Their major achievement was the design and construction of the Lac Saint-Jean Railway—though neither lived to see the completion of the network of railways they'd planned. In 1870 Thomas Angelo married Susannah Parke, whose family was Irish. Her father was a doctor, considered by many the best in Québec City. As newlyweds, they bought #83 St. Louis Street— one of a row of comfortable stone houses whose front doors opened onto the Plains of Abraham. Dad and his four sisters were born there, the survivors of nine children.

Our grandfather was a shy man with an uncanny resemblance to Edward VII. The king liked to travel incognito, so when he boarded a train it was emptied immediately of passengers. When our grandfather was in England, the same thing happened to him, who wished to go unnoticed. But why was there such mystery about this family—so many silences and gaps and none of them mentioned?

If my parents knew of Willy, he was never mentioned. I heard about him from my cousin Alfie Bailey, whose mother was Dad's first cousin. We met in Ottawa when he was attending a conference in 1957 and became good friends. Alfie was the dean of history at the University of New Brunswick then, and a poet fascinated by family connections. Willy, he told me, lived in Montreal for years, then moved to Arizona and disappeared without trace. Alfie brought his friend Roy Daniels, head of the English department at UBC, to my attic studio overlooking the Rideau Canal. We ate, drank good wine and talked well into the night. I had just resigned from the Department of Northern Affairs to paint full-time. Alfie wished he'd had the courage to do the same.

Grandfather Piddington, a successful businessman in Québec City, had an uncanny resemblance to King Edward VII.

Of Dad's mother's side we know less except that since the 1700s they built ships and sailed back and forth in them, from Ireland to Canada—with many of them established in Québec. Gradually we are pulling details out of the black hole they'd fallen into. For example, we now know that the two sets of silver candlesticks left to me by my godmother, Dad's sister Vivian, once belonged to her great-aunt Mary Anne, who is buried in the cemetery at Saint-Sylvestre. And their names, Thomas, Arabella, Mary and James, keep appearing on both sides of our family. Many of them, grandparents, aunts and uncles, were living in Québec while Dad's parents were there too. Many more are buried there but for some reason were never mentioned.

Mum's father's family, on the other hand, could be considered *pure laine* as it stretches back deliciously to the founding of Québec. The first Drouart de Carqueville arrived in the early 1600s and probably married an Aboriginal woman. Our first known descendant of this family, Josette Drouart de Carqueville, married John Porteous in 1771. Another young Scot, James McGill (the founder of McGill College, which became McGill University), was witness at their wedding. John Porteous was from Scotland's border country—a place of skirmishes and cross-border raids. Accused of stealing a sheep and fearing an unfair trial, he and a brother left in a hurry to avoid hanging. Perhaps they slipped across to Ireland, boarded one of Dad's ancestors' sailing ships and hightailed it to Canada. Those two young bachelors reached Québec in 1760. We think the Drouart de Carqueville family was Huguenot. Would they, otherwise, have allowed their daughter to marry a Presbyterian? Later James McGill and John Porteous were buried together under a ginkgo tree in the grounds of McGill University. Mum was at least fourteenth-generation Canadian.

Another of our ancestors, the Baron de Tessier de la Tour, was an officer in the Swiss Guard at Versailles. During the French Revolution, he escaped the Terror by walking out of Paris with his wife. Disguised as peasants, they pushed their young daughter, Jeanne, in a breadbasket, surrounded by baguettes, a *gros pain* on her head. Bartholomé Gugy, a young officer in the same regiment, helped them. By 1795 all four had made their way to Québec. Later Jeanne married Bartholomé Gugy, and their daughter Amélie married the

*Mum and my daughter Arabella share a love of France
and the French language: here, Mum is snowshoeing at the island
ca. 1935, her ceinture fléchée about her waist.*

second John Porteous. Both Amélie Gugy Porteous and her mother-in-law, Josette Drouart de Carqueville Porteous, had flaming red hair, and neither spoke a word of English all their lives. They must have been a comfort to each other.

This hair reappears from time to time. I know of an aunt, some cousins and two nieces with the same glorious red hair, and our son has a reddish beard. But there is something else. No one that I know of in our direct line of descent had black eyebrows and lashes—brown maybe, but not black. It is the same in Dane's family, yet our two children have them. I always wondered where they came from until I saw miniatures of the Baron and Baronne de Tessier de la Tour with their powdered white wigs and startlingly black brows and lashes. Of course they might have been painted. Or are our children throwbacks? I prefer that idea.

The name "de Tessier" has been given to various members of our family. Mum was Helen Mary de Tessier Porteous and our daughter is Arabella Monique de Tessier Campbell. They, of all their generations, have a greater love of France and the French language.

Mum's mother was Frances Eliza Drury of Saint John, New Brunswick. A Drury arrived in England with William the Conqueror in 1066. Later his descendants moved to Dublin. And eventually, around the time the first Drouart de Carqueville reached New France, some of the Drurys went to New England. As Loyalists they moved north to Canada and intermarried with the Hazens, another English family who went to New England, then moved north earlier on. Granny grew up in a lovely house called Newlands outside Saint John.

Like everyone else's family, our tree grows and spreads with each marriage, each child born—its trunk, twigs and branches forming a dense mat to protect and strengthen us. I love this human tracery—spreading forever forward, outward, backward—always reinvented, with relations met and loved, the soil and light of Québec—our *home place*—keeping connections strong!

(I should add that when our parents came west in 1924, Montreal was the major business centre in Canada and one of the important English-speaking cities of the world. Educated people spoke both languages, as they did in Québec City. It was in country towns and villages that French predominated. These days this is sometimes forgotten.)

In 1910, Mum and Dad were married at Sainte-Pétronille on l'île d'Orleans. Montminy & Cie photo

5. ARRIVAL

My parents reached Victoria just before Christmas in 1924 with six young children, ranging in age from thirteen years to three months, and all that was left of their belongings after a house fire in the Eastern Townships of Québec. Dad had always had horses—growing up in Québec City, as a young man, and before and after the Great War—so among their possessions were saddles and tack, a cutter, a horse-drawn sleigh and a pony trap. Most of their books, furniture, silver and Mum's jewellery had burnt, as had their rugs and a great deal of clothing, but by no means all. There was still enough to fill a railcar. A second private railcar carried the family en masse.

They came expecting snow and bright winter days. They found rain and greyness, and the only place available to house them was a cold and uncomfortable family hotel near

Dad poses with Sylvia and Peter after moving to Wychbury, 1925.
H.M.P. photo

Beacon Hill Park. Houses in the east are kept warm. This place was dank and chilly, and the owner's family hogged the best spots around the fire—leaving their guests to shudder in corners.

So Dad stepped out to look at houses and chose the first place that caught his eye. For twelve-thousand cash he bought a large and imposing house. It had high ceilings and large rooms: a drawing room, library, dining room, breakfast room, five bedrooms (four with fireplaces), a large dressing room, bathrooms—a lavatory at the front door, a sink and mudroom by the garden door, and up on the third floor another bedroom with its own sink—a billiard room and a large box room. Down in the basement was the laundry room and comfortable quarters for the cook. Dad was charmed by the long driveway curving up through woods to the house, then circling a huge arbutus at the front steps, plus the large and private garden, the lawns, the orchard. But the selling point was the stables, complete with stalls and loose-boxes for horses and cows, a tack room, feed shed, chicken house and large paddock. Beyond, to the east, were open meadows stretching to the edge of the golf course. It was in that house the last three of us were born, lived, played, fought, laughed and had our being. There was space and freedom all around us—and always, wherever we were, the scent and sounds of the sea. Dad couldn't have made a better choice!

6. WYCHBURY

The house Dad bought had belonged to George F. Mathews, who commissioned Samuel Maclure to design him a house to be called Wychbury after a place he knew in Worcestershire, England. It was to have stables, a paddock, an orchard and a large garden on over two acres of land in Esquimalt. The property was L-shaped and stretched from Lampson Street east along the length of Wychbury Avenue and across to Rosemead, the place next door, which was also designed by Maclure. Both were built in 1909.

Samuel Maclure was Victoria's most highly regarded architect at that time and part of the Arts and Crafts movement—an important force in architecture and design in Great Britain, Canada and the United States. The Mathews family had the good sense to allow him a free hand with their house, for he designed them a structure of simplicity and elegance—perhaps the finest of all his houses.

The rooms in Wychbury were spacious and beautifully proportioned with high ceilings and large windows. The deep overhang of the roof was painted light grey with a tinge of turquoise, which kept the rooms cool yet flooded with light. On the main floor the drawing room, dining room and library led directly from a massive central hall with its vast brick fireplace and wide staircase leading up to another hall on the second floor. Almost every room had its own fireplace with carefully chosen coloured tiles, and windows that took advantage of Esquimalt's magnificent scenery: the Olympic Mountains, the Sooke Hills, Wychbury's own garden and, beyond it, the Macaulay Golf Links with sloping grassland and large Garry oaks. Most of those windows were lead casement or double-hung sash. A few were of stained glass in simple art nouveau forms and muted colours. Wherever colour was used—like the dark green panels above and between the fir timbering on the dining room walls—it was perfect. The house itself sat comfortably on a large hummock of rock that sloped downward to the west, with flat land to the east.

Designed by a Canadian architect for that particular place, the house *belonged* there—surrounded, but not squeezed, by five vast Douglas fir, several tall Garry oak and cedar, and the massive arbutus by the front steps. It was an extraordinarily comfortable house to live in—its only flaw a lack of bathrooms, with just two upstairs for six bedrooms. Our parents remedied this, in part, by adding another after they bought the house.

As for the garden, Maclure left all the land along Lampson Street wild and untouched, other than two stone gateposts at the drive's entrance. This made a buffer between the house and the street and a magical place for children to explore—full of trees, wild flowers and native bushes that gave endless hiding places. The rest of it was standard Maclure. While he always made good use of what was growing on site, he liked a rose garden, a tennis court, a croquet lawn, a holly hedge along the street and an avenue of red and white may trees interspersed with laburnums and a high laurel hedge—giving privacy along the property line. My sister Sylvia claims that if you know one Maclure garden, you can walk around another with your eyes closed.

The stables, at the far end of Wychbury Avenue, were almost out of sight of the house, snuggled behind trees and bushes. To get there one crossed the croquet lawn and the tennis court or took what we called the Bluebell Path edging the holly hedge that stretched all the way there from the house. Behind the stables were the orchard, the kitchen garden, all the berries and a large paddock that Dad turned into his Riding Ring.

When they left Wychbury, the Mathews family must have moved to a smaller place, for they sold much of their furniture and a number of handsome Persian rugs, stuffed chairs and a large oak dining table with leather-seated chairs to match. All these attractive things were in scale with the rooms and made the move so much easier for our parents, who had lost most of their possessions just a few weeks earlier. What was saved was brought west—like some mahogany chairs with leather seats that were used in the dining room when we had lots of guests. Otherwise, whatever was lacking Dad found in the local auction houses—places he loved to haunt.

I have two rugs from Wychbury, two armchairs, two wing chairs, the old sideboard from the dining room, the dining table from their first house in Montreal, Mum's rosewood tea table and her small desk. And the living room curtains in our log cabin are made from the heavy raw sienna velvet cloth that once hung in the library.

Many years after we left Esquimalt, when I moved back from France to West Vancouver—a printmaker now, rather than a painter—I met another printmaker, Alistair Bell, and his wife, Betty. They were extremely kind and helped me find and install a heavy press bed in my studio. To my great surprise, Betty knew exactly who I was. "Your family bought my aunt's house!" she said. She had often stayed there as a child.

For all of us, that house gave a precious lens through which to view the world. So I bless Samuel Maclure for designing Wychbury and our parents for choosing it. We lived there for twenty-one years with great pleasure and might have stayed on indefinitely but for the Great Depression and the Second War. I write of it in the past tense because it no longer exists. In 1945 the War-time Housing Board transformed it into nine apartments, with the rents frozen at forty dollars until the late fifties. This was wonderful for those living there but made it impossible for us to maintain and heat the place—let alone pay the taxes. So in 1958 the house was torn down and sold as scrap, the land sold and subdivided. All that remains is a small bundle of grooved panelling from the upstairs hall—just enough to frame a small painting. A classmate of Hilly's, who watched the demolition, thought she might want it. She didn't so he gave it to me.

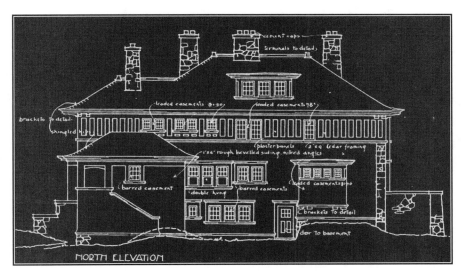

*The northern exposure of Wychbury looked across the road to Royal
Roads School, up the hill to Lampson Street School and Esquimalt
High, or down into the intriguing garden across Wychbury Avenue.*

Thanks to the late Michael Hanna, who was with me at Royal
Roads School and also at Esquimalt High, I have a copy of the plans
of Wychbury. They were given to him by Madge Wolfenden—Victoria's archivist for many years and the youngest sister of Nellie, Mrs.
George F. Mathews. Michael gave copies to the Esquimalt Archives
and they gave a set to me.

To discuss a house you loved in detail is as difficult as describing
a person. It is such a private matter. While those of us who lived
there can move around it in our mind's eye, others can use the plans.

7. ESQUIMALT

The municipality of Esquimalt is connected to Vancouver Island by
a narrow neck of land between Portage Inlet and Thetis Cove and,
for a short distance, abuts Vic West to the east. To get there you
must cross one of four bridges over the salt water that almost sur-
rounds it. Or drive along the highway from the west through View
Royal to the Gorge, turning right at Admirals Road through the

Songhees Indian Reserve, then on into the village. But for those of us who lived there, or who live there now, it seems far more like an is-land—remote and glorious, cut off from the world at large. And whenever we approach from any direction, especially when crossing one of those bridges, we feel relief and pleasure settle on us: we are coming home! It is our own magical *presqu'île*, run by a reeve until quite recently and utterly unlike its neighbour, the City of Victoria. Those who've not lived in either place sometimes insist they are one and the same. How wrong they are.

It is surprising how many people I come upon have some connec-tion with Esquimalt. Only yesterday I sat chatting with strangers on our wharf in Loughborough Inlet. This far-flung place is rather like a bus or a train, for people like to sit and talk about their lives, their past and present—eager to share things they mightn't be willing to in town. These two were retired schoolteachers, both somewhat puz-zled and concerned by all the changes in education.

"Did you have inkwells and desks with flap-up seats?" I asked, trying to gauge their era.

"Yes!" the man said. "And I walked along Grenville, through the Transfer, to school."

Ha! I knew instantly he meant the Transfer Woods and Lampson Street School. So he was there in 1943—as I was. And just two years younger. His wife, who was considerably younger, grew up in Oak Bay. When young she was not allowed to cross the Johnson Street Bridge. Her parents thought Esquimalt a rough and dangerous place.

I spent my childhood years in that "dangerous" place, though our time was divided in two parts, one up, one down. For July and Au-gust we were up the Malahat at Savira, our summer cottage on Shawnigan Lake, named after the two Moloney girls, Sarah and Vir-ginia, whose parents built it as a hunting lodge in the 1880s. In sum-mer it teetered on dragonfly legs, right on the edge of the lake—the verandah leaning out over the water. But in very wet winters, if the outlet stream flowing down to the sea was blocked, the lake might lap against its floorboards.

For the rest of the year we were at sea level—living near, but not in, the village of Esquimalt. Close by were deep woods, parks, beach-es and a marvellous rocky shoreline we could run along unimpeded.

At the end of our garden were the golf links, and on the other side of the links was a high ridge of glaciated rock, begging for explorers, that broke our view of Work Point Barracks on Peters Street, complete with living quarters, parade ground and jail—all hidden behind high brick walls. To the west was Esquimalt village, with churches, shops, a beer parlour, a movie theatre, Naden—the west coast base of the Royal Canadian Navy—and the world-famous drydock.

Esquimalt was full of surprises. For one thing, when out for a walk you never knew where you might bump into Mr. Potts and his Holsteins grazing along the edges of roads. Others were equally enchanted by the passage of Dad and those riding with him: either people having lessons or some of us out exercising horses. Dad would be singing—not just humming to himself but SINGING in a loud voice—or shouting encouragement: *Sit straight there! Shoulders back! Mind your seat! Rise with your horse! Knees in to your horse's side and elbows in to your own!* I found his singing especially embarrassing when passing people we knew or classmates, who'd often shout out, "Hallo Major!"

But whenever people asked why we didn't live in Oak Bay or the Uplands, we would gasp and ask, "Why would anyone live anywhere else—if they could live in Esquimalt?"

8. EARLY SCHOOLING

Mum arrived in Victoria with six children—Tom, Jamie, Peter, Sylvia, Joan, Frances Mary—and over the next seven years she had three more—Phyllis (better known as Hilly), Michael and me. Help was hard to come by. There was usually some sort of governess, a nanny, a housemaid, a cook, faithful Tim the gardener, and possibly someone to help with the horses. Mum was expected to make and receive social calls and entertain with tea parties, dinners and dances. She went to lectures, plays and concerts and belonged to various cultural groups besides doing a considerable amount of painting in oils. I don't suppose it ever occurred to her that she might teach her children. She was much too busy.

In January 1925 my two eldest brothers, Tom and Jamie, who were fourteen and ten, were packed off to Shawnigan Lake School at the north end of Shawnigan Lake, some twenty-seven miles up and over the Malahat, north of Esquimalt. Auntie Bella's sister-in-law, Winifred Morres, was a matron there, so Mum and Dad went to see the school. They liked the look of the place and the headmaster, Christopher Lonsdale, so the boys were sent there after Christmas, within weeks of arriving in Victoria.

Peter followed them later, but he started off at local schools. When that didn't work very well, he and Sylvia studied at home with a tutor, their younger sisters in the wings—learning how to embroider French dots.

Joan claims she wasn't taught to read until she was eight. And that only happened when she, Sylvia and Frances Mary were sent across the street to Royal Roads School, founded in the early thirties by Jas and Betts Burchett and sold the following year to Ruth Johnson, a young English woman who had spent a year in a one-room school on the Prairies. When our last governess, Helen Roach, went across the road as her assistant, Phyllis and Michael went too.

By then Sylvia was a weekly boarder at St. Margaret's School in town. In their mid-teens, the next two joined her as day girls, as did Hilly later on. Michael went to Lampson Street School.

In the spring of 1937 we all had measles and chicken pox and were quite sick. I began Grade One at Lampson Street School that fall and loved it, but because of constant earaches was kept home for most of that year. I spent hours with books or up trees, exploring, or on the swing, thinking. It was a good year for me—a necessary one. Yet some of the others never forgave me. They thought I was malingering.

9. BROKERS

Dad's advice to his daughters was 1. Avoid the mix of men and alcohol. 2. Never trust a smiling man. The first was to protect our virginity; the second to protect himself from yet another poor investment.

Mum claimed that in Montreal, where they lived before the Great War, Dad was an astute businessman—someone who took care of

*Mum took this photo of Dad while returning from
their honeymoon in 1910.*

his holdings and his appearance. He changed investments as warranted and his clothing three or four times a day. He was up-to-date and dapper. Somehow he lost both his business and his clothes sense during that war—managing in the same garments for days and weeks. Or was it the crossing of this country that changed him? If so, I like to think his conversion happened in the Prairies—somewhere in that immensity of rippling land covered, as it would have been in late November, by snow of shifting colours with golden stubble poking through. And then the sky, that vast arc of brilliant blue. I can hear him calling out across their train car: *Helen, Helen, look! Isn't it marvellous! Children, look!*

Then, from far out on the plains, he would have caught his first glimpse of the foothills and the Rockies rising to the sky. Next the softer Selkirks and the Coast Range—all snow-clad with great knobs and rocky fingers jutting upward. Not to mention the size of the trees! He would have been absolutely *ébloui*—dazzled by the scale of it all, after the gentler landscape of Québec.

And then, of course, the sea and the misty islands. After that, why would anyone care about the best tailor in town? No, henceforth he would appear at special events appropriately clad in dinner jacket, morning coat or tails—those ancient garments that had, by some magic, escaped the fire in the Eastern Townships and the moths. And he did so to his dying day. Otherwise he wore his old Royal Field Artillery blazer with Viyella shirts, grey flannels or his riding coat with britches, jodhpurs, drill slacks or his favourite tan drill shorts with knee socks held up with the brightly coloured garters we'd knit for him. To many he looked bizarre. Yet whatever he wore he had an almost electric presence one could feel when he entered a room.

But how can one explain the turnaround from clever businessman in Québec to gullibility in BC? For as soon as he reached the coast, Dad fell prey to sharks. He sought advice from local brokerage houses, invested heavily in short-term bonds promising high interest, bought stocks and then a share in a ranch. That was fine until the crash of 1929, when those bonds, without backing, were worthless and the stocks of almost no value. In those days, brokers made house calls. Dad's favourite came often, taking up a lot of his time and infuriating Mum, who didn't trust him. He was a prosperous-looking man with a warm smile, a mellifluous name and sleek mustachios. He persuaded Dad to sell his remaining blue-chip stocks for more "exciting" ones. Mum hung on to hers and later did well.

After a long string of investments that ended in failure, his resources dwindled to next to nothing. Then his broker suggested an absolutely *surefire* gold mine. For the first time, and at Mum's urging, Dad said NO!

After that, whenever we drove through the Uplands, the smartest, most expensive part of Victoria, Dad would point to the grandest of the new houses and say one word: *Zeballos!*

10. BUTCHERS

Mum had three pieces of advice for her daughters: 1. Never put off today what you can easily put off tomorrow. 2. If you want help, ask the busiest person you know. And my favourite: 3.If you want good meat, you must always be a little in love with your butcher.

Esquimalt had two butchers: Mr. Young, on Esquimalt Road in the village, and Mr. Lock, also on Esquimalt Road, but near Head Street, about a mile away. And then in Victoria there was #9 in the meat department of David Spencer's department store. Mum went to them all. They treated her with deference, as if she was someone special—a customer with many to feed and someone who expected the best. Often she'd phone in her order. Until I went to school full-time, I'd walk with her to Mr. Young's or Mr. Lock's. While I liked both of them, I loved their shops, each with its dry, clean smell and great carcasses hanging on hooks—the sides, the quarters, were sometimes cut before our eyes—and then all the fascinating things displayed on, or under, their counters. And Mr. Lock's shop had sawdust on the floor! When I grew up, I'd be a butcher too!

When shopping in Victoria at David Spencer's, Mum and I would often have a frosted malted as a pick-me-up toward the end of the morning, sold at a counter in the basement. Then we'd take the few steps across to the butcher shop. You didn't see much there other than a few sausages, chops, kidneys or meat pies on the counter. Most of the meat was behind the scenes in some inner sanctum.

There were several butchers but Mum always asked for #9. Summoned, he would come rushing out with an enormous grin. He was by far the most flirtatious of her butchers. They would chat for a bit and Mum would give her order; then she'd tease him with "You'll give me good meat now, won't you?" And he would bow or throw up his hands and say, "Now, Mrs. Piddington—you know I always save the best for you!"

If we were meeting Dad and driving home, we'd probably take our order with us; if we went by streetcar, it would be delivered. Deliveries were expected in those days. When things arrived, the deliveryman would ring the backdoor bell. If no one answered, he'd pop whatever he'd brought right into the large wooden icebox on the back porch.

For me, meat was the *plat de résistance*, the centrepiece of a meal. Whether a delicious roast of beef, lamb chops or chicken, it was what I looked forward to—that, and fruit.

I couldn't wait to grow up and start butchering!

11. THE RANCH

To be on a ranch—to own one—had been a boyhood dream of Dad's. So when his broker suggested he buy part of one for *next to nothing*—all his deals were to cost *next to nothing*—Dad said, "Yes! Certainly. Go ahead!"

That was at the tag end of the twenties. In no time the other partners, all in Vancouver, began to renege on their shares. So to save his, Dad bought them out, one by one, until he was sole owner of the largest sheep ranch in the Chilcotin. A place he knew nothing of, with a vast herd of animals he knew nothing about. *Well*, he thought, *we'll move there. Why not?* But Mum balked. She loved our house in Esquimalt and she loved our summer place. Why in the world would we move up there? She drove up to see it, though—the car filled with gear and Tom and Jamie and as many of the babies as could fit in.

The journey seemed endless. First came the overnight CPR boat to Vancouver and cabins for everyone. Then the long drive through Vancouver and up along the Fraser Canyon to Pavilion Mountain.

Jamie snapped this photo in 1930 before Dad took him and Tom in the Packard to the ranch for the summer. Peter, who wanted to go too, is in Jamie's seat.

Crossing over it still strikes terror in the bravest heart! Then all the way along and down to Jesmond—marked on the map, but nothing more than one house. From there, left and southward, driving down and down to the Fraser again, only now it wasn't just a few feet from the road but hundreds of feet below it. A sign pointed left to Big Bar Ranch.

The ranch house and land clung to slopes that fell abruptly down to the Fraser River. To get there you followed a track around a bluff—a track so narrow the outer wheels of the car were in the air much of the time. Mum had to be blindfolded. No wonder she vetoed this venture. For her the only positive thing about the ranch was Lucky, the tiny puppy she saved from drowning and took back as a present for Peter, who had longed to go there with them. But Dad was undaunted. He was thrilled by the place.

The two older boys stayed on all summer—Tom to look after the accounts and run a commissary for the ranch hands, and Jamie to act as shepherd, high in the hills above, where the view, in all directions, was nothing but sky, rippling hills and sheep. Was it those dreamlike empty spaces that gave him the urge to fly? It was a wonderful summer for them. Then it was time for school or college.

Dad's problems were just beginning. He had to hire managers or full-time shepherds—often sight unseen—and buy horses as needed. The ranch was a bottomless pit. Sometimes those recommended for jobs were excellent; sometimes they were punk. One charming manager pretended the ranch was his and invited all his friends to come up from Vancouver and stay—at Dad's expense. Another, when told to buy quarter horses, chose Thoroughbreds instead—then swaggered around on them, with his friends. When money was needed and amounts weren't specified, Dad sent blank cheques. In those days there was no other way, unless he delivered funds in person.

The last days of the ranch coincided with my birth, so I've always felt a certain affinity for sheep and an urge to see the Chilcotin. In 1968 I drove up there in my Peugeot 203—a wonderfully manoeuvrable little car with front-wheel drive. A friend came with me. There was no real problem getting there, other than Pavilion Mountain, which we crossed twice by mistake and overheated. But the track around the bluff, on that last stretch to the ranch, was still so awful the charm of the place vanished and I was glad to get away.

We spent that night in Jesmond in a lovely old farmhouse full of several generations of one family. When the grandfather heard my name and that my father had once owned Big Bar Ranch, he became agitated. *"Piddington!"* he roared. "That fool! He shouldn't have had sheep! This is *cattle* country! And all those animals were destroyed! Wasted!"

Poor Dad. He was no rancher. Had he lived there and run the place himself, he would have realized this mistake and changed to cattle, as the current owners had. But I was distressed about the wasted flock.

As soon as I got back I asked Mum about this terrible loss. "Don't worry," she said. "The sheep weren't wasted. I made a deal with Mr. Lock on the q.t. If he paid for their transport down to Esquimalt, the entire flock was his. He had his own slaughterhouse in those days and was delighted!"

So that's what happened! All those years she had kept that secret to herself. No one, not even Dad, knew about it. I was the first to ask.

Soon after we lost the ranch, Joanie remembers going to Mr. Lock, the butcher, with Mum and being *given* legs of mutton. Perhaps from our own sheep.

We ate a lot of mutton in those days and it was delicious. The only time I remember having lamb for sure was when Granny asked us to lunch at the Empress and we had tiny lamb chops with paper frills on the tips of the bone. They were delicious too.

12. BIRTH

No one can remember which room Hilly was born in, but Michael arrived the day after Christmas 1928 in the blue room facing south and east. I came two and a half years later in the yellow room, looking west to China and the Sooke Hills. A new bathroom had just been installed next to that room.

I was born to hoofbeats galloping over hard ground. This is something I know—not what I've been told. I know it because running horses thrill me—running in the distance or approaching across a field. And this makes sense. With both Dr. McCallum and a nurse, Mum was in good hands. Fathers didn't hang about in those days, as they do now, but Dad liked to be there when, or soon after, his babies were born. With both Tom and Jamie working at the ranch, Dad would have been short-handed—his only helpers Peter, not yet twelve, and Sylvia, just ten. He'd have been up on that wide expanse of flat land opposite the Buxtons' house, exercising horses—a soothing lovely place to be on a summer's night, especially when anxious, as he must have been. Peter would have been on guard, ready to deliver the news—on foot or on horseback. *The doctor says come home!* Hence the hoofbeats, the ki-yi-ing and the whoops.

Dad loved babies. When he got there, caresses for Mum—then he'd have lifted me from her arms and danced me round the room, crooning, as he had to all his babies. I must have appeared just before midnight because Dad had it firmly in his head that I was born on the twelfth. Then, as she had after each birth, Mum stayed in bed for a month with a trained nurse in attendance.

Babies were such a common occurrence in our house my siblings scarcely noticed my arrival. To be the *tenth* child was nothing special, but at ten pounds I was their largest infant and, born in July, aggravated everyone by stalling the family's annual migration to the Lake. Not only that, I appeared exactly a week before my sister Joanie turned eight. Mum, exhausted by the whole ordeal, had forgotten to buy her a present, so she made one of those gauche moves we parents are prone to: she offered her *me*, instead. Joanie was appalled and said, "Who in the world would want a real baby?" This gaffe was resolved a week or so later when my parents bought her a large and special girl dolly. But the damage was done. It took years for her to accept me as anything but a bally nuisance.

Joanie holds me on her eighth birthday, just a week after I was born.

Joanie had been a beautiful baby, much admired by her maternal grandfather who had an eye for beauty—until he remembered that each child he found special died young. Grandpapa had adored his daughter Diana, who died at twelve of appendicitis. Then he had a passion for Anna Cicely, Mum's first daughter, who died aged two. So to save Joanie, he turned his back on her. Then thirteen months after Joanie was born, Mum produced Frances Mary, a demanding child— her first and only baby with hazel eyes. So Joanie was put on the sidelines again. What a shame it is that we, parents and grandparents, aren't granted divine understanding and must flummox and flounder through the lives of our young, distressing and embarrassing them with our well-meant gestures.

13. GRANNY

Our maternal grandmother, Frances Eliza Porteous, née Drury, was beautiful, gentle, gracious and kind—the perfect Granny. When she said, "Be sure and look up my dear friend Madame So-and-So," you could bank on a warm reception. Her circle of friends was vast and included Colonel James Peters, once the commandant at Work Point Barracks in Esquimalt. Her home, Les Groisardières, was considered a local showplace, so in summer there were many visitors—

Although he adored her, Grandpapa was sometimes put off by the imperturbability of Granny Porteous, ca. 1886.

including the Governors General, who would bring their families down to the island during their obligatory month at the citadel in Québec City. It was much cooler on the island than in town, so many of them came often and became good friends.

Much later, when the Allied leaders met in Québec City in August 1943, Granny was eighty-eight and her house was filled with relations of all ages. Franklin Delano Roosevelt phoned to ask if he might come to tea. He had met Aunt Fran in Warm Springs, Georgia, while both were taking a cure for polio. He arrived with a large entourage that included Clementine Churchill. Mr. Roosevelt was delighted by Les Groisardières, which he said resembled his own home. So when he signed the guest book he put "Hyde Park" instead of "the White House."

Granny was not fazed by floods of visitors, whether relations or friends. She was almost imperturbable. So much so that when she was shipwrecked (history doesn't relate where or when), she gathered together a parasol and a folding chair and stepped from the sinking ship onto a sandbar, where she sat in comfort until rescued. "It was all rather amusing," she said.

This calmness of spirit must have been a godsend when surrounded by her eleven children, especially during their annual migrations from Kingston down the St. Lawrence by steamer to their summer place on l'île d'Orléans in those years when most of her children were small. My cousin Patrick, in a letter in June 2006, described these journeys, which would have tried a saint: "During the 1880s and '90s when Grandpapa was manager of the Bank of Montreal in Lindsay and Kingston...the family—many children, maids and Nanny—went by boat to l'île d'Orléans for the summer in the original cottage called HOLMWOOD bought by great Grandpapa John de Tessier Gugy Porteous...The boat trip took a few days, so to provide milk for the children they took a cow with them. At the end of the summer back came the cow! Grandpapa could not stand the thought of this voyage, pleading urgent business he joined them later by train." (Patrick explained that Les Groisardières "was built in 1903 as a silver wedding present. Only two rooms, the morning room...and the library...are from the old cottage.")

Legend has it that sometimes Grandpapa was put on edge by Granny's steadiness. Although he adored his "Nance," as he called her, and had two magnificent houses built for his beloved princess, if the cook served lukewarm soup, or if he disapproved of a menu, he might fling a fork or a spoon at her from his end of their very long dining room table all the way down to hers. Let's hope he was a poor shot, but whether this actually ruffled her serenity, I don't know.

Apparently this happened so often it was scarcely noticed. Children are apt to consider their parents normal. Our mother thought her father a godlike figure, which is curious as such behaviour does not mesh with her view of "God the Father, God the Son, etc.," to whom we were urged to give thanks and praise—but his wife and children loved him dearly. Besides being a clever businessman, he was an accomplished painter and spent a lot of time, money and effort supporting Canadian artists. Mum always spoke of "my father's house," never her mother's, as we always did.

These Victorian, then Edwardian, parents travelled, if not all winter, at least most of it, and often spent Christmas in Europe or, later on, at their house in Nassau—without young. So except for the eight years when Les Groisardières was first built and they stayed year-round at the island, they were rarely, if ever, at the house for holidays, except in summer.

It was Bessie Baine, the nanny, who saw to their children's needs and mothered them at Christmas and birthdays, helped dress the girls for balls and parties in Québec City and arranged that they be taken there and back by horse-drawn sleighs across the ice bridge—edged with small firs to mark safe passage. And she was there to greet them on their return a day or two later, listen to the highlights of their stay and share their joys. She arranged sugaring-off parties and outings with their island friends—snowshoeing, skating or skiing. Knowing Mum's great love of Edward Lear, Bessie Baine gave her a beautiful sterling *runcible spoon* for a wedding present, having told Mum often that she was her *favourite*—something good nannies tell each child in their care, I'm sure, especially when their parents are far away.

Apart from Grandpapa, the only others aggravated by Granny's calm were her daughters-in-law or daughters—those who felt aggrieved, for whatever reason. But Granny seemed blissfully unaware of their plaguing and kept smiling sweetly.

She came west to see us every other year, which was wonderful—yet I was only in her house once while she was alive. That was on my way to art school in London, when I stayed for about a week. In those days when you visited someone, especially a relation, you took a signed photographer's portrait of yourself in its folded cardboard case. I hated this practice but our parents thought it essential, good manners, the decent thing to do. On the way to Granny's house I stayed with my godmother, in Montreal. This was our first meeting. She was Dad's sister, warm but frank and quick-tempered. She had wanted to be Joanie's godmother, not mine. She took my photo. Glanced at it. Then tossed it away. "You look like a tart," she said. "You have lipstick on! I much prefer the last one of you—as a schoolgirl." I was twenty-one, had just graduated from university. Of course I wore lipstick!

I went down to Les Groisardières from Montreal, spinning in my seat—so eager to see the countryside we were passing through, places I'd only heard of or dreamt about. Later, when I presented the same photo to Granny, she said, without looking at it, "Oh! What lovely thing have you brought me, my dear?" I couldn't help admiring both of them: one for honesty, the other for charm.

In her late nineties Granny was still the perfect hostess. She showed me places in the house and garden that Mum had loved particularly, and together we drove around the island to see her favourite spots. There were two other guests: one an old friend of Mum's, Alice Russel, a person I liked immediately; the other was an aunt who kept criticizing me and saying *out loud*, to all of us, how grotesque it was for anyone to have more than two children! I don't know about Mrs. Russel, but Granny had had eleven children and I was Mum's tenth. Granny smiled and ignored her. I tried to, too.

On the day she turned ninety-nine, Granny died in her beloved house, right in the middle of her birthday party—surrounded by family and friends. Some of her children had predeceased her, exhausted from waiting to inherit either the house or her possessions. I came back to Canada that fall, found a job and was preparing to go to the Arctic, so I went to the west coast for a quick visit to see Mum and Dad, then returned to Ottawa. No one wanted to be alone that

Christmas so Aunt Phyllis, Mum's eldest sister, gave a huge family party on Christmas Day. She rented a hotel ballroom and, wearing a red woollen dress of mine, disguised herself as Santa Claus. There were masses of aunts and uncles and fifty-five cousins. It was a grand affair and lots of fun!

The next time I went down to the island, the siblings were dividing the last of the spoils. It was not a happy time. Without Granny there was no structure, no decorum. The house seemed a mere shell. Grandpapa's plan—that each of the siblings tag what they wanted most, then buy it from the estate—did not work. First-comers marked almost everything or funnelled things away to their immediate families. Others kept changing tags. There was such bickering and squabbling, Bessie Baine would have been shocked. And I suspect even Granny might have said a thing or two. Mum was appalled how her siblings fought over the valuable things. When I got there she had made her choices: a painting she very much wanted, some wooden chairs from the drawing room, a few sketches on small wooden panels, and two of the presents Grandpapa had bought for Granny in Paris. Luckily no one else wanted them. But she decided then and there that there must be a better way to divide possessions. So over the years she made a detailed list of who was to get what of her things—with a proviso that anyone making a fuss would be *disinherited*. That almost happened!

In Grandpapa's time, churches paid no taxes. He considered this was an unfair burden on the citizenry so decreed that his house and land not go to *any* religious group. But whoever was in charge of the sale flipped the property quickly, and the house became a retreat for Roman Catholic priests. Now, I gather, it belongs to a worldwide organization that welcomes elderly Roman Catholics to stay as long as they like.

It seems a good solution for that lovely place. But how would Grandpapa feel about this? Do spoons and forks fly about sometimes in the dining room? Does he haunt the house and gardens—roaring and ranting—with Granny at his side, smiling her sweet all-encompassing smile?

14. GARDEN FÊTES

What could be more exciting than to have a village fair right in your own garden, or next door, or down the street? That's what Garden Fêtes were like, and they were a common event in the 1930s. And where but Canada would you find such a name?

The first fête that I am aware of at Wychbury was in the summer of 1931. It must have filled the garden, sprawling over the croquet lawn and the tennis court and extending around the house to the front lawn, then down to the stables and the Riding Ring. There would have been lots of little stalls selling all manner of things or offering games that one could play for a penny or two, and trestle tables set out for tea and cakes with all the good women of St. Paul's

Sylvia, Joanie and Lucky are pulled in the pony trap, ca. 1931.

Women's Auxiliary bustling about, being useful, especially that year, because Mother had just given birth to me. Of course the family would have helped as much as they could, but it must have been hard on her with all the noise and confusion swirling around her.

The centre of attraction that year was a life-sized wooden rocking horse built by the ships' carpenters at Naden—the navy's contribution to the affair. And the army? They probably supplied manpower, folding chairs and tables, and possibly cups and saucers from Work Point Barracks—just a step away on Peters Street. Children would pay for a few minutes' rocking on that huge horse or being led about on our Shetland pony Bingo. My brothers, especially Peter, would have organized all sorts of games and sports events—sack races and the like. So if that Garden Fête was anything like any of the others I attended later on, it would have been great fun. Everyone dressed in their best, greeting friends and neighbours and strangers too, happy to have the chance to be in someone else's lovely garden—and not just to be there, but be welcomed—something especially important in those difficult times when so many people were unemployed and hungry.

A few days after this event came Joanie's eighth birthday, and just as she was given the infant *me* that year, she was given the wooden horse. Exciting for a few weeks but not easy for a small girl to mount and dismount alone, even with a mounting block. Eventually it was seconded by Dad and used to practise polo shots—the shifting horse making them seem all the more real.

That Christmas all our relations in Québec were sent photos of our family on horseback on the lawn with Michael astride the wooden horse and Hilly on Bingo. Weeks later, questions started arriving: *And where is Ba?* Only then did they realize what they'd done. Apparently I was having a nap when the photographer came and they had forgotten all about me! Some existing copies of that photo have a cut-out snapshot of a baby gummed on. So much for the tenth child!

There was one more Garden Fête at Wychbury that I remember and enjoyed enormously. Another was next door at Rosemead, and others were in Harold Pooley's beautiful garden on Old Esquimalt Road, at the Barnards' Clovelly in West Bay and at a large half-timbered house in behind Wilmot Place, in Oak Bay.

During the 1930s the proceeds of these events went to a church or some far-flung mission, but in the 1940s they helped the war effort. I wonder if Garden Fêtes still exist. I hope so.

Apparently, I was having a nap when the photographer came and they had forgotten all about me, so some copies of the Christmas photo have a cut-out snapshot of a baby gummed on, as above!
Knight on Fort photo

15. CHAPPIE

The Reverend Frederic Colbourne Chapman was the rector of St. Paul's Naval and Garrison Church from 1922 until 1933. To many of his parishioners and all who loved him he was simply Chappie. Unfortunately I can't remember him at all, except from stories, as I was, at best, two years old when he left Esquimalt. Nevertheless, he had an enormous effect on my life.

St. Paul's Diamond Jubilee year was 1926, and Chappie had *A Historical Sketch* written and printed for the occasion. On September 12 a festival was held to celebrate the church's first sixty years, the date chosen to coincide with a visit by the Bishop of London. A photo was taken in the grounds behind the church with as many

*To celebrate St. Paul's Diamond Jubilee in 1926, a festival was held
with as many parishioners as could be gathered together.*

parishioners as could be gathered together. Chappie sits in the front
row, and to his right is Archbishop de Pencier, the Metropolitan.

To the right of the archbishop is one of the eldest members of the
congregation, Mrs. Charles Pooley, née Elizabeth Fisher, who was the
second bride to be married at St. Paul's, in the new church that was
erected in 1866 near the sea, on the south side of the road, at the base
of Signal Hill. Before then, services had been held in an old schoolhouse close by. Mrs. Pooley was married in her teens, and in a quote
from the above-mentioned sketch she remembers her wedding day:

> The church was but recently completed and it was lavishly
> decorated, and looked very pretty. In those halcyon days of
> the old port a beautiful wooded road led from Esquimalt to
> Victoria, and it was always busy with busses coming and
> going, officers riding into the city to some function, or
> crowds of brilliantly dressed folk coming out to tea on the
> Flagship, or to watch cricket. There was always something
> interesting to see in Esquimalt, for, besides the men-of-
> war, liners were constantly coming and going on their way to
> the gold fields, or returning with small fortunes.

That 1926 photo shows, as well, our friends Major and Mrs. Sisman and her daughter, Francie Price; my father, Arthur Grosvenor Piddington, and mother, Helen Mary de Tessier Piddington. In that same row is my eldest brother, Thomas Angelo, fifteen. In the back row, two other brothers stand side by side: James Arthur, about to turn twelve, and Peter Grosvenor, who had turned seven two days before the photo was taken. He is wearing a pullover crocheted by Mum in Cannes in 1918. It was striped of gorgeous colours and was always known as "Jamie's jersey." Perhaps Tom had found it too gaudy so refused to wear it. But I remember wearing it with pride in Grade Two at Lampson Street School in 1938.

At the far left-hand side, in the front row, sits the Honourable Harold Pooley, the Attorney General for BC. Perhaps his sister, Alice, is seated behind her mother in the second row. If so she looks young and pretty—not the ancient woman I remember.

In that photo, Chappie looks puckish. He was no beauty but a very funny, wise and charming man. Mum and Dad both loved and admired him. Eventually he christened the last three of us—Phyllis and Michael and me. By my christening, in the summer of 1931, my parents were utterly exhausted. Dad had lost almost everything in the crash of '29, and as a result, Mum had almost no hired help. Both were working extremely hard, and here she was with her tenth baby! Neither had the time or energy to think of names.

"She reminds me of the pink dahlias growing in the round bed by the croquet lawn. Let's call her that," said Mum.

"Right-oh," said Dad, probably thinking of some horsey matter. So the decision was made.

But Chappie would have none of it. Whether he rebelled at the font, or beforehand, history does not relate. Perhaps he knew that the correct pronunciation of "dahlia" was hideous, or maybe he wouldn't allow me to be called after such an ugly flower. Who knows? But he is reputed to have said to Mum, "If you can't think of a decent name give the child *your* name, for heaven's sake!" And they did. Adding "Vivian" for Dad's youngest and favourite sister, who became my godmother. Like so many from eastern Canada—who call Ontario *central* Canada and Manitoba *the west*—she refused repeated invitations to come out to the coast to stay with us. She thought we should go east! Or she preferred Europe.

When small, I often wished Chappie hadn't interfered. I would have loved my own name. Not my mother's name and my big sister's first name. But now I bless him. I can't imagine being called Dahlia. Ivy, Pansy, Poppy, Violet, even Rose—but not Dahlia!

16. THE GREY MORRIS ROADSTER

Whenever Mum was asked what she would like for her birthday or Christmas, she would say, without hesitation, "A car and chauffeur!" Sometimes, if feeling either frivolous or exhausted, she might suggest to Dad that he not bother to buy her a pair of new gloves or an Easter egg this year—a car and chauffeur would do nicely. But of course *she* was the one who bought presents for *us*, not Dad. In my day he gave nothing but "good-fors" or a few shares—to teach us the value of money!

To us, her request was outlandish. Ridiculous. Extreme. So absurd it was a joke we all enjoyed. But to her it seemed a normal state of affairs. Her mother had a car and chauffeur at the ready on l'île d'Orléans. Her eldest sister had a chauffeur in Montreal. And her twin in Saanich owned a car. But Mum had to wait until someone could drive her or give her a lift, or else take the streetcar. This vexed her. She yearned for freedom—to be able to pick up her paints and go sketching somewhere, or perhaps go shopping or to see a friend when she had a spare moment, or just tootle off alone. All her friends had cars, hadn't they?

So at some point, soon after they arrived in Victoria, Dad bought a large touring car for himself and a grey Morris roadster convertible—a two-seater with rumble seat—for Mum. Driving lessons were not considered necessary in the twenties. You rode a bike—you drove a car. And there was no such thing as a car licence. The salesman told her how to drive and sent her home. He was considered something of a marvel already—at least by Peter and Sylvia—for every time the family went to skate at the arena, they and everyone else accepted the hard and fast rule: *No one go out on the ice until the*

Tom poses by the grey Morris roadster with a rumble seat, 1936.

lights were lit. But every single time, though they and everyone else stood with their skates on, waiting impatiently for that moment—when the lights came on, there was our car salesman, that same round and dumpy little man, hands clasped behind his back, twirling in circles in the middle of the rink! He must be a magician.

Somehow Mum drove herself about, unscathed. Then one day, hurtling down the long hill on Admirals Road, below the village, she lost control. She crossed over a ditch and found herself upright but well up the muddy bank. That was it. Probably pregnant and feeling vulnerable, or remembering her brood at home, she walked back and bequeathed the roadster to her sons. But to her dying day her top choice for birthday or Christmas remained the same: *A car and chauffeur would be perfect!*

For us, the last three, a rumble seat was magic enough. We didn't need the little car salesman. We didn't really need a driver. Once we clambered up from the running board onto those special little rubber foot pads fixed onto the mudguard, then stepped into the luxury of that small compartment and sat ourselves down on the soft squishy leather seat, we were alone—free—away from everyone else and able to see in all directions—behind, above, to each side—and also a little of what was ahead (but who really wants to know the future?). The sensation was wonderful, even when the car stood still. But when we moved—the wind rushing at our faces, flattening our eyelashes, our hair streaming out behind us, as on a bicycle, on a sailboat. And we could sing or yell into the wind! Then, if we needed anything, all we had to do was tap on the window. What could be more glorious?

In retrospect, the rumble seat seems the essence of the thirties and forties and the freedom we had in those days. Most of it is quenched nowadays by fear and restrictions: the seatbelt, the bicycle helmet and the life jacket. We managed beautifully without any of them. We took care, we paid attention—we were responsible. And if we weren't, we suffered the consequences. No one considers responsibility anymore. It is not even thought of, nor mentioned in our Constitution. Instead we are given *rights* and are constrained by laws and hemmed in by expensive gadgets that encourage mindlessness. Is this progress?

17. THE RED CANOE

𝒟ad was so at home in a canoe, he might have been born in one. Both paddle and boat seemed an extension of his body. They moved as one. He could keep a straight course in strong wind, travel at great speed or slip along slowly, silently.

As soon as our arms were long enough, he taught us how to handle a canoe, to use a paddle, with competence and force: *It's not a feather to be dipped through the water. Use your strength!* So it wasn't surprising that when his sisters found a beautiful red canvas-covered Peterborough sailing canoe in Québec City, called *Trente et Un*, they could not resist buying her. All they needed was an occasion. So, liking the juxtaposition of numbers, they saved it for Jamie, who was nearly thirteen.

In early October 1927, the *Trente et Un* arrived in Victoria by CPR express—as Jamie's birthday present. It was extraordinary what could be sent across the country in those days, with ease and for very little, either by freight or express. The Royal Mail, too, came at least twice a day, with the postmen bringing the mail up our long drive and leaving it at our front door. They were good-tempered men, glad of their job and doing it to the best of their ability—like solving incomplete addresses. In Québec, Dad once received a letter from overseas marked only *Pidd—The Plains of Abraham—Canada*. And telegrams were phoned to you, then would arrive in written form by bicycle shortly after.

Jamie's birthday present arrived in Victoria by CPR express, and he christened his new craft The Red Canoe. *H.M.P. photo*

Jamie named his new craft *The Red Canoe*. She came complete with mast, sail and leeboards. As Dad would say, she was a splendiferous present! Sylvia was six then and remembers how the canoe was hauled down to Fleming's Beach for her maiden voyage, sitting in state on a small wagon hitched to the pony Bingo, in a procession of anxious children and adults, all terrified the canoe would slide off—especially on the steep hill near the end of Lampson Street. Then she was manhandled over the rocks and slipped into the sea.

The Red Canoe made it there and back safely, but it wasn't a performance anyone wanted to repeat. So after that she was moored at Rodd's Boathouse in the Gorge. That meant driving whoever was going to use her back and forth, and though it was fun paddling up and down the Gorge, there was scarcely enough room for sailing.

Mum and Dad had been looking for land on Shawnigan Lake ever since they first saw it. Soon after the red canoe arrived, Mum was in bed with a cold and, for once, had time to comb through the *Colonist*—even the want-ads. And there she found a notice:

> *For Sale: a small hotel or summer house for a large family with lake frontage—large Living Room with balcony, Dining Room, eight bedrooms, two kitchens with china, cutlery, utensils, pots and pans, bed linen, towels, fully furnished throughout plus a launch and several rowboats and its own whistle stop for the CN Railway.*

Mum was very excited. She saw immediately how super it would be to have the canoe on a lake—with no tides and no 250 feet of steep steps down to the St. Lawrence, as at her father's house. Dad agreed. They drove up the Malahat, motored across the lake, saw Savira, as the property was called, and bought it on the spot—the perfect place for *The Red Canoe*. It was one of the cleverest things they ever did.

A little later *Tippy Canoe* was bought from Rodd Brothers. Also a Peterborough of cedar—later canvas-covered—she was much lighter and very tippy, hence her name.

In 1929, when Sylvia was eight, there was a regatta at the Forest Inn where the Shawnigan Beach Hotel once stood. The reigning champions and popular favourites for the canoe race were the two Kinlock boys—huge muscular lads whose family farm was on Cliffside Road opposite the store. Tom and Jamie were in *The Red Canoe*. Dad and Sylvia were in *Tippy*. The two all-male crews were convinced that one or other of them would win, but to everyone's amazement, Dad and Sylvia came first. *Tippy Canoe* was so much lighter they got up speed right away and kept it. Sylvia was given a huge

Mum saw immediately how super it would be to have the canoe on a lake. They bought Savira on the spot. The Red Canoe *is tied to the left of the wharf.*

box of chocolates with a winter scene on its cover. She claims the chocolates were a bit stale, but that picture inspired all her subsequent school art projects.

Jamie had fun sailing his *Red Canoe.* There are photos that show this—the full sail, the tilted hull, the beaming young face—but in actual fact she didn't sail very well at all. So after a while the sail, mast and leeboards were stored in #2 bedroom at Savira along with Dad's lake tools, hardware, varnishes, paints and often a small boat needing repair. When we went there for a hammer, a screwdriver, oil for an engine, or a tin of white lead to prime a canvas to paint on, we couldn't help but see the sailing gear leaning rather forlornly in a corner. It became a sort of shrine to Jamie, who was so very far away. Only on rare occasions did *The Red Canoe* use the wind.

For us her main advantage was stability. *The Red Canoe* was wide but wonderfully manoeuvrable and a joy to paddle, even with three or four aboard. So we explored the lake in her, took picnics out in her—changing positions as paddlers tired. But we had to keep going or drift—unless there was a good wharf to tie up to—because the canoe was so heavy, and beaching her was a problem. If we planned to go ashore, we took a rowboat instead.

Sometimes Dad used *The Red Canoe* for trout fishing and would take me with him. I loved those pre-dawn jaunts. We'd leave in the dark, using the dim outline of the eastern hills to plot our course, both of us paddling and chatting. I'd want to keep on talking in the worst way. It was rather scary out there—in that deep dark nothingness. But when we neared our chosen spot, Dad would whisper, "Hush now, Ba! Ship your paddle. I'll manage from here. We don't want the fish to know we're coming." So I'd sit and stare ahead as wisps of mist curled around us. And in the stern he'd slice his paddle back and forth through the water without raising it—the only sounds small purring bubbles against the hull or the plop of his baited hook entering the lake.

Sometimes a loon, sensing an intruder, would cry out—*Who is this entering my territory? Go away!*—his yodelling call echoing back and forth, back and forth across the lake. And then, once again, just the bubbles—and our breath.

Only when we had some trout for breakfast would we talk and sing again as we paddled home. But if daylight came and still no fish, we went home perfectly happy.

In the evening, after we were tucked in our beds—sometimes three beds in one room, sometimes each of us in a separate room or, if the house was packed to the gills, out on narrow cots on the verandah (as "cougar bait" we'd say)—Dad would take Mum out for what he called a "canoodle." The house was built on stilts right at the edge of the lake, so we would hear them passing below us—their voices soft in conversation, the ring of drops falling from his paddle. And he'd sing to her. Sometimes we'd hear snippets of his songs all the way around Bunny Island. It was so romantic. *I'll only marry a man who can handle a canoe*, I promised myself, way back. I forgot to wish for a singer!

Years later, when Mum and Dad were living year-round at Savira, they heard of an auction to be held at the far end of the lake, near the village. Dad loved auctions and was intrigued about a canoe that was up for grabs. So they paddled the five miles up the lake in *The Red Canoe*. Of course he fell in love with this long, elegant, varnished craft, complete with a cart and system to wheel her in and out of the lake. The only hitch: to get the canoe he had to buy the cottage! But it was cheap and somehow he scrounged the money and bought both.

Like Savira, this new place, Sootsus, came completely furnished with china, pots and pans, sheets and pillowcases, towels and everything else you could imagine. The house consisted of one large main room with medieval curtained nooks along the walls instead of bedrooms. There were steps up to a narrow kitchen and bathroom with sliding doors to separate the rooms, a small porch at the back and a long one overlooking the lake—and on all sides, gardens.

Now the new owners, Mum and Dad locked up the house and towed the new canoe down the lake. Then, whenever they wanted a change of scene, they'd paddle up again and spend a few days at Sootsus. Mum said it was a lovely diversion—and so small it was like staying in a dolls' house.

Sometimes Sootsus was rented—once to Derek Hyde-Lay, a master of Shawnigan Lake School, and his bride, Mary, the school's nurse. It was a perfect place for a young couple and an easy walk to work. The only inconvenience was his granny. I believe she had brought him up, and I'm not sure whether she was there when he married or arrived later, but she was part of the deal and shared that one room with them—going to sleep in her own curtained nook, with them in another, across the room.

Perhaps our mother had "the sight," as long ago she foretold that if Savira were ever rented, it would burn. After she died the property was subdivided into four lots and Hilly ended up with the house. She decided Mum's prediction was hooey so rented the place to a charming couple. The first night they had it, the house burnt to the ground and so did *The Red Canoe*—hanging in *safety* from the rafters under the bedroom annex. That couple was a front for a biker gang.

But *Tippy Canoe* escaped. Dane had always wanted to re-canvas her, so he drove down to Shawnigan with a friend in the spring of 1976 and brought her up-Island on the roof of our Land Rover, then by sea on the deck of our sailboat and here to Sidney Bay.

It is one of those extra jobs he's never had time for. So poor *Tip-py*—waiting for a refit almost as long as I can remember—is now up the hill in a loggers' drying shed, stuffed in with other treasures needing help. This shed, re-shingled once, needs doing again. But *Tippy* waits on. Has she forgotten the feel of water?

18. MUM

Mum was born in January 1888, in the manager's quarters above the Bank of Montreal in Lindsay, Ontario, the fifth child and first-born of twins. This position meant nothing to her, yet rankled her sister Arabella, whose expression, even as a toddler, was somewhat sour. When their family moved to Kingston three years later, the twins were amazed to see their bank draped in black cloth. They watched from an upstairs window as a river of horse-drawn carts and mourners shuffled along the street below. Even the horses were black, with fluffy black feathers stuck between their ears.

"What is happening, Mum?" they asked.

The Porteous Twins, "Sweetie" and "Goodie," pose for a portrait on their third birthday. Kingston, 1891.

"This is the funeral cortège of Sir John A. Macdonald. He was our first prime minister and a wonderful man. He's to be buried here."

It is hard to describe one's mum. Ours was gentle and fun. She tried her best to be fair and realized early on that silence is much more effective than scolding, thus making every misdeed impossible to forget. They hang in the air forever—lurking. I much preferred a scolding or a spank that's over and done with quickly, but I never told her. She had lots of good points, though, and took joy in what she called "small blessings": sunlight on fresh leaves, a cat on the knee, a smile on a stranger's face, sweet-scented air. I knew she longed to paint but can't remember her complaining, however tough things got. She loved music, conversation, debate, brisk argument, but also silence. She was the brain of our family, Dad the passion.

Convention did not concern her. We understand she was the first in Victoria to ride astride. We could see from old photos that she always dressed well, yet after the crash of '29 she managed with what she had or with hand-me-downs from relations. Her dressmaker could adjust things or whip her up something special, if needed. Yet if she found something exceptional she bought two! That, she felt, was good sense. If she had an indulgence it was for shoes. She bought elegant, expensive, sometimes bizarre shoes, took good care of them and kept them going for years. "With beautiful shoes," she'd say, "you can wear almost anything and get away with it. They will make you feel wonderful—so that's how you'll look!" So I studied the shoes we passed, and the faces, as we walked our way around the village or the town. At crosswalks she'd run. "Why should cars have to wait for people?" she'd say—then zip across, even in her eighties!

Who knows what Mum might have done, given her druthers, but she respected Dad's ideas about makeup, perfumes and perms and went without. All she used was a little powder and some eau de cologne. Yet when she entertained, female guests who left their coats in her bedroom found her dressing table replete with hand cream, some lipstick, perfumes, eau de cologne, powder, fresh powder puffs and handkerchiefs—even a bottle of smelling salts. There was so little space in evening bags.

Whenever I could, I'd sit beside her while she did her hair or powdered her nose, and I'd inspect those powder puffs. They were beautiful: orange, mauve, blue or pink—some of marabou, others velvety—the size of an orange but flat, like a tea bun, with a band on their backs to slip your fingers through when you dipped the puff into the powder to do your face. Sometimes she'd put a teensy bit of perfume on my temples or twist the glass stopper off the smelling salts and, waving her hand over the opening, let me sniff. Even the tiniest amount was far too much. But how I enjoyed those rituals!

Mum paid cash. She would not borrow money or be in debt—yet insisted we borrow a small amount so as to have a good credit rating. Books were her delight. She read constantly: short stories, poetry, novels, history, magazines, political articles. But her own books, clean books—not from the public library. For the ten or so years before she died, when she was comfortably off again, she bought almost every Canadian book as it was published. Ivy Mickelson, of Ivy's Books in Oak Bay, would bring them to her—chat about what she'd brought, have a glass of sherry and go her way.

When I was born, nannies were becoming extinct, so I was Mum's *last* child and her *first*. Of all her brood, I was the only one she dealt with. She had breastfed all of us, of course, but had never changed nappies, washed, bathed, dressed or seen to a baby's everyday needs. Perforce she fed and washed me, spanked and hugged me, read to me and took me for walks. Between us grew a friendship and a bond the others ached for but never experienced. They had a series of nannies. I had Mum and occasionally Lolo—a governess who drifted in and out of our lives, more a family friend than a servant. In all my growing up I don't remember Mum hugging the others. She loved them dearly and kissed them morning and night and thought of them all incessantly, yet they did not seem intimates. There was remoteness between them. How very sad for them. What a great gift for me!

Our brave little Mum, the survivor, adaptable and strong, could swing with the punches, yet when she had to push or lift something heavy—beyond her strength—she made noises: exhalations, grunts, almost animal sounds. When I complained, she said, "That's my secret! They help. Give me strength when I need it. Try it sometime!" And I do.

To me, she seemed immensely wise—but with a touch of naivety. For instance, when a young unwed woman we knew had a baby, she was amazed. "But she's not married!" she said. As if somehow a wedding enabled procreation. Had no one told her *the facts of life*? We discussed this amongst ourselves and thought her innocence rather sweet.

Mercifully she did not give advice or inflict her ideas on us—felt we'd learn best by osmosis, a good example. When we went to a party or away for the weekend she might say, "Be good and you'll be happy!" But once, bothered by a letter from a friend in the Eastern Townships, she said to me, "Never imagine that country people are necessarily kind and good." What was I to make of that? But I never forgot it.

19. TIM

Grape hyacinths have pushed through the earth again. Their flowers are appearing, at first solid, all of a piece—then, as they grow, separating into clusters of tiny round bells of a startling cobalt blue, shot with violet, each bell fringed in white. Grape hyacinths seem the essence of spring and remind me of Tim, my first love, my first best friend.

Tim came to us several mornings a week, and as soon as I could walk I'd be outside early, trailing along after him, joining in whenever I could and chattering the while. Tim and Mum had their differences about flowers. She claimed he preferred weeds and would tend them, alone, if he could. One year Mum planted a bed of montbretia near the front steps. Tim and I disliked them intensely. They were spiky and scentless. One day he pulled them up and replaced them with French marigolds he got from a friend's market garden. The offenders were dumped on the compost heap. Mum was dumbfounded but did not make a fuss. Tim was too precious to lose. In theory she was chief gardener, with Tim her assistant. Often it seemed the other way around. But there were many time-consuming things he did well that compensated for the odd lapse. Anyway, like me, she was enormously fond of him. We all were.

When Dad's resources vanished after 1929, corners had to be cut in all directions but Tim was kept on. His family depended on us. His earnings fed and clothed them and financed his regular trips back to China to see them. In between those visits, I was his child. Almost every hour he spent in our garden, I was with him, by choice—looked after, safe and sound.

There were at least five huge Douglas firs that grew around the edges of the back garden with its croquet lawn and tennis court, so Tim spent a lot of time raking the inevitable cones and twigs that fell from them onto the lawns and paths. A row of round lavender bushes stretched along the path above the croquet lawn, alternating with Mum's beloved standard roses, Madame Edouard Herriot. They and other shrubs needed annual pruning, so Tim disposed of all those clippings too—wheeling them down the path and around the corner, near the Riding Ring, to burn or compost. When I grew a bit bigger I was given a wheelbarrow of my own and would follow along behind him, carrying my share.

We were kept very busy and had fun together. And no one interfered. Then, when weary and hungry, Tim and I would sit under the Douglas fir beyond the southeast corner of the tennis court, near Mum's grape hyacinth bed, and share his lunch. He ate before noon and we around one o'clock so, knowing I'd be starving, he always brought extra. How I loved the subtle flavours of his food: rice cakes and exotic steamed buns, their tops stamped with red marks telling what was in them—all delicate, delicious. But he never shared his tea. He carried it cold, in a whisky bottle. I'd say, "Tim, I'm thirsty—please won't you give me a sip?" And he'd say, "No, no, no, you take cream and sugar in your tea. You know that. You won't like this!" I used to wonder why he drank his tea cold, but when I asked he'd just grin and take another gulp. It seemed to warm him.

The others had loved Tim too. Had watched or played around him, but always in twos or threes or more—never alone with him as I was. And certainly they never shared his meals. But if ever I mentioned what Tim gave me at noon, jealous as all get-out they would call me a Cupboard Lover or a Greedy Hog—which in our parlance meant someone sneaky, with no manners at all. But couldn't they see? Couldn't they understand? He had to slip down to the Sismans' after eating his lunch. Otherwise I'd have had him sitting by me in the dining room—sharing mine! We were best friends after all.

Dad wouldn't let anyone help with the vegetables in his kitchen garden or with the fruit trees or the berries. They were his preserve entirely. He refused help with the holly bushes too, and with the holly hedge that stretched from the red garage, three hundred yards or so, all the way to the stables. But there was always more than enough for Tim to do. Our garden was large—two acres of it at least—with so much lawn to keep cut, with a rotary mower of course, then flattened with a great iron roller. Tim was faithful and honest, and he radiated contentment—a deep and profound happiness, rare in those difficult Depression days. And he would tell me over and over how lucky he was to be here, working in gardens.

There was a short gap in our relationship when I was three. Perhaps Granny sent a cheque with a note saying: *She needs an education, that girl. Send her to kindergarten!* So for a while I went across the road with my siblings to Royal Roads School, where Lolo, our ex-governess, went to work when our numbers dwindled and she was no longer needed full-time. Then the best I could do was wave to Tim on the way to school, or we'd cross paths at noon. I was busy learning to sing in French and struggling with modern dance and other esoteric subjects.

When that money ran out, I rejoined Tim in the garden and he'd tell me about his family in China and how well they could live with what he sent them. Whenever he came back after visiting them, he'd bring me a present—like a doll all dressed in silk with frogs on her jacket instead of buttons.

In Victoria the Chinese were considered valuable citizens, hard-working and honourable. They helped and looked out for each other and were employed all through those terrible years, earning enough to live on and still send money home. If only the federal and provincial governments had been as caring. The vast majority of males in Canada, whatever their education or experience, were searching endlessly for work and food, riding the rods across the country, living on hand-outs or on the dole. They were anything *but* happy or contented.

What would you say about the head tax, dear Tim? My guess is: *We didn't have to come. That price was small for the benefits gained in Gold Mountain.* Then you'd grin your radiant grin and talk about your family.

Curiously enough, we had to leave you in the end—not the other way around. But how did your family manage, I wonder, through those long and ghastly years of war, then the Cultural Revolution?

Thank you, Tim, for that precious time and for teaching me to love weeds as much as flowers. I have a bed of grape hyacinths in my garden and each summer, I edge my raised beds with those bright marigolds we so admired. Gentle, happy Tim, how I loved you!

20. MADAME STANNER

Anne Stanner was Mum's hairdresser. Yet she was more than that. She was our family's avenging angel. Her small fierce house sat across the road at the far end of Wychbury Avenue where it petered out into a muddy track. As we walked downhill and past the woods toward it, her house faced us. Stared at us. It seemed to me she was aware of everything we did and said—and stood in judgment over us.

I never discovered why she called herself "Madame"—she didn't seem a bit French. Perhaps it was to exalt herself a little, if only in her own eyes. She was proud and severe, very tall and slender, flat-bodied and stiff with strong hands and large narrow feet—a plain woman with a stern expression and thin tight lips. Usually she wore dark clothing and blouses buttoned right up to her neck, as if she were a widow. If she smiled, it was only with part of her mouth—never her eyes. I couldn't understand that either. A lot of smiling went on in our house, and more laughter.

Madame Stanner lived beyond the Big Woods, all alone in her house on Fraser Street, surrounded by trees with more woods behind her. But she hated the woods, and whenever she met us anywhere near them she would growl, "Never go in those woods! You are not safe there! They are full of BAD people!" But we loved them and went there often to explore. And we rarely, if ever, saw anyone else.

Sometimes we went to her place to leave a message for Mum. Or she came to us. Once she actually stayed several days—looking after us, the three youngest, while Mum and Dad and all the others went up to Duncan with the horses for a polo match and a gymkhana. I was very small and don't remember much of that visit except that on

Sunday morning, instead of going to St. Paul's Church, as we always did, Madame Stanner, who was agnostic, took us down toward the sea to a brown and white house we didn't know at all. It belonged to friends of hers. The man was supposed to have sleeping sickness but, as it turned out, it was the woman who was in bed. There were always intriguing inconsistencies with Madame Stanner.

What I remember best was going to her salon to watch Mum being murdered. Madame Stanner believed hair should not be washed with water but should be dry cleaned instead. She would massage powdered orris root into Mum's scalp—that was pleasant. Then she poured

We never discovered why my mother's hairdresser called herself Madame Stanner— she didn't seem a bit French.
H.M.P. photo

handfuls of dry oat bran into her hair and brushed *hard* for thirty minutes, at least, to remove the dust and grease, while Mum squeaked and squealed and sometimes cried out, "You're murdering me!" Then in a week or two she'd go back for more. Sylvia, my eldest sister, had her hair bran washed too sometimes, but I missed her sessions.

The salon was upstairs, rather small and dingy, facing south on lower Fort Street. I would sit there drawing my usual tree and birds and perhaps a cat, wishing I were deaf. Next door there was a dressmaker who, if she remembered, would save her scraps for me. On those days, surrounded by bits of beautifully coloured cloth, Mum's cries weren't quite as frightening.

This bran washing sounds archaic and may well be, but, like organic gardening, it is a good idea and still in use. Recently, while sitting waiting for my daughter, who was having her hair done in the smartest salon on Vancouver's South Granville Street, I was amazed to see that powdered oat bran was sprinkled into her hair, massaged gently, then fluffed out. When I commented on this, some was put in my hair too, and I must say that both head and hair felt wonderful afterward.

The best thing about Madame Stanner was her Skin Food, a marvellously nourishing, subtly scented cream she made from dear knows what. It was the only cream Mum would consider putting anywhere near her face. "I'll never tell what's in it," Anne Stanner would say, one of her rare almost-smiles flitting across her face. "No, by Jove, this recipe will die with me." And it did.

I make a healing cream too, nowadays—of herbs and beeswax with olive and lavender oils—and, thinking of Madame Stanner, I delight in sharing the recipe with whoever wants it. Sometimes, for my own amusement, I call it Skin Food.

Only now, thanks to Sylvia, do I know what ailed the poor woman. Years before I was born, she and her husband ran the beauty salon and barbershop in the Empress Hotel, the most prestigious in town. Until, that is, he ran off with the profits and a younger woman. Poor Madame Stanner—no wonder she looked grim!

21. WATERING THE GARDEN

Mum's days were so full she hadn't time to do the pleasant things—like watering her plants early in the morning, when they needed and expected her. We came first and they a distant second. However, below the night nursery she made a new garden bed for plants that didn't mind partial shade. They did, of course, need water. So on spring and summer evenings we would fall asleep to that peaceful yet urgent sound of watering going on for ages. To this day, whatever the hour, the night songs of robins and spraying water mean bedtime.

Sometimes, if I couldn't sleep, I would get up out of bed and peek down. And there she was—in gumboots and raincoat, standing absolutely still, water spraying from her hand. I don't think she would have heard had I called down to her. She was miles away, lost in her own thoughts. Who knows—perhaps she was solving problems, figuring how to pay bills, stretching, in some magical way, our scant finances. Was she thinking of her beloved father, who'd had the wit to make that rich young man sign a marriage settlement that protected those dividends we lived on for years? Or was she lost in the past—with the *could-have-beens*? The *what-ifs*? Like the handsome young man who'd asked her to marry him, years ago, at a ball in Québec City? Or was she grieving, perhaps, for her first daughter— her sparkling darling, Anna Cicely, who died so suddenly when two years old? She and Tom and the baby, Jamie, all came down with flu shortly after Dad left for England to rejoin his regiment in 1914. Little Anna seemed to be getting better so Mum and the nurse concentrated on the other two. Then suddenly, inexplicably, Anna was dead! Mum was haunted by guilt. What could she, should she, have done? And there was no one to talk to. Dad broke down at the very mention of his darling. Tom didn't want to hear about her either. The rest of us didn't even know of her existence until much later. Poor Mum! What a burden to deal with, on top of everything else.

This quiet time of watering calmed her, gave her solace and strength to carry on the next day. It went on and on and on until it was quite dark. The wonder of it was that Dad understood this need and let her be. Then he would call out gently, "Come on in now, Helen. Come and sit by the fire and warm up."

There are many mindless repetitive things that one can do—like sweeping floors, washing windows, even hand-washing garments— that allow the mind to wander. Gardening is good for this, and church sermons, too. With the mind freed, in a meditative state, you can, sometimes, hit upon solutions—or at least feel rested, calmed.

I like to think this was the case for the woman I observed in northern Greece years ago, when approaching Turkey. I was hitchhiking on a bullock cart, moving slowly with plenty of time to watch her sweeping her yard. There was no sign of a garden, nothing growing, just a huge expanse of packed earth around a house and a lone woman sweeping—clouds of dust rising around her, rising and falling. As we clomped past she made me think of Mum. There was no way she could get rid of that dust. It kept billowing up as she moved through it. Nothing was accomplished, except, I hope, in her mind. I had a strong urge to go and give her a hug. Would she have thought me mad? Probably.

*Little Anna waves goodbye as her Daddy leaves
to rejoin his regiment in 1914.*

22. THE GHOST

Families often have ghosts. Ours was no exception. It was not seen, that I know of, but it was there all right, biding its time. There'd be an allusion to a certain occasion, a date, a day, and the whole comfortable jolliness of our family would crumple in a heap.

Tom and Mum were the ones to remember. Jamie, at two, three and four, was too young. But Tom kept it—as ammunition. Dad had put him in charge, after all, when he left in 1914 to go off to fight: "Tom, my boy, you are the man of the family now—you are in charge. You must look after your Mother, Little Anna and the baby. You must take my place." This was music to his ears. Just three years old and *in charge!* Then, at the first test, he failed to save his little sister.

There was always a tinge of jealousy between father and first-born—for Mum's love. But after the war it blossomed and grew. So on occasion, to win a point, to strike a blow—*the ghost* would be hinted at and Mum was in Tom's thrall.

In 1916, after Dad had been fighting in Salonika for two years and Mum was still grieving for Little Anna, she and her sister Evie heard that women were desperately needed to help nurse the troops in Cannes. Almost no one answered this plea—not in Canada, nor in France. French women wanted nothing to do with foreign troops, especially the sick or wounded. Nursing was nun's work! But Mum and Aunt Evie were game to help and could pay their passage. So off they went with Tom and Jamie in tow, and a maid called Hilda. Promising their father they'd avoid *the wicked city*, Marseilles, they boarded a ship in New York and crossed the U-boat–infested Atlantic in terrible November weather. Most of the way the captain managed to keep the ship down in the troughs of huge waves, where it rolled about and made many seasick. Nearer the coast of France the sea was calmer but the ship at greater risk, so Mum, with her far sight, spent the daylight hours on deck helping the captain look out for German U-boats. She was prepared to do anything useful to help others, and perhaps, when they were in Cannes, Dad might be able to join them for his leaves.

It was a ghastly journey but they reached Bordeaux and caught a train to Marseilles—a long circuitous route with three changes. They arrived at two in the morning only to find their hotel had been taken over by the military. Their cabby took them to another. This one housed British officers, but Mum recognized two of the names posted over the desk, one well-known to Dad. So she wrote him a note. In the morning there was a knock on their door and a Sergeant said the Colonel would like to see her. And there he was, in person—remembering Dad as a fine rugby player. She explained that her husband didn't know she was in France, and could he stop him going to England on leave.

It turned out Dad was there already, visiting his mother and sisters, who spent the war years in London to be near him—in Greece. And he was planning to go on to Montreal to see Mum and the boys. But word was sent that they would be in Cannes, so he came to them as soon as he could. It was Christmas time. Dad stepped off the train as a human Christmas tree, his body dangling with tiny parcels. They were hanging from his ears, his epaulettes, all his buttons, his wrists and his fingers. There was rejoicing and a sharing of sorrow. This was their first meeting since Anna's death. After that Dad managed to get leave from Salonika at least once more.

Going to France seemed perfectly sensible to Mum and her sister. Mum was strong, fit and determined to nurse. But Evie, with a bad heart from rheumatic fever as a child, planned to read and write letters for the troops. Instead she was commandeered to nurse forty men! As for Mum, the authorities said *Non*—her duty was to her sons. Disappointed but undaunted, she found a comfortable *pension* where delicious food was served.

One day *the ghost* appeared on her balcony. Seated at her dressing table, brushing her hair, Mum felt someone staring at her. She looked up and found a wild-looking tousled man in some sort of filthy uniform standing on her balcony—gazing at her. Furious, she rushed down and complained to the manager. He apologized, explaining that the Marquis de —— had been up to his armpits in mud for months. Now he was in Cannes being nursed back to health by a nun. (A nun for one?) Would she forgive him? She would, of course, as long as he kept well away, and the manager blocked access to her part of the balcony.

A day or two later, the nun came to apologize and plead his case. Would she come to tea and meet this young man? She would not! But the invitations kept coming. Eventually she agreed to meet him— but only if Tom came with her. She found the Marquis utterly charming, a handsome young man, tall and blond with singing blue eyes. From the start he was determined to marry her and take her and her boys to his château in Normandy. He could not accept the fact that she was married already. Non, Monsieur le Marquis could not be dissuaded. At his first glimpse of her he knew *she* must be *his* wife. He would give her his love, his château, all his land and wealth. Would that not do? *No! It would not!*

After that they met occasionally and she began to enjoy his company—but there was no question of leaving Dad for him. It was a mutual attraction that amounted to nothing more than a few pleasant afternoons and some gentle flirting. She felt desperately sorry for him, and it does one good to be admired. But at the end of her memoirs, written fifty years later, there's a little plaintive note: *We moved away to spend the winter at the seaside and I never saw him again and I have forgotten his name! (And) I never became a Marquise!*

Mum (with parasol) and Aunt Evie (centre) stroll along the Corniche with friends, ca. 1917.

On the beach one day, Mum met two women from Normandy, aunt and mother, with a young boy about Tom's age. He'd been ill and their doctor prescribed the Riviera—as if it were peacetime. They became friends, going on jaunts to the hills or walks along the Corniche, or having tea at Rumplemeyer's. Yet in photos Mum looks pained. She'd come to help, not amuse herself.

One day on her way back from shopping in the market, she happened to be at the station while two trains, full of Allied troops, were sitting on sidings. The men gazed out, frightened, weary and desperately sad. So she walked along the platform and gave each one some fruit or whatever she had. The next day she got hold of a little cart, took it to the market and filled it with fruit and flowers, pencils and writing paper. From then on she met all the troop trains passing through Cannes and gave each man his choice of whatever she had.

No one would help her—but on her way to the market, people thrust coins in her pockets so she always had more than enough money to fill her cart.

The troops, she said, seemed so pleased to be given something, and when asked what they'd like—most of them chose a flower. And they behaved beautifully, appreciating the attention of this pretty young woman, sometimes with her two small boys. Only once was she frightened, when a trainload of Serbs got overexcited and mobbed her. It took a lot of effort, this meeting of trains, but it was her way of helping and bringing a little pleasure, perhaps, to those frightened young soldiers—so many of them going off to die.

Mum and Tom buy flowers in Nice for the soldiers passing through Cannes on the way to the Front. April 27, 1918.

There were quite a number of women from different countries *doing their bit* in Cannes at that time, plus a few other Canadians, and the Serbs, in their demonstrative way, wanted to say *thank you* to all of them. So they chose a handsome but officious English woman with her fingers in many pies, and they made her a saint. Before Aunt Evie fell ill, nursing her forty charges, and was sent to hospital in England and then back to Canada, she and Mum attended the ceremony, trying not to giggle "as this appalling woman became a saint before our very eyes!"—canonized by an archbishop of the Serbian Orthodox Church.

Eventually, when the war was well and truly over, Dad reappeared. Now *he* seemed a stranger—as unkempt and wild-looking as the Marquis had been, terribly troubled and almost unable to speak. And they began their long, slow journey back to Québec.

Years later, it might happen in the dining room, with all of us at table, chatting and happy. Then suddenly silence. Tom would look at Mum, then at Dad. He'd start to say something. Then stop. Mum's

Miss P. being canonized by the Serbian Orthodox Church, Cannes 1918.

face would go ashen. We'd feel a ripple of fear. Then Dad, who missed nothing, would break the silence by saying grace or telling a joke. And we'd all relax. *The ghost* had been laid again. Dad was no fool. And *he* was in charge.

In my collection of treasures I have one I consider particularly precious. I noticed this small rectangular leather box sitting in Mum's medicine cabinet one day and asked her about it. "Ah," she said, "that's the first-aid kit I took to the South of France." And she got it down, opened it up and showed me what was inside. As a treat, sometimes, I was allowed to open it myself and take out the little glass-stoppered bottles containing medicines, or hints of them, and all the tiny boxes with pills inside—labelled by a pharmacy in Montreal or in her hand. Later on, she gave it to me. It is made of heavy leather covered with fine morocco leather so it seems padded. Inside the lid is a tiny tortoiseshell spoon and a brush of squirrel hair with tortoiseshell handle. The main body of the box once held six glass-stoppered bottles, seven centimetres high, which sat snug in loops of leather. Two of these have broken, but one is still labelled in her hand: *Honey and Almond* (her favourite hand cream). A tiny tin is labelled *salve for eye lids and nails*, and a jar of white glass with a lid of French ivory still has a trace of Vaseline in it. Under them are two paper envelopes marked *Court-Plaster*. One of these she marked *Nox Vomica Pills—in this envelope*. Ninety-one years later these seem to have melted into the paper. But the smaller envelope contains *EUREKA Court Plaster, Three Pieces in Each Envelope— FLESH, WHITE and BLACK made in the U.S.A.*, and there they are—Band-Aids and untouched. The front of this box flaps down and holds another leather box in excellent condition because it has been closed up all these years. It holds two little glass bottles: one of *Balsam of Pine* and the other *NEW-SKIN—waterproof liquid court plaster*, dated 1906. There are two cardboard boxes; one labelled by her *Boracic Acid Powder and Dobell Tablets*. The other contains black and white pills. Both are in perfect condition. Underneath is a recipe for cough syrup to be made of "special wine, water and brown sugar." The box itself is marked *MOYNAT—Fabricant—PARIS—5, Place du Théatre Français*. Unfortunately both street and shop seem to have vanished.

23. ARCHITECTURE

*E*very afternoon, when Mum and I went for a walk, we'd discuss the houses we passed. Esquimalt had a great variety in size, shape and style. Some had Victorian gingerbread around their windows and verandahs, finials on their roofs, and cut-shingle patterns on their eaves. I loved these, but Mum, who hated anything Victorian, preferred the plainer ones, especially the comfortable-looking houses sitting squat on their foundations. But many of Esquimalt's houses didn't look or feel comfortable at all.

One of these was Fernhill, Miss Alice Pooley's house. It sat almost at the top of the Lampson Street hill on land that sloped right down to the corner of Lampson and Esquimalt Road. It was built of wood painted grey, yet was shaped like a castle, complete with towers and crenellated roof. It loomed over everyone living below it, a structure so high and rickety at its southern end it seemed perilous climbing the steep steps to get in. It was a huge place yet Miss Pooley lived there alone, with a few retainers. Castles demand retainers. She had closed the rest of the house and lived entirely in the south end to take advantage of the sun and the glorious view of the Olympics. Mum and I would go there for tea sometimes. Miss Pooley was a dear but her house scared me. I felt it might collapse around us if we so much as sneezed. Luckily it didn't until after she died.

Other houses clinging to the tops of rocky ridges, such as those above Esquimalt Road to the east of Lampson Street, must have had glorious views too, but I wondered how it felt inside them during storms—with wind roaring in off the sea. Even Wychbury seemed to sway sometimes in those winds.

Some lucky people had widow's walks on their roofs. Others had *portes cochères*—like the tiny house at the bottom of our street, built at a jaunty angle across its lot, and of course Rosemead, right next door—so their coach and horses or their car could drive up in comfort to their front doors—wonderful when raining. There were lots of *old dogs* in Esquimalt too—those tall narrow houses with long narrow windows that accentuate their height. Others had broad flights of steps to wide verandahs with stout pillars, often narrower at their base, to support the roof. These made me feel uneasy. I much preferred the low wooden bungalows with verandahs stretching right around them, or the square newer bungalows with sparkling stucco walls. They were ugly—but fun, I thought.

Quite a number of houses were painted dark brick red, like the old Pullen house across the road from Fermoyle, which became the site of Royal Roads School, and also Bryden House between Head Street and Lampson. Perhaps at some point there was a stash of this paint "going begging," as we used to say. Some were bright blue—almost a Ricketts blue or rich yellow. I liked those, but most houses were brown, dark brown or black, white or cream, white and black, grey or green.

Mum chose handsome houses with good views, large rooms with high ceilings and big windows, and, of course, a lovely garden. Just what we had—so she had no desire to move. But my ideal was a house so small that I could lie in bed and see and hear all that was happening. How I envied my school friends who lived like that— with flowery Congoleum rugs on all floors and oilcloth-topped tables. No need for them to wonder what was being said downstairs. Or suffer the terror of mounting long dark staircases *alone,* then crossing unlit halls—the fate of the youngest, off to bed first!

Mum liked to talk about her father's house in Québec. She would describe the rooms, the furniture, the murals and paintings. I had her far sight, she said, so whenever we were on a hilltop I would peer eastward, hoping that I might see something of that magical place. But try as I might I never quite managed it.

One of the most exotic houses, and one I loved dearly, still stands. Captain Jacobson's House on Head Street, in West Bay, is a child's delight—built rather like a wedding cake with each storey slightly smaller than the one below and with so many fancy details it boggles the eye: bay windows, stained glass, a fringe of fancy metal spikes along the edges of the first floor, complicated eaves over each window, cut-shingle gingerbread galore, ending up with a tower on top for sighting the return of the Captain's sealing fleet—right to his wharf at the end of his garden. Perhaps this house had a chequered past, or maybe Mum knew that questionable things were going on in it then. Whatever the reason, she would not go near it, so we had to view it alone—on foot or on bicycles—which made it all the more intriguing. And it kept changing colour. Sometimes it was white or bright Ricketts blue. Now I believe it's white with blue trim. To me it always looked about to collapse—but it seems to have extraordinary staying power.

At the beginning of the war a new house, an entirely new sort of house, sprang up like a mushroom at the foot of Lampson Street. I was entranced. It was stark white and square, with a *completely flat roof!* I loved it. And I liked the people who lived there. I'd met them while gathering fat with Mike for the war effort. But Mum was appalled. It was our first real difference of opinion, architecturally. Then, as if overnight, the Lady's Mile, a delightful unpaved stretch, exactly a mile long, that our family and others had always used to clock the speed of their galloping horses, became dull old Colville Road. Then, to add insult to injury, all along both sides of this new yet ancient road, strings of small houses appeared. They sat cheek by jowl, row after row of them, almost identical in shape and size and looking like overgrown dolls' houses—all of them designed for some unknown eastern place where it never rained. These were the first of Victoria's wartime housing.

Captain Jacobsen's house on Head Street is a child's delight, built to look like a wedding cake.

Worse still was the day when the Big Woods, which once covered almost all the land between Wychbury, Fraser, Munro and Lampson streets, were felled and all those glorious trees were hauled away. Then, once again with terrible speed, that huge stretch of land was covered with houses not much bigger than wartime housing but more pretentious. For us, this was almost as bad as losing our brothers. Esquimalt seemed defiled.

As those woods came down, a large imposing half-timbered

*A mysterious house overlooking the sea near Macaulay Point appeared
suddenly during the war.* H.V.P. photo (2002)

house sprang up on the edge of the cliff near Macaulay Point—far
from other houses and right above the beach. We watched in amazement as it went up. We had never been in a house actually under
construction, so after school we clambered through all its rooms as
they took shape. It must have cost a pretty penny. In wartime, building materials were scarce and expensive, workmen hard to find and
wages high. Yet in no time it was finished and a family moved in.
How had they managed to build there and to build so quickly? Their
view was incredible: across and up and down the Strait of Juan de
Fuca. But wasn't this military land? And hadn't we been warned to
expect bombardment by sea? There were all those gun emplacements tucked in the rocks close by, some of them there since the
Great War—once active, their noise would be appalling! It seemed
an extraordinary site to choose, especially then. At about the same
time, others managed to build two houses right in the middle of Saxe
Point Park. One sits there still, looking surprised and embarrassed.
And so it should.

But one of the most intriguing houses was close at hand, just across
the road from us. It was the Ismays' house on Wychbury Avenue:

rather low—of pale yellow and brown wood with very little of it showing behind a dense high hedge. The best I could do was peek through their gate or look down at it from my attic bedroom. Their private garden fascinated me. I longed to walk all around it and go inside their house. There were two boys, John and Alan, both around Mike's age. I would say hello to them, walking or biking past, but I never did see their house. If I'd had any wit I'd have knocked on their door and said, *Excuse me. May I please see your house?*

Unfortunately a great many of Esquimalt's most interesting old houses, like Miss Pooley's castle and our own beloved Wychbury, have been torn down. But recently I went exploring with my school friend Cicely Meek, née Rossiter, who once lived on Greenwood Avenue, just below our place. In those days their house had an extra treed lot on either side and, tucked away in its woods, it seemed rather small. Since then both those lots have been cleared and built on. So their old house stands out in the open, tall and proud, and looks almost majestic among the smaller, newer buildings surrounding it. And to my great delight there are a number of lovely old wooden gingerbread houses around about—still lived in and obviously loved. Most of them are freshly painted and beautifully maintained. Some with monkey trees in their gardens! That, to me, was the ultimate chic—something I always wished for. Long may they last!

24. VEHICLES

Among the family's possessions brought west by train from the Eastern Townships was a pony cart, a sleigh with runners, a trap and an elegant cutter. The trap and pony cart were used often. Once, during one memorable snowbound winter, our pony, Bingo, hauled the sleigh and a host of children across the golf links and along by road to the army barracks on Peters Street, then home again. But the cutter sat forlornly all those years, outside or in the old red garage-cum-shed, waiting for Québec winters. I don't think it was ever used except by dreamers—those of us who took long cold journeys in it without ever leaving the garage.

As well, Dad had a series of cars. One, a grey touring car, had gone *over the edge* on the Malahat, then was hauled up again, relatively unscathed. Lonie, as my parents called Christopher Lonsdale, the founder of Shawnigan Lake School, owned it for a while and then sold it to Dad. The grey Morris roadster was bought for Mum, and she drove it occasionally—until her accident on Admirals Road.

One day Dad's broker produced a custom-built Packard convertible with an elegant chrome bowsprit. It had been a special order for someone very rich. The exterior was black with scarlet trim and the upholstery was soft black leather. Behind the wide front seat, which held three at least, were two little fold-up chairs, close enough together so that three could use them, in a pinch, with the middle person straddling an edge of each (Mike was often that *pig-in-the-middle*). All told, the Packard held ten comfortably. The overflow could travel in the roadster or, for a certain distance, on the running boards. Whenever possible, which meant almost all the time, Dad drove with the top down. Only if it were raining hard or snowing would he snap the roof in place. And whenever he drove—he sang. If he passed

Dad's broker produced a custom-built Packard convertible with an elegant chrome bowsprit, which, all told, could fit ten passengers.
J.A.P. photo (1939)

people waiting for the streetcar, he'd offer them a lift. That meant we hardly ever got to town without the car full of people, with more standing on the running boards holding on for dear life. And if Dad weren't singing, he'd be discussing politics or whatever was on his mind.

People often waved when we passed. I used to think they knew Dad or enjoyed his singing—but more likely they admired his car. Others called out, "Hello Major!" It sounds silly now but I found this really embarrassing and would cringe down in my seat.

Not long before my birth, Dad had a two-car garage built at the back of the house. I wonder what Samuel McClure would have thought of this addition, but we deemed it splendid. It sat well on the ground and had two huge doors and a roof with a slight swoop to match the house. The exterior walls were of pale pink stucco—not the multicoloured glinty sort that I admired when young, but matte—very modern. One half was for the car, the other for one of the sleighs.

The Packard, as all our cars, was serviced at Thorburn's Garage on Esquimalt Road. Dad wasn't as careful with cars as he should have been, so an exasperated Mr. Thorburn would repeat, whenever Dad appeared, "Major Piddington, you always forget the oil. You must feed your car as you do your horses. You give them hay and water and your car gas and water. But you can't forget the oats. Oil is like oats! It's essential!"

One of my favourite childhood events was the drive home from the Lake each fall. Tucked in, as I'd be, between my parents, I felt safe as houses as we zoomed along Shawnigan West Road, clouds of dust rising—then we'd curl up the paved Cut-off to the highway. Once there it was all downhill and we'd pretend we were riding or on a sleigh, leaning into the curves but always on the outlook for that snatch of the Saanich Peninsula from Scenic View Café or the first glimpse of the Olympics or, better still, the Rock of Gibraltar at Goldstream—singing, excited about seeing friends, sleeping in our own beds and school. Little did I know that Dad was coasting all the way down the Malahat—to save gas. Safe indeed!

But the fate of the Packard when we left Esquimalt? Some say it was sold to Plimleys, an English car dealership on Yates Street in Victoria, as an antique treasure for their display room; others that it was given away. Gas was still rationed in 1945, and the Packard used a great deal. We watched, as strange hands drove it away, and wept. A large part of our lives went off with that car.

25. SAINT PAUL'S NAVAL and GARRISON CHURCH

$\mathcal{E}$squimalt had a number of churches of different denominations, all trying their best to be Christian. We went to St. Paul's, the Anglican Church on Esquimalt Road, which was known officially as St. Paul's Naval and Garrison Church as both the navy and the army attended—at least in theory. Our parents believed in the creed; they prayed, studied daily lessons and observed the church's seasons and ceremonies. At home we all said our prayers separately and went to church en masse on Sunday: early communion and/or matins at 11 a.m., or sometimes evensong, a lovely service. Either way, we'd all stuff into the Packard or we'd walk. We never went to Sunday School but had *the real thing* instead.

St. Paul's Church has a long history. At first it sat on the rocky shore near where Captain Cook may have anchored between 1772 and 1776, Captain Vancouver between 1790 and 1795, and Sub-Lieutenant Quimper of the Spanish Navy in 1790 on the confiscated British sloop *Princess Royal*. But it wasn't until 1849, after Vancouver Island became a Crown Colony and was leased to the Hudson's Bay Company for seven shillings a year, that the first British man-of-war came to Esquimalt. Later, because of the Crimean War in 1856 and the attack on Petropaulovski, the fleet anchored in Esquimalt Harbour to tend the wounded. Then the colony's governor, James Douglas, had three buildings erected for the navy's use on Duntze Head: a prison, a school and a hospital. And though the official creation of the naval establishment in Esquimalt took place only in 1865, wherever British sailors were stationed there had to be a church. So the first services were held in that small schoolhouse.

In 1866, St. Paul's Church was built near the Dockyard with a grant of one hundred pounds sterling from the British Admiralty. In 1904, because of the increasing risk of damage to the church from gunnery practice at Signal Hill, it was dismantled and reconstructed at its present site on Esquimalt Road. And in 1911 it became the garrison church for Work Point Barracks as well. From then on both the army and the navy used it for their church parades.

Long before I was born, my family was asked to use the front, left-hand pew—the Admiral's pew—whenever it was empty, probably because Dad's singing encouraged the congregation to sing with the choir. His voice rang strong and true and sounded glorious. Both Mike and I loved the liturgy, the hymns and all the responses and sang almost as lustily as Dad. For some five years, Mike was a server, assisting the parson, so wasn't often with us. But the whole family sang—some "in their beards," as we'd say—or with more or less gusto.

When they attended without the Admiral, the navy sat directly behind us, and as a small child I disgraced myself by twiddling my hat and making young officers laugh. But laughter was acceptable in our church—as long as you meant well. As Mother would say, "As Anglicans we must think for ourselves while accepting the rights of others to different opinions. Our purpose," she insisted, "is to give thanks for all our blessings. We are *High Church*—not *Protestants!*"

But once I really wanted to protest. At the age of eleven I was becoming agnostic and hated the preparation for confirmation led by a man I did not admire, though I was fond of his wife, and his daughter was my friend. Because of them and my parents, but against my better judgment, I relented. But I did not feel ready to make such momentous promises.

Dad wasn't strong on group affairs. Mum had more tolerance. One of the groups she belonged to was the Women's Auxiliary or W.A.—women who did good deeds, sent money to missions, made things for and ran the rummage sales and such like. Because she had no one to leave me with, I was made a Little Helper. My "help" consisted in sitting through those tedious meetings with a pad of paper, a pencil and crayons, and I would draw. One of our ever-changing parsons had a daughter about my age. She was a Little Helper too, and sometimes we were allowed to go off and play by ourselves. The rectory, where she lived, had a south-facing wall, and along it grew a splendid grapevine. One day, when the two of us were about four, we noticed that the grapes were almost ripe and we feasted on them. When he found out, her father was furious. "Those rascals have eaten MY grapes!" he roared. And I was blamed. He yelled a lot, that man, both in and out of church. But he didn't last long—thank heaven.

The rectory had a splendid grapevine, and one day, we noticed the grapes were almost ripe and feasted on them.

St. Paul's rummage sales were held in the church hall. They were lots of fun—especially the Christmas ones. There was always a Lucky Dip filled with mysterious wrapped parcels. You paid five cents, put your hand in the barrel and took your pick. Perhaps it would yield something you could give away as a *tilly* on Christmas Day, or it might hold a treasure for you. There were Curiosity Stalls, too, covered with things people had found in the Lucky Dip in other years or that they gave from their own possessions, or, possibly, something homemade.

Mum spent months making what she called her Châtelaines: little cloth-covered cases for scissors and needles, a small round flat pin case and a bag to hold threads and a thimble—all of beautiful upholstery cloth strung together with silk cord. You wore the cord around your neck and everything you needed for sewing was dangling— right there—at hand. Mum charged much more than the materials cost—then bought all of them from the stall herself and sent them off as presents to her friends and relations in the east. ("The east" in our house meant Québec—*the centre of the world.*)

There were food stalls, too, with cakes and jams and chutneys made by village women, and book stalls, and others selling homemade toys, knitted garments, doll clothes, tough mitts for boys, balaclavas, in case of snow, and the perennial pen-wiper for clogged nibs—all them possible solutions for the difficult people on your list: cousins, elderly uncles or godparents.

There would be so many people pushing and shoving and poking about—those rummage sales were as much fun as a fair. And of course there'd be lots of little tables set about for afternoon tea—served with plates of shortbread, cake and cookies—all homemade.

For the Christian church the year begins on the first Sunday of Advent. While Advent was an exciting time, with each week bringing Christmas closer, Christmas Day was much more thrilling. The church was beautifully decorated, with boughs of fir and cedar, holly branches, poinsettias, chrysanthemums, Christmas roses and other winter flowers, and the pews packed with excited people smiling and greeting each other. And then the service was punctuated with the most beautiful carols! In those days Christmas carols began on Christmas Day and carried on until Little Christmas or Twelfth Night. Only Advent carols were sung beforehand.

After Advent and Christmas, the most important church ceremonies were Easter, Ascension Day and Thanksgiving, and each had its own charm—its own music, liturgy, vestments and decorations. My favourite was Thanksgiving in October, what we called our Harvest Home Festival, when the church was spilling over with flowers, fruit and vegetables—all from the gardens of the congregation.

There were private ceremonies too, a great many baptisms and occasionally funerals, like that of my brother Peter—who went down with his ship at Scapa Flow—on October 14, 1939. That heart-rending service was followed, three years later, by a joyful one: the wedding of Jamie to Phyllis Maude Heath Parkes in August 1942. Then, a year later, as an RAF Wing Commander and bomber pilot, Jamie was shot down over Hamburg. It took six months to verify his death, so there was no funeral at St. Paul's. His widow could not bear it.

All through our time at Wychbury, the church year was a strong thread—more like a rope really, binding our weeks and months. To leave St. Paul's was as much a shock as leaving Esquimalt.

26. BUSINESS

Mum was always trying to instill a little French in our systems. When she heard the theories of Dr. Wilder Penfield of the Montreal Neurological Institute on developing the brain, Mum tried speaking French to us when outside and English in. We were incensed, hated it! Refused to answer her. How silly we were! She had more success with occasional words or phrases—these we absorbed without realizing it. Some got a bit anglicized, like *As tu fait ton besoin?* (Have you done your business?), which meant "Have you had a bowel movement?" and to my ears sounded like *bizné*. When we were small, "business" meant that alone.

One day, walking along Lyall Street, Mum surprised me by saying we'd just pop in to see the Cranes for a while. They were a kind, elderly couple who went to St. Paul's Church, but they weren't friends. Theirs was a high house, square, dark brown and white—a comfortable-looking place with a tidy garden near the clubhouse of the Macaulay Golf Links. Mrs. Crane let us in. I was told to wait in the hall, and Mum set off up the stairs with Mrs. Crane. Partway up she turned and explained to me that she had some business to do with Mr. Crane.

Business? That was something you might do with a friend in a two-seater outhouse at the lake, but not with someone you didn't know very well. Especially not with a man! What was she thinking of? Should I rush up and rescue her? Or go home—alone? Instead I sat anxious and fidgety in that intriguing front hall—unable to enjoy the treasures hanging around me.

Eventually she came back down looking weary and a bit grim. "That took longer than I thought," she said. "We'd better get a move on."

We bought milk from Mr. Potts, down the street a bit, then scurried home via the golf links. Did she find me strangely silent? That's how I found her.

It took me a while to ask why she'd done her business with Mr. Crane.

"Oh my darling, no! It was church business—something rather dull and complicated—about money, but I think we solved it."

Grownups were full of mysteries!

27. KINDERGARTEN

Why are some periods of one's life crystal clear and others murky? And why is it I remember kindergarten above all other school years? Was it because I longed to go to school, like my siblings, and when I finally managed to get there, at the age of three, felt enormous pleasure? Or was it because that was the first and only time in my life I've felt really old, grown up, sophisticated. For there I was—*in school*—a real and proper schoolgirl, not just that brat called *Ba*!

There were quite a few kindergarten children, and Lolo was our teacher. Most of us had big brothers and sisters at the school who had to wear uniforms, but we wore our ordinary clothes: woolly dresses and knee socks in winter, cotton dresses and ankle socks in summer, or knee pants, shirts or sweaters for the boys. We were an equal mix of girls and boys but not equal in development. I don't remember girls crying when their mums left, but a number of the boys did for the first few days. Then turned into tough braggarts. But one darling little boy, with a head of bright red curls, wept each day when his mother tried to leave. So she stayed for weeks on end until

This is my fifth-birthday party. My guests are friends from school, plus Mike and Hilly, 1936.

we scarcely noticed her. He, it turned out, was at the advanced age of five! By then most of the boys were hustling, making deals with marbles, swaggering about and teaching us girls how to hurl spitballs into the fire—to hear them sizzle. One boy wore elegant dark brown velvet shorts, the colour of his eyes, with three little pearl buttons up their sides. He was timid and shy at first—then, when adult, became a hotshot lawyer. His beautiful mother had such a sad expression. Was it because she was forever mending those trousers when he ripped them, climbing trees?

Of the girls, only one stands out. She was the youngest in her family too, and a year older than I. Weeks before her birthday she began to pressure us: *If you don't promise to give me such and such* or *do what I say—I won't ask you to my party!* "Who cares," I told her. "We all have birthdays." Nevertheless I went to several of hers. But they weren't much fun. The wilder kids weren't there.

Our schoolroom was large and bright—designed as a library or a study, with a fireplace and many glass-covered cupboards and bookshelves and a wall of windows. We sat at low tables: painted pictures, counted beans, made words with wooden letters, learnt the elements of sewing using coloured thread and stout printed cards, and spoke a few words of French. Reading wasn't forced on us. We spent more time listening to stories or telling our own—or singing French songs or dancing. Occupations to stimulate the brain. Little did I know that Lolo had never ever taught before. But she loved children and became a marvellous teacher.

28. HELP

Once the Great Depression struck, Mum found herself alone in her own house. Not a bad situation in good times but somewhat tricky with a family whose numbers kept increasing plus a large house to keep clean and tidy.

From time to time she had help in the kitchen. There was someone called Nerty, who was sweet but fey, and a cook called Mrs. Luff, who would come and go, but the one I remember best was Mrs. McTavish. She was a good cook with an ancient air about her. Her black dress was long to the ground and rustled like silk. The only thing she wore that wasn't black was a pleated strip around her neck. It was pure white and hid her goitre. I used to beg her to take it off so I could see her lump. But she wouldn't. Instead she'd shriek from time to time, "You'll get one too! If you go on eating snow!"

Peter learned to drive while she was with us. On her days off he'd offer to take her wherever she wanted to go. Her choice was always the same: to the cemetery to see her plot. And off they'd go in the roadster.

From time to time we had Chinese cooks, and they were wonderful. But for household help we were all dragooned to dust, sweep, carpet-sweep and tidy, especially our bedrooms. One year I was given my own little carpet sweeper. Most were wooden in those days. Mine was metal and bright red and it worked!

We made our own beds daily, but we tidied only for special occasions or when guests were coming. This made it a pleasure, not a chore. Otherwise Mum relied on faithful Mrs. Findlay, who came once a week and gave the house a good cleaning—that is, the floors and as far as she could reach, which wasn't very high as she was short. A merry rosy-cheeked woman with dark shiny eyes, she lived at the far end of Wychbury Avenue—in those days a muddy track through the woods. I knew that walk made her nervous, so sometimes I'd wait for her at the corner or watch her going home. Whenever Mum needed something extra for a tea party, Mrs. Findlay would whisk up her wonderful scones—hundreds of them, as light as feathers. She didn't mind me hanging about as she worked and loved to boast about her son, Jimmy. Sometimes she brought me things he'd made of wood, like special hangers for my pigtail ribbons—wooden cutouts of terriers looking around over their shoulders at their tails, which stuck out behind.

The one thing we could do, and did regularly in between cooks, was wash the supper dishes. But that was entirely thanks to Miss Johnson, or Johnny as we called her, who came to supper one night when she first took over Royal Roads School, when Michael and I were still eating upstairs in the nursery. The meal over, she watched as the others sat on at the table, talking and laughing, while Mum washed the dishes. Mum's theory was that we shouldn't have to do anything that she had never had to do as a girl. Johnny, bless her, told them it was shocking that they lazed about while Mum, having cooked and served our food, washed all the dishes too. "Henceforth," she demanded, "we must help Mum in every possible way!" She marched them all into the kitchen and insisted that Mum retire to the drawing room. Then, good teacher that she was, she showed them how dishes were done. After that we did them religiously, taking turns. There was the occasional shirker, but if someone slipped away without helping one night, Sylvia made sure she did her fair share another time. I say "she" because Mike was dependable—always doing his bit or more.

There were always scads of dishes but, like Mum, we found it an agreeable job. Luckily she believed a good cook had all her pots washed before the meal was served, and she usually managed that. For everything else, Sylvia was in charge and had us all organized. Some of us would clear the table, others rinsed the worst off the plates, others washed or dried or put away. Dishwater had to be near the boil and changed frequently and, of course, the rinse water was crystal clear from start to finish. My specialty was drying glasses. With a fresh dishtowel, each one was polished carefully, inside and out, then checked against a light. I do this still and, as I check each glass, can almost hear my big sister's muttered praise: *Not bad!*

29. MAJOR SISMAN

Our swing hung from a large oak near the northwest corner of the house in the front garden—the part least used. Sometimes we rolled down that steep slope of lawn, spinning like logs to the driveway. Or we explored the rocky hummock, knee-deep in polypody ferns and covered in scrub oak. It rose along the western edge of the lawn all the way down to the front gate. Once I found an Easter egg there, tucked in a tree, still perfectly good in June! This part of the garden was relatively sunless until mid-afternoon, so we spent much more time east of the house where there was far more space, and more warmth. Was it just convenience that made Dad choose that particular limb for our swing? Or did he remember swinging as a private affair akin to contemplation—soothing for one; a rowdy hazard for more.

The oak that supported our swing rose high above the house, and its many branches made it difficult for anyone inside to see the swing or the swinger. Even on the terrace you'd have to lean far out and peer down. So though whoever was swinging might hear shouts from the lawns on the other side of the house, or scraps of conversation from the terrace above, sitting there, you felt hidden—in your private world.

Once Mike and Hilly went off to school, the swing became mine, at least during school hours. I spent a lot of time there—swinging and thinking—thinking and swinging—each backward swoop passing over the spot where Mum flung her faded cut flowers from the terrace above. One day this accumulated heap produced a hellebore—a pale mauvey-pink Lenten lily! When I showed it to Mum, she was dumbfounded. She had never grown this plant nor had it inside as a cut flower. We decided it was magic and left it untouched. Its faithful reappearance each spring remained a mystery and a joy.

Sitting on the swing one day, a question struck me. If I needed help, and my local heroes weren't around, where would I go? It didn't take long to decide. Yes! I would trot down the wooden sidewalk to the end of Lampson Street and turn left around the corner to 1024 Munro Street where Major Sisman lived with his wife and step-daughter. They were kind people—family friends. If he could, he would help me. I knew that. And if they were out, Tim might be there, cutting the grass.

Major Sis, as we always called him—*Sis* like *fizz*—was one of the constants of our lives. What Dad called not only "an officer and a gentleman" but "a consummate gentleman"—someone you could rely on at all times to do the right thing, without drawing attention to himself. He was not, Dad insisted, a *Jumped-up Johnny*—those reserve soldiers who rise quickly to high rank in wartime, then preen like peacocks, never letting you forget that they are *colonels* or *generals*—though their war is long over. There were lots of them around the town.

Major Sis was a respected citizen of Esquimalt. We saw him every Sunday at St. Paul's. He was at our christenings, our confirmations, Peter's funeral and Jamie and Big Phyll's wedding. So from 1924 to

1945 he was part of all the most important ceremonies of our lives. What I liked about him was his kind and gentle face and the way he treated children just as he did grownups: with patience and care. He would look at you, head tilted, ears raised, like a large intelligent dog, eager to anticipate what you were trying to say as you mumbled shyly. Yes, if I needed help, I would go to him!

Their house had a certain stiff elegance. It was tall and narrow, like his stepdaughter, Francie, whose father had it built in 1895, on the cheap—as a rental property. Hans Ogilvy Price's own house at 1820 Dunsmuir was almost a carbon copy. As we understood it, when he died, sometime before the Great War, Mrs. Price rented both houses and took her daughter to live in England. They returned to Esquimalt after the war with Major Sisman, her new husband. Some spinsters were jealous. They felt she had had more than her fair share of husbands.

When we went to the Sismans' house we felt a pervading sense of kindness, of three people living happily in each other's company. Francie, somewhat taller than her mother and stepfather, was a warm and pleasant chatty person. Mrs. Sisman was rather pretty. She stood straight and proud and seemed to us a softer version of Queen Mary—even to the black velvet ribbon around her neck and the cameo pinned to her chest. But she held the purse strings tightly and would not allow any changes or repairs to her first husband's house, even when sorely needed.

Their home was what Mum called a "look at me!" house. It was built on flat land high above Fleming's Beach with a glorious view of the Olympics to the south, the Sooke Hills to the west, and eastward to the golf links (designed by Mr. Price) and beyond them the woods of Macaulay Point. A path led from the front gate straight across the lawn to the front door. There was a formal garden on the west side of the house while a narrow lawn led around the other side to the orchard at the back, where fruit trees seemed to stretch forever—on and on, in rows—all the way to Bewdley Avenue. There was no basement so the ground floor, only inches above the soil, could be both dank and cold. All the windows were tall and narrow and so were the rooms. Warmth, if any, came from sunlight, the people in the house, the kitchen stove, open fireplaces or a heater in the front hall. The rooms must have been glacial when cold winds blew in off the Strait of Juan de Fuca. We went there, as a family, for formal teas at Christmas, and in between I'd go sometimes with Mum. Whatever the season we always wore an extra cardigan and, in winter, a woollen vest. I believe they had servants before I knew them, but in the thirties and forties there was no sign of anyone—except for Tim, who looked after their garden. Mrs. Sisman and Francie were good cooks and served delicious food.

A *maison à trois* can be difficult but there were no sharp edges in the air there, as there were in other houses I knew, and even in ours when Mum and Dad argued fiercely. No, when talking together their voices were like distant birds or the soft buzzing of bees—warm and contented.

Seven years after we left Esquimalt, Mrs. Sisman died. Soon after, Francie and Major Sis moved to Oak Bay. Since then that house has been repaired, adjusted and added to. It has changed hands many times and has even been a bed and breakfast. But for us it is, and always will be, the Sismans' House. Mr. Price, and his widow, will have to lump it!

In the end I never needed to go for help. But as a child who spent a lot of time alone, it was comforting to have a plan and know there were neighbours nearby who were both wise and kind.

30. LAUNDRY DAY

Laundry Day was on Monday: the gathering of sheets, a slow and stately dance with Mum as soloist. Sometimes she had an audience of one and sometimes a helper, me.

In our house the top sheet was removed and set aside. All the covers were stripped off and the bed aired. Then the top sheet was turned and put back as bottom sheet. All the bottom sheets, whether cotton, linen or flannelette, and sometimes the pillowcases were stuffed into a large cotton bag. A drawstring at one end was pulled tight and tied. Then, my favourite part of the day, that bag would bounce, fat and heavy, down, down, down and around the back stairs to arrive with a terrific thud in the downstairs back hall. Soon after, a deliveryman would collect it and take it to the Sam Kee Laundry in Victoria, where they were washed.

A few days later they would return, all neatly folded and wrapped in paper, our laundry bag tucked in. If someone were home the deliveryman would carry the parcel upstairs and leave it by the linen cupboard in the back hall.

Everything sent to Sam Kee had to be marked. Mum had a smooth boxwood disk for this, about five centimetres in diameter. Cloth would be spread over it and cinched tight with a wooden ring—then with pen and nib she would write *Piddington* and the year in black indelible ink. A long name like ours had to be written in a semi-circle. I have this device hidden away somewhere and a few pillowcases, made from the good ends of old sheets, with name and dates still perfectly clear: 1934, 1938 or 1943.

If everyone was home there could be twelve or more beds to unmake and make up again. I find changing four beds arduous. Imagine having to do a dozen or more!

Washday happened on Tuesday, weather permitting, with the same players performing. But this was quite a different dance: fast, frenetic, with a lot of gesture, bending, turning and twisting. Clothing to be washed was kept in a large covered wicker basket in the upstairs back hall—each of us dropping our grubby garments there during the week. Towels and facecloths were gathered from the bathrooms. Each person in our house had his or her particular colour—two sets of everything. Mine were pink.

On the appointed day all would be sorted into whites, colours, darks, things needing a rub with Sunlight Soap on cuffs and collars, or perhaps a dollop of Ricketts blue for whitening. Then each lot was carried separately in wicker baskets down two flights of stairs to the laundry room in the basement. There Mum spent hours manipulating a cranky wringer washer, electric but cumbersome. Frequently clothes would jam, so she'd hit the release bar. The wringer would explode with a terrific crash and come apart so that stuck garments could be removed. Then, of course, it had to be screwed tight again—but not too tight.

The laundry floor was concrete and sloping. Used wash water would gush out onto it and gurgle down into a hole to vanish into the bowels of the earth. For me, the small observer-cum-helper, the heat and steam and rush of water were thrilling. Other than Mr. Maynard's greenhouses across the road, it was the closest I'd come to the Jungle. Mum looked grim sometimes and exhausted, but I don't ever remember her complaining.

She had always hand-washed a few things, like woollens, undies, cotton gloves, silks or baby clothes. But both these major functions—the changing and making of the beds and the washing of the family's laundry—were new to her, tasks thrust upon her by the combination of Dad's investments and the crash of '29. Before that, servants had done all this.

No one had dryers in those days. So the second act of her Tuesday performance took place with more grace and less speed. The wash was hung outside in wind, if possible, on long clotheslines strung from the back porch to trees or on a free-standing spiral device made for that purpose, whose support was jammed into the ground. All I could do, in either case, was pass the clothes pegs.

In a pinch, during wet weather, clothes were hung on clotheslines in the laundry room or sometimes on a ceiling rack in the kitchen, which could be raised and lowered liked a sail. Luckily there was almost always some wind in Esquimalt, for even if it is raining, clothes will dry, at least partially, in wind. And how exquisitely sweet everything smells when dried outside in the air.

Years later when Hilly and I stayed with our cousin Amy Drury, in England in the mid-1950s, she lived with her lady's maid in a little Elizabethan hotel, the Hayes Farm Hotel in Sussex. They always ate at separate tables in the dining room but otherwise spent most of their time together, and Miss Emeny hand-washed all Cousin Amy's clothing in a washbasin in their apartment. Cousin Amy, who was in her mid-nineties, would watch, fascinated, and often said to us, "You know I have never washed a garment in my life! Do you think I should try?" And we'd say, "Yes! Do! It's fun!" But I don't think she ever did. She feared it would bother Miss Emeny, who might consider it a question of *crossing the line*!

31. THE CBC

Mum was really keen on buying a radio when they were first available. But Dad was not. He felt we should be content with newspapers and magazines for news, and with books, the piano, his beloved player piano or gramophones for entertainment. It was only when he heard that King George V was to address the outposts of Empire via radio that he relented. Once he had one, he was hooked and wanted several. So our parents were ready and eager for the Canadian Broadcasting Corporation long before it became fact in 1936. They were tired of the limitations of American stations, much as they enjoyed some of the plays on Lux Radio Theatre.

On Sunday evenings, when that program was broadcast, Mike and I would slip under the dining room table after high tea so as not to miss any of it. Those plays distracted our elders too, so sometimes no one noticed that we hadn't gone up to bed—until the play was over. There was so much talk in our house about having our own Canadian radio programs that the names of those who lobbied successfully for the CBC, like Graham Spry, Alan Plaunt and Brooke Claxton, seemed as familiar as relations.

Our first radio was wooden and tall, up to an adult's waist at least. There was another, slightly smaller, for the breakfast room and another for Mum's bedside table. All were made of varnished wood, about a metre high by half a metre and about thirty centimetres deep, with a churchy look about them from the Gothic arched cutouts in their fronts. Coarse brown cloth was stretched across these openings, where the sound came out. And there were all manner of knobs that we weren't supposed to touch. When we did, coloured lights came on, stations changed and the volume went way up or down. We would sit in a ring in front of the radio, quite close—staring at it, as if *seeing* whatever was happening.

Mum insisted all our radios be kept stuck on the CBC. We didn't have our own radio corporation in order to listen to foreign stuff! Then we got a portable radio too, so it could go outside with us if need be—which meant if important news was expected. The covering on this one looked like leather and seemed to be waterproof. It was light brown with green and orange stripes and weighed at least ten pounds. In summer it would travel with us up to Shawnigan Lake. How modern we felt, listening to loons *and* the news, while sitting out on the rocks under cedars or pines.

But at the Lake I much preferred listening to our windup gramophone. For one thing, it was an elegant piece of furniture with pale pink pleated silk inside its fretted openings. It, and the records that came with it, were from the early days of the twentieth century, if not the nineteenth, and they were played with thorns. The others would wind and wind and wind the crank. When they could turn no more, they'd place the record on the turntable, turn on the switch and lower the thorn to the record's outer edge. Then, depending on the record played, out would come a strong tune or ancient sounds: tiny little human voices squeaking and whirring, and music that would rush and slow of its own accord. This was the past. Radios were the future!

After the initial excitement, we young ones didn't listen to the CBC much except for the plays—for some of them were really well done. But if we were sick in bed, radio was a godsend. The always over-eager Happy Gang came on daily and the "Just Mary" stories— even the news and the farm programs helped pass the hours when eyes got too tired to read. As years went by the CBC's programs got better and better, like John Drainie's plays, and *Rawhide* and Allan McFee. Mum and Dad felt the country had come of age at last, and even when money was really short, they paid the fee for their radio licence promptly.

Each Saturday night when the hockey game was broadcast, Mike would pull on his hockey sweater, closet himself in our parents' bedroom and enjoy himself hugely. Foster Hewitt gave the play-by-plays so well he made the game come alive, and we'd hear shouts from Mike—of delight, rage or sadness. Mike considered these sessions his alone so the bedroom door was shut tight. However, amazed that my otherwise mild and gentle brother was getting so excited, I'd peek in sometimes and I swear he used to dash about wielding a hockey stick, making appropriate gestures. But he says, "No! Never ever!" The Aunts, Dad's two eldest unmarried sisters living in Montreal, supplied those sweaters, and it didn't occur to them that he might want anything but a red Montreal Canadiens sweater (they weren't called "the Habs" in those days), whereas Mike backed the Toronto Maple Leafs. As embarrassed as Roch Carrier, he never wore his hockey sweater outside. Too bad they couldn't have switched.

But there was one given in our house, and no question about it: Radio meant the CBC.

32. THE PEACE

Since we moved to Loughborough Inlet in 1975, my husband does the shopping—makes the long journey in by boat and then by car to buy supplies. I give him a list, some vague ideas, and he elaborates. He has a good eye for quality and bargains and comes home, the boat laden—with enough, sometimes, to last a month. We like to think of ourselves as independent, growing much of what we need to eat and drink. But there is a lot we can't manage: wheat, dairy products, oranges and bananas, manufactured things and honey.

It was last week's honey that caught me off guard. There, sitting on the breakfast table, was a yellow pot of no-name honey from "the Valley of the Peace." And I was back again in mid-Depression, wide-eyed and wondering: *Why is Mum obsessed by this place?*

My brothers and cousins go off, one by one, to join the Royal Air Force, the Royal Navy. There is nothing happening here. There is no money for university, no careers, no jobs in Canada. Things are grim. The population is holding its collective breath, waiting. Yet while our parents are working harder than they ever dreamt of doing and many people are suffering, there are others far worse off somewhere way up north in the Peace River Valley. It is the suffering of these people that preoccupies Mum, and her bizarre attempts to cheer them filled my early years. Everything imaginable would be packed in boxes so large I could barely see into them. When full, they'd be sent north to the Peace. While everything she'd known began to crumble around her, Mum held fast to the belief that others were desperately in need and she must help them.

Somehow our eastern relations were not affected by the Depression. Perhaps they held on to their blue-chip stocks. Dad's two eldest sisters continued to flood us with presents. And at Christmas and Easter they sent enormous fruitcakes, all iced and decorated, large boxes of chocolates and special bittersweet mice for Dad, who remained, forever, their baby brother. They had been born, like Dad, at 83 St. Louis Street in Québec City and lived there long after their parents died. At some point in the early thirties they went up to Montreal to cut coupons and never returned. The Québec City house was left as is, jammed with furniture and things, much to the chagrin of neighbours. The Aunts' delight was buying and sending presents. We understand that duplicates of everything they sent us went to "83."

While working in Fort Chimo in northern Québec in 1955 I got an infection in my left hand that wouldn't respond to treatment. I had been working with raw sealskins. Was it Speck's disease? When the chief public health nurse flew in for her annual inspection of northern nursing stations, she was concerned and insisted I fly south with her to Québec City for further medical care.

We arrived late at night and shared a taxi from the airport. I was to stay at the Château Frontenac. She was to be dropped off first. Imagine our combined astonishment when I discovered her house was right beside the all-too-familiar 83 St. Louis Street—unlived-in for years, but jammed with things—even, perhaps, a duplicate of the red canoe!

In our house "The Family" meant Mum's relations. Less generous, perhaps, but more sensible—they had written us off years ago. Anyone choosing to live outside Québec was suspect. They sent us hand-me-downs but lovely things: dinner dresses fit for supper at the Ritz Carlton, elegant evening gowns, opera cloaks, long kid gloves with pearl buttons at the wrist, and ancient cashmere sweaters, sometimes mothy. One year an almost unused chestnut-coloured riding coat arrived. It was perfect for Sylvia. But usually very little fitted us in any way. No matter; anything we couldn't use was snapped up by Mum and popped into her Peace River box. "Who knows," she'd say, "where these people came from or how they lived before. They might be glad of some gorgeous impractical things—if only for dress-ups." And then she began to intercept new incoming gifts.

Upstairs in the main hall of Wychbury was an armoire some eight feet tall. It was a place of mystery—which we were not expected to explore. And rarely did. Its many shelves held wrapping paper, ribbon, and presents too. When its doors were open, two adults could stand there, hidden from view from the thigh up. The nursery was nearby in those days. Before Christmas and birthdays, we young ones would fall asleep to the exquisite rustle of wrapping paper. Once, when I was creeping barefoot back to bed from the bathroom, I passed behind Mum holding up a beautiful white rabbit and saying to her companion, "Isn't this a beauty! Ba won't miss it a bit. I think I'll pop it in the Peace River box. They'd love something absolutely new!" Sure enough, there was no rabbit for me that Christmas. But later, to make amends perhaps, she bought me a rabbit from a man who came to the door, desperate for money for food. It was real fur too, and wonderfully soft, but it was grey and gutless and difficult to love. A empty sewn-up rabbit skin—nothing more. For years I dreamt of that white rabbit. Where was it? Who had it? Did they like it? And worse: who should I have thanked for it, sent, as it had been, "To Ba—with love"?

Another Christmas I unwrapped my heart's desire—a chocolate brown, curly-haired dolly with scarlet velvet pants. I was in heaven. Then, distracted by another present, I put him down among the wrappings and never saw him again. Had my mother, or her scouts, whisked him away and into the Peace River box?

What actually happened in the Peace River Valley in the 1930s? Was life as desperate as we thought? Books in our library give no clue. Was it really a disaster area? Or was it all an invention of the Women's Auxiliary at St. Paul's Church to help some far-flung mission? Did Mum's boxes ever reach anyone in need and "do the trick," as she'd say—bring comfort and solace? One thing is sure: by concentrating on others she believed to be worse off than herself, she was somehow strengthened.

As for me, ever since childhood, at every meal a message flickers from the past: *Eat up your food, my darlings! Think of the starving Armenians and the people of the Peace!* And in the wonderful circular way of things, on this isolated west coast inlet we too received boxes of treasures when the children were small and we were on our uppers. They came from people we scarcely knew and were full of toys—some brand new, others rare and old-fashioned—plus puzzles, clothing, even pieces of cloth: something for each of us, charming and delightful things, chosen with care—all of them a complete surprise. Had the donors been really hard up once? Were they perhaps from the Peace River Valley?

33. THE ELEPHANT'S CHILD

History relates that when Mum first held the heft of me, newborn and rosy in her arms, she announced to those present: "This is the Elephant's Child!" Loving Kipling, she read his stories aloud by the hour. Perhaps that's where this name sprang from—who knows— but it stuck.

Later it became "My Elephant's Child," though I was christened Helen Vivian and called H.V. by relations to distinguish me from Mum, who was Helen Mary. At home my name was *Ba*, but when people came to tea, all of us children would be lined up, clean and tidy, to shake hands and say, "How do you do, Mrs. So-and-So." And Mum would present each of us by name, with mine last: "And here's my Elephant's Child." This didn't bother me at all, when small, as I loved the story of Toomai, the Elephant Boy, who'd been lucky enough to watch elephants dance.

One day a tea salesman came to the door (was it Salada Tea he was selling?), and Mum tried to explain that she preferred China tea and bought it from a friend whose brother imported it directly from China. Somehow she let my name slip and the salesman heard. He excused himself, went out to his truck and came back in with a little ebony elephant—for me! I was thrilled and of course she bought some of his tea. After that, each time he came he brought me another elephant—until I had five or six.

But whenever a shipment of her favourite tea arrived from China, Mum and I would go together across town by streetcar to Mrs. Garrett's house. It was full of fascinating things and I liked her, for she treated me as a person, not a child, and she called me Helen. We'd go early enough to have tea and talk. Then Mum would buy some China tea. It came in wooden boxes—red or blue-green and painted all over with flowers, dragons and designs (I have some still). Each one was bound with heavy bamboo rope, to protect its exterior, and inside the tea was sealed in an inner box of lead and sealed again in a bag of thick rice paper. Those boxes were heavy, so when we were ready to leave, Dad came for us in the car.

I asked Mum once, if I was the Elephant's child, didn't that make her an elephant too?

Unfortunately I can't remember exactly how she wiggled out of that—but she did. She was dainty, small boned and fragile, while all of us were big boned and buxom, at least when young. As for Dad, while he might roar and trumpet like an elephant, and he loved to dance, he was also gay in the old-fashioned sense of that word—a joyful man. The gist of Mum's answer was this: *When you reach the point of wanting to marry a man—insist on seeing his sisters in bathing suits—for that's what you'll get when you have his children.* When she was engaged to be married, skirts were to the ground, so she had no idea Dad's sisters had such heavy legs!

34. THE STORM

Our front hall was a fine example of Samuel Maclure's specialty: the large central hallway. From the front door one entered a vestibule, passed through a doorway with a stained glass window and went on into the front hall. The effect was rather like entering a church. The space seemed extraordinary in both length and height. And though the wall panelling was of fir and fairly dark, it seemed a wonderfully bright and airy room with a huge brick fireplace along one wall and recessed inglenooks on either side, with storage under the seats and more above in recessed cupboards. A wide staircase led up one flight to the first landing, then turned left up to the second, and left again and on up to the upstairs hall. The hall windows were in three parts, beginning at the first landing, with the other two following the rise of the stairs. This meant that the first segment was almost a storey and a half high. They were of leaded glass shaped in elegant Arts and Crafts designs, mostly clear but with some muted yellows, pinks and greens—beautiful in their simplicity. The curtains that covered them were heavy cotton of burnt orange with stripes of purple, blues and greens with simple geometric flowers.

We loved those windows in all the different lights and seasons. They were awkward to dust and wash but not impossible—especially on the outside, as there was a balcony that stretched two-thirds the width of the house, formed by the roof of the back verandah. This roof was a deviation from the original plan, so to get to it one had to climb out a bedroom window.

On the day in question our parents had gone to an afternoon lecture. Before they got home a strong wind blew up. It came from the east, an unusual direction, and it struck those windows with terrific force. As the sky grew dim, the wind gathered strength. There were only six of us at home—the five girls, aged fifteen, thirteen, twelve, ten and five, and Mike, almost eight. All of us were anxious about that howling wind. Then someone noticed that the hall windows were rippling—bellying in slightly and out again, in and out. As Mum put it later: "Blowing in and out like muslin!"

Sylvia organized the four older ones with long-handled brooms, mops or their hands, and with the curtains pulled they stood there, for what seemed hours, supporting all that space and weight of rippling glass. Mike and I were anxious to help but were told we were too small to be of any use. So while he acted as gopher, I stood at the bottom of the stairs watching, feeling cut out of the action, licking a butterscotch all-day sucker but finding no pleasure in it.

When Mum and Dad got home, probably about an hour after the storm began, they couldn't do much more, but it was a comfort to have them there and they could take turns holding up the windows.

That wind howled all night while Mike kept watch at his bedroom window. We were used to night winds roaring around the house, but that particular wind was far stronger than most. Somehow our lovely windows survived intact. But as soon as possible they were double-glazed on the outside.

35. MEALS

Until we were seven we ate in the night nursery—sitting by an open window if the weather was fair, or before a crackling fire. Meals were brought up to us and not always supervised, so we could eat in peace, laughing and chatting, as raucous as we liked—Hilly, Michael and me. We sat at a small white wooden table on chairs of varying size, like the Three Bears. When all were finished we'd play a bit, have our baths, all three together, brush our teeth, be read to, say our prayers, be sung to and then be tucked in.

By degrees we ate breakfast in the day nursery, also known as the breakfast room. I can remember my delight at being there, eating with the grownups and feeling very grand—sitting in my high chair at the big table.

When I joined the family in the dining room for special occasions, I had a tendency to spill my water glass. This happened so often the others would hold their breath until I did. And Dad, who'd be carving at the far end of the table, too far away to see what was happening around vases of flowers and candlesticks, would call out to Mum: "Has she done it yet, Helen? Has she spilt her glass?" When it happened, the drill was simple: plates, knives and forks would be pushed aside; the tablecloth, and the silence cloth under it, would be raised and table napkins stuffed underneath to soak up the moisture. You'd think they'd have been annoyed by my clumsiness, but for some reason it was a ritual they all enjoyed. I would be sitting in the high chair but with my plate on the table—eating with a small spoon and fork, my food cut up by Mum or my neighbour. I don't know why I wasn't given a mug but, like everyone else, I would have to manipulate a delicate goblet of pale green glass, bulb-shaped with stem and narrow base. Rather tippily, as Mum would say, but they went with our best green dinner service.

The dining room was green too, and the table oak, as were the chairs—their backs and seats of dark green leather stuffed with horsehair. The fireplace tiles were deep green, and in between the fir panelling the walls were lined with cloth of the same dark forest green with a touch of blue. Above, between the dark beams, the ceiling was creamy white, and the curtains covering the French doors were of a subtle deep blue velvet. It sounds rather dark and gloomy but it wasn't at all. At night, with a fire in the hearth and the table laid on a white linen cloth, and on it water and wine glasses, silver spoons and forks, silver salts and peppers, a bouquet of flowers in the centre, lit silver candlesticks at either end—or two bouquets of flowers and the great silver candelabra between them (bought by Dad to brighten their last house in Québec, where there was no electricity, after Mum complained it was rather hard to see)—plus the lights from the brass chandelier overhead, everything glittered and twinkled and shone.

During the day there was plenty of light from the French doors that ran along the entire west wall, plus light from the casement windows above the inset sideboard opposite the fireplace on the north wall. These were mostly clear with just a touch of stained glass. And light came through the hall door, which was almost always left open in daytime.

Behind Mum's chair was another wooden open sideboard—a place to serve from, if someone was waiting at table. Beside it was the baize swing door to the pantry, and then another one into the kitchen, so you could back into the dining room, hands laden, carrying food in—or dishes out. If there was a cook or someone serving, they could be summoned by pressing a small bell under the carpet, placed conveniently near Mum's right foot. Long before my time, Mum had two black cats—a mother and daughter. They sat on the arms of her chair all through meals and, breaking all rules, she fed them.

On special occasions there were eleven of us, plus Stoko and possibly Granny and Aunt Fran when visiting from Québec, and/or Auntie Bella and our four Nixon cousins from Hill Farm on Wilkinson Road. Luckily the oak table had several leaves so could be extended to great length.

What I remember best of those dinners, apart from the wonderful play of light across the table reflecting on all the faces around it, was the sense of contentment from all of us being there together, the satisfaction from the good food served with conversation crackling back and forth, and then, when the meal was over, sitting in drowsy state on Dad's knee, listening to his stories—until carried off to bed.

Often the adults would sit on at table—chatting or discussing serious matters or sipping brandy after we younger ones had been excused. Or they'd sit in comfortable chairs at the far end of the room, listening to the radio.

When we had guests, Mum would make coffee, and the coffee pot and demitasse cups would be carried on a brass tray to the drawing room—to be enjoyed before the open fire.

In our house, suppers, and especially dinner parties, were ceremonies attended by the entire family. The only exceptions were small children or those dashing off, like Peter, going to Sea Cadets in the evening, or some college course or lecture, a concert or the theatre. They might eat a special meal earlier, perhaps in the kitchen. But in the dining room, everyone waited to eat until the last person was served. Then, at the end of the meal, everyone stayed seated at table until the last person was finished. Only then might we ask to "Get down." The exceptions were breakfast and lunch—when we had to rush back to school.

I remember dinner parties held in honour of godparents and such like. My Victoria godmother came to tea quite often—but I don't remember her at dinner. My godfather came though, with his sons. He was a silent man with no interest at all in other people's children. Mike's godfather, Christopher Lonsdale, the head of Shawnigan Lake School, was much more fun. Sometimes he'd slip down the Malahat on Boxing Day for Mike's birthday. He was a loud and jovial man who loved to eat, drink and roar with laughter. His presence was embarrassing for my big brothers, boarders at his school, and terrifying for Mike, when small, as he'd be placed beside him. Mike's christening present from him was a pewter beer mug with pieces of Maundy money rattling in its glass bottom. Perfect for a teetotal parson!

When Granny's visit coincided with the twins' birthday she would order the Bird's Nest dessert from Mr. Notte's Bon Ton Bakery—in Victoria in those days. It was a splendid sight and delectable: large eggs of meringue and ice cream nestling in a huge golden nest of spun sugar. When Mum and Auntie Bella turned fifty, there was an even grander dinner with invitations sent out announcing *The Twins are One Hundred!*

On Sunday morning, before we stepped out the door for church, a huge joint of beef would be popped in the oven of the electric stove. That meal amounted to dinner, so we'd forego afternoon tea on Sundays but have high tea instead at about 6 p.m.—a collection of cold dishes, salads, cheeses and perhaps hot soup, followed by cake, a trifle, a homemade fruit jelly and lashings of tea. This meal was served on Mum's favourite Indian Tree china.

On weekdays we ate our "brekker" in the breakfast room. It faced east so got all the morning sun. If it were chilly there'd be a fire in the grate. Sometimes, when Dad had lumbago or sciatica, we three stayed on after breakfast—my parents talked, discussed the paper and the morning mail, while I played at their feet—drinking it all in.

On Sundays breakfast was served in the dining room and we'd have hot brown and white buns from Durrant's Bakery with butter and jam, along with coffee or hot chocolate and fresh fruit.

For elevenses Dad and Mum might have a glass of logana—a wine made from loganberries by Growers Winery on Quadra Street—or a cup of coffee with digestive biscuits to give them strength to carry on till lunch. There was no specific place for this ceremony. In fair weather it might be in the garden, or Mum might carry a basket down to the stables.

Lunch was served in the breakfast room at about 12:15 on school days so we could race across the road from Royal Roads School or down the hill from Lampson Street School or Esquimalt High and back up again by one o'clock. But on weekends it would be in the dining room, as we'd all be home. Then it was served at 1 p.m. It seemed to me Mum spent her entire life making meals.

Afternoon tea would appear in the drawing room at 4 p.m., pushed in from the kitchen on a tea trolley—everything snug on a large silver tray with silver grapes near the handles. Dad never missed teatime. I think it was his favourite meal. Whatever he was doing he arranged to be free to have tea with Mum. He'd come in from the stables in his riding boots and breeches, often a bit horsey. Some guests might sniff—others loved it, or so they said, and he'd entertain them with tales or chat while downing endless slices of brown bread and butter, then countless pieces of cake. In between he'd take seven cups of tea—each one poured on his saucer by degrees so he could drink it quickly—hot, but not scalding. But much as he loved his tea, he was always in a rush to get back to his horses. In warm weather tea was served less formally on the terrace, with guests sitting on cushions along its wide concrete edge.

Supper was between 7 and 8 p.m. and served on our willow pattern china. Our terms and times weren't the same as some of our friends, and that made it awkward for them to accept invitations to meals. My friend Cicely, who lived just around the corner, was asked often—but never came. As she told me recently, "I had to be in bed before your supper began!"

Our meals were plain but copious, our food organic—homegrown or local. Dad's corn, picked minutes before it was cooked in a huge tureen, seemed limitless. My brothers built cob log cabins on their plates, their structures rising to considerable heights. If anyone disliked a certain fruit or vegetable cooked, it could be eaten raw. Milk and cream came from our own cows or from Mr. Potts' dairy down the street. In the first half of the twentieth century it was not at all unusual for families to have a cow in their stables. To have your own source of good whole milk was considered sensible. When I was born we had two cows: a Jersey named Daisy and a Holstein called Bunch. I have vague recollections of Daisy but remember Bunch clearly, her silken flanks, her grinding jaw and that swinging tail—long and hairless until the scraggy tuft at its tip—all of her seen from behind.

No one remembers what happened to our beloved animals. Dad loathed killing anything and couldn't have butchered them either. He enjoyed carving though, but spent so much time gesticulating with carving knife and fork in hand that our food would get cold, so at some point it was decided that Mum should do it. She was an excellent cook, which is extraordinary because until the crash of 1929 she had cooks, kitchen maids, housemaids, cleaning women and nannies. But, she'd explain, she knew good food, so it wasn't difficult to make. "It's like grammar," she'd say. "If you grow up hearing correct English, French or whatever—then grammar is easy. You may not know the reasons for the rules but you know exactly how to speak and how to write." Still, it amazes me how she managed to adapt so quickly from a fleet of servants to almost none at all and still have time to do a lot of extra things. For example, once Mum and Auntie

Bella came home for tea in a state of collapse after a reading by Stephen Leacock, their eyes red and swollen, still weeping with laughter. At night there might be lectures, concerts, dances, skating or dinner parties. It was not a dull life.

Nevertheless it was impressed upon us: *Meals were at set times with no snacks in between.* So, like active children anywhere, we were always hungry—"Starving!" we'd say—and when nothing was edible in the orchard or garden, we'd stave off the pangs by nibbling sour grass or chewing rhubarb leaves.

36. THE BAKER

I love the smell of flour—the touch of it. Perhaps because as a child I spent so much time in the kitchen playing with it, making little messes that became buns and cakes. I learned early on that if I cooked something for Dad, he'd scarcely notice when I didn't turn up for riding lessons. (For some reason the eldest and the youngest in our family were not horsey.) "The way to a man's heart" certainly worked with him. He ate my inventions with gusto, some of them low-carb: like peeled grapes dipped in cocoa.

One of my favourite walks was to the village, where we'd pop into Durrant's Bakery. The smell was delectable and there'd be flour in the air, on arms and faces—what could be more appealing? Mr. and Mrs. Durrant, their son Ernie and daughter Rose, ran this bakery— a blessing for the village. Mum asked early on if they were French; when told they were English, she pronounced their name in the English way—with almost equal stress though a little more on the first syllable. They, however, preferred stress at the end but were far too polite to correct her. So we grew up saying it wrong. It is hard now, having used this word so often and with such happy memories, to think of it the other way.

Their Eccles cakes were better than any I've ever tasted. Of their breads, we loved their round Coburg loaf with its four crusty peaks, which we cut in chunks, not slices—having a large piece with butter and raspberry jam when we got home from school. Next came their oval malt loaf and a flatter, rectangular brown one. Then their long square sandwich loaves, which Mum bought for tea parties. When she made sandwiches we'd hang about in the kitchen to snaffle those crusts when they were sliced off. Best of all, though, were their rolls: round white or brown buns and their Parker House rolls. We bought dozens of each for Sunday breakfast and more again in summer for lunch on the lawn. But the *plat de résistance* was their meat pies. They were scrumptious! Two or three dozen would be needed for our family and hangers-on. I've had a great many meat pies in my life, but none came close to theirs. Even during the war, when meat and butter were severely rationed, they were full of meat and as good as ever. I just wish they'd made a cookbook.

37. HEALTH

There was talk of public health care in BC in the thirties but nothing much came of it. If there was a scare of an epidemic, Miss Morrison, the nurse at Lampson Street School, took care of us—jabbing our arms so gently we scarcely noticed. Penicillin, invented in 1928, was available by 1938 but reserved for those in the armed forces until after the war. If you were injured, with broken bones, or terribly ill you went to St. Joseph's or the Royal Jubilee Hospital. Otherwise you saw your doctor in his office or his home. But more than likely he made a house call. For all of this you paid: with money, a chicken, a sack of potatoes or a promise. Some never paid. Times were tough. It was very much worse for the unemployed—those poor men who spent years crisscrossing the country on the tops of trains, searching for jobs. If they caught flu, pneumonia or measles living outside in their Hobo Jungles, they sought help where they could. An historian puts it rather coldly—*Indigents flooded the hospitals*—as if this was their fault. Health was considered a family affair. Tough luck if you were hungry, on your own and out of work.

We were lucky. Mum was a patient, caring nurse. She would sit with whoever was sick, sewing or darning, if we were feverish. Or reading to us by the hour when we were getting better. She never made us feel a nuisance—quite the reverse, she seemed glad to have this private time with her "sick one," as if this was somehow her treat. How she coped I can't imagine, but she did, keeping the whole house functioning smoothly: cooking for the family as well as her patient.

In between our bouts of illness she insisted on personal hygiene. Not the "pink toothbrush" we read about in magazines—to be treated only with "Ipana and massage" (Ipana toothpaste and gum massage to prevent bleeding)—nor the dreaded B.O., which could be cured only with LIFE BUOY Soap. No, much more basic. We washed our hands frequently and we each had our particular towels and facecloths that were hung separately in our own spot. If any of us fell ill, we were isolated immediately, unless it was something like mumps—considered easier to endure as a child than an adult. I shared a room with Mike when he caught mumps, poor guy—moaning and groaning for weeks with vast puffy cheeks—but never did catch them myself. Was there some magic then, to disease, that some became sick and others didn't?

In between sickness, Mum dosed us with Scott's Emulsion or cod liver oil—that appalling stuff that claims to be "pleasant tasting—of course." The only thing I liked about it was the vast cod on the fisherman's back, printed on the box and embossed on the bottle. The cod was almost as long as the fisherman and so heavy that one of his feet came off the ground! Far more pleasant was malt extract and something called Castoria. Was it really made from beavers? These doses were "in case." If we had colds she rubbed Vicks VapoRub under our noses or put hot mustard plasters on our chests. Those with trouble breathing inhaled steam with eucalyptus oil floating on bowls of hot water—our heads smothered in thick towels. For anything worse there was always a purge with the dreaded castor oil—made from the castor bean.

When I was three I experienced the noise and smell of Hospitals—something you never forget. Hilly and Mike needed their tonsils and adenoids removed. "Why not throw Ba in too?" our doctor said. "She'll probably need hers out sooner or later." So off I went with them to the Royal Jubilee. We were put together in a small room and told over and over by a bustling nurse, crackling in her starched uniform, just how lovely it would be *afterward*, when we could eat as much ice cream as we wanted.

Hilly was wheeled away first and Mike and I called, "Goodbye!" After a while she came back prone—absolutely silent. Was she dead? Then they wheeled Mike out. He came back prone too. Were they both dead? I was desperate. Then they came for me! The operating room nurses used the same line about *ice cream* and *afterward*. And Dr. Duck, the anesthetist, arrived whistling and told jokes that weren't funny as he put me out.

Later, when I came to, Mike and Hilly were chatting wanly. But none of us felt like eating ice cream, or anything else, for weeks.

(To keep out of the hands of doctors, the important thing is to climb lots of trees, run as fast as you can and keep breathing in the salt sea air! Then you'll stay healthy. Thus sayeth the Elephant's Child.)

38. THE BENEFIT of FRESH AIR

Trips to Esquimalt village were always exciting whether in a push-cart, held firmly by the hand or walking smartly under one's own steam. There was so much to see and I never knew who I would meet en route.

I loved looking at the houses—wondering, as we passed, about the families who lived in them, how many people there were and how they all fitted in. Our house was large, but even so we had to share rooms, and if someone went off to college or some such, we all shifted about. Most of the village houses were far smaller than ours, so I always wondered how the occupants managed—and just how many they could squeeze in if they had to.

There was a house on the northwest corner of Lyall and Fraser that gave me a glimpse of what went on within—for on the balcony that ran across the front of the house was a bed, and on that bed lay a young woman. Was it a question of space? Why else was she there? Whenever we passed that house she'd be there, lying comfortably, watching all the passersby. She was so close to the sidewalk we could see her well and she us. She seemed to be almost on our laps. Did she spend the night there too? I didn't go to the village after dark in those days, so that mystery remains.

Each time we saw that young woman I'd ask Mum about her. Was she ill and, if so, who looked after her?

There was little Mum could or would tell me, other than that we must respect her privacy. "Smile and say hello—but don't stare. Whatever the situation, she must benefit from the fresh air."

I longed to know more. Was she really sick? Was she comfortable?

Once in January 1936, when I was four and a half, Mum and I met people we knew as we were passing this mysterious house. They told us the king had died—King George V. Mum was visibly upset. But all she could say seemed curious: "This is the third king to die in my lifetime—but the first in yours." Was I to expect a long line of dead kings?

At last, after many years of wondering, thanks to Marjorie Hawker, née Coton, whose parents ran the shop Round the Corner, which sat across the street from that house, I have an explanation. The young woman was Anne Kennedy and she had TB. Perhaps she chose to stay home—for even if her family could have afforded Tranquille, BC's sanatorium for tuberculosis in those days, her treatment would have been pretty much the same. There she would have had rest and mountain air. In Esquimalt she had rest and *sea* air. So she was nursed at home and kept outside. When she got really ill she was moved inside. And, still quite young, she died.

But during that long and difficult time, whenever she could, Marjorie would hop across the street and visit her friend. Afterward, so glad to be well—to be alive, to be outside and moving—she'd leap right across the open ditch on her way home. That was quite a leap—from death to life! And those ditches were wide. Damp fascinating places, rich in strange plants, insects and animals—or full of rushing water.

As for the king, we had three kings that year, for George V died in January; Edward VIII followed in succession, then abdicated in December to marry his fiancée, Wallis Simpson, a commoner and twice-divorced American woman; so his younger brother, Albert Edward Arthur George, became George VI and was crowned the following May.

The British Empire had been in turmoil for over a year, so that coronation in 1937 was greeted with delight. In Victoria, to commemorate the day, ships of the Royal Navy, stationed in Esquimalt and anchored in Esquimalt Harbour on that vast piece of water known as Royal Roads, put on a magnificent display of fireworks for all to enjoy.

We sat on rugs on Beacon Hill with thousands of others—waiting for the sky to darken. Then from all those ships below us, adrift on the Strait of Juan de Fuca, came the most amazing fireworks I have ever seen. They weren't just blasts of coloured light but whole scenes of royal families, ancient and modern—of battles and victories well before and during the reign of the House of Windsor. We, all of us, oohhhed and ahhhed and squealed with pleasure—thrilled and delighted that this shy and stuttering prince would be our king and, together with his beautiful wife, Queen Elizabeth, and the two young princesses, Elizabeth and Margaret Rose, just a little older than I was, would reign over us for a time that we hoped would be both long and glorious.

I have never seen fireworks to compare with them since. They must have cost a fortune. And this was during the worst of the Depression. So I wonder how the hungry felt—all those unfortunate people without work, without shelter, with little or no food to eat and no prospects at all, in threadbare clothing and little or nothing on their feet. Did they rejoice?

And as for young Anne Kennedy, had she been awake and looking in the right direction—over the treetops and the low hills toward Beacon Hill Park—she too could have seen much of that miraculous display, right from her bed.

39. WHEN GRANNY CAME

When Granny came to stay she always brought her youngest daughter, Frances Esther Dudley, with her. Aunt Fran had polio at eighteen and spent the rest of her life in a wheelchair, at home. When she wasn't gadding about with her mother or going on painting trips, the two of them would cross the country by train. They would take the overnight CPR boat in Vancouver to arrive in Victoria the next morning, where Dad would meet them.

Once at our house, Granny would walk up the front steps with us, while Dad drove Aunt Fran around to the back of the house. There he'd had a long gravel ramp built especially for her, edged with a stone and concrete balustrade. It sloped up from the basement door to the terrace, where she had easy access to the main floor of the house. The slope was steep, so I don't know how in the world he managed to push her up, because she was large and heavy and quite demanding. But even with his sore shoulders and sciatica he never complained—in fact, he insisted that he be the one to push her, both up and down.

Our lives changed considerably for the month or two Granny was with us. Knight photo (ca. 1935)

Granny came to see her twins and their children, so she preferred staying in our house. But Aunt Fran came to swim. Swimming was her joy and delight, and the seawater in the Crystal Garden pool was world famous. For people like her, who sat in a wheelchair with iron braces on her legs, the buoyancy of seawater gave her a grace and ease of movement she found nowhere else. She much preferred staying at the Empress Hotel, where she could be pushed across the road to swim—several times a day, if she wished. None of us can remember how she was lowered into the pool, but the hotel was expecting people in wheelchairs and knew exactly what to do.

Wherever they stayed, for the month or two they were with us our lives changed considerably. For one thing, Granny insisted we hire a Chinese cook—to come for several months before she arrived, to get the hang of things, and then stay on afterward so Mum could readjust. Granny paid for these cooks. In theory this was to give us a treat, and Mum a bit of a holiday, but in actual fact Granny wanted her entire attention. She and Aunt Fran expected to be taken on jaunts—if not daily, at least several times a week, with or without Auntie Bella. This meant that both Mum and Dad were tied up for the duration of their stay.

The year I turned seven, Granny wrote suggesting that I join them for a week at the Empress. That was pretty heady stuff and I was enormously excited. I had eaten at the Empress but had never stayed there. Most of all, though, I loved the idea of all that time with Granny. Two pairs of pale yellow and pink flannelette pyjamas were bought for the occasion, and a new bathing suit.

But when they arrived, Aunt Fran said, "*NO!*" She didn't want a *brat* around—is how she put it. So when they got home to Les Groisardières, on l'île d'Orléans, Granny sent me a present. It was an old ivory jewellery box lined with purple velvet and filled with trinkets and treasures—things she thought I might enjoy, including a silver bracelet I've worn most of my life. It was a dear, kind gesture that didn't blot out my disappointment. But by that time I was eight years old, grown up, and didn't mind so much.

40. CLOTHING

Mum's childhood spanned the end of the nineteenth century and the beginning of the twentieth. In those days clothing was made of natural fabrics: fur, leather, rubber, silk, cotton, linen, wool or Viyella—a mix of wool and cotton. Girls were covered up, even in summer, with high collars, long sleeves and hemlines ankle-length or to mid-calf, their legs in long stockings, their feet in button boots. When they went out they wore hats with wide brims. The important thing was to protect their skin from the sun. They were considered *ruined* if their flesh was browned, even a tiny bit. How modern that seems now—how sensible. But I used to look in horror at photos of Mum and her sisters swaddled in all that cloth—when they could have been running free as we did in shorts and T-shirts, our arms, legs and feet bare or in sandals or simple runners of the kind one can climb in—the kind I still wear. Or even better, sunbathing by the hour—soaking in the sun till our skin turned golden brown or was

Aunt Evie in wool, holding Tom, with Mum in silk at Les Grois-ardières, Québec, in 1913.

covered in freckles. We felt strengthened, empowered by the sun. Only now do we suffer the consequence of that delicious freedom.

One thing always surprised me in those early photos. Once girls of her era reached their teens, off came the boots, at least in summer in the country, and on went those same simple runners. I can see them in photos of the girls out sailing with friends, playing tennis or sitting about chatting on the verandahs of their family home. But was this just in Mum's family? They were always a little different, if not rebels. Those shoes look so sweet, peeking out from under their elegant long skirts.

In Mum's youth, women wore extraordinary bathing suits: long puffy pantaloons with ruffles to mid-calf, a dress-like shirt with elastic at the waist—the hem reaching well below their hips—and three-quarter-length puffy sleeves. Topping all this was a gathered cap of the same cloth. Gradually bathing suits were made of wool and far less elaborate. They still had legs that extended several inches beyond an overskirt to approximately mid-thigh. This skirt affair was part of the main body of the garment, with narrow shoulder straps and a series of curious open holes under the arms. Men's bathing suits were similar. Mum and Dad wore such things when I was small. There was an advantage, they said, to woollen suitings. They kept one warm, whether wet or dry.

At Savira there was a whole collection of ancient bathing suits that came with the house, left there by the previous owners who ran the place as a small hotel. The suits hung from antler hooks in the hall between the annex, where the bedrooms were, and the main part of the house—a weird yet rather splendid display. I wish we'd had the wit to keep them. They would be treasures now.

As Mum's life got more hectic—and she the only *cook and bottle washer*—she designed smocks to be worn over bathing suits: knee-length, with long sleeves, a collar and open neck, with smocking across the chest and around the wrists. She ordered two of cotton crepe: one blue, the other green. After a dip in the lake she would undress on the beach inside a vast terry cloth tent with a drawstring around the neck—then

Dad swims in the rain, Rivière du-Loup, Québec, ca. 1899.

slip on a dry bathing suit and then the smock. Thus she was able to take a dip whenever she felt the urge. That way, though always preoccupied feeding her family plus friends and relations, she felt a certain delicious freedom: ready to swim at all times, yet dressed well enough to receive anyone.

My first bathing suits were woollen too, hand-me-downs undoubtedly, and I can remember the cosy feel of them. Then the excitement of my first new cotton suit of mauve and blue print with its gathered skirt and puckered elasticized bodice. Later they were nylon and simpler in design but always with a tiny residual skirt across the crotch. That bit of you never to be seen!

Once on the coast, Mum realized her daughters wanted to join their brothers climbing trees, so she bought them boys' brown overalls. Then they could explore in comfort, fill their pockets with stones,

Mary and Helen model new bathing suits at the lake, ca. 1939.
Netzer's Island is in the middle distance.

conkers, marbles or apples, and climb or scramble anywhere. I think Michael was the last to wear these treasures. When I came along I was put into Jamie's old sailor suits (he and I were the same shape), still quite fresh and new: striped navy blue and white for mornings, white for afternoons—complete with lanyard and whistle. In those days it was obvious. I would be a sailor.

In the mid-thirties, long pants came into vogue for women. They were called "beach pyjamas" and had very wide legs. The first pair handed down to me was of deep beetroot-red linen. I loved them and would swoosh around feeling very grand and grown up, convinced that I would be a torch singer—some day—and in the meantime practising "Moonlight Becomes You," "As Time Goes By," "Dancing in the Dark," "The Nearness of You" and other songs. By this time, clothing of rayon, nylon and other artificial fabrics was becoming commonplace.

Underwear has changed a lot too. Mum came west with vests and underpants for her daughters—all of fine cotton lawn edged with embroidery or lace. Sometimes the tops buttoned onto panties. Or the panties and tops might be of one piece—buttoning under the crotch. That presumed someone, always at the ready, to undo these pesky buttons—a nanny or a governess—when the need came. Sometimes they wore "waists" of wool with little tabs coming down to button onto woollen panties.

By the thirties these were phasing out. We wore modern panties with elastic at the waist, sometimes made of the same cloth as our dresses, and pulled separate vests of cotton or wool over our heads. Women wore the same sorts of things underneath, but to keep their figures trim and to hold up their stockings they also wore suspenders, girdles and bras, corsets or corselettes that combined girdle and bra, plus suspenders to hold up stockings. Some were boned with whalebone inserts—set in narrow slots so they could be replaced when they snapped. (I remember seeing a group of elderly French women buying these whalebone strips in the Notions Department of the Galeries Lafayette in Paris in the early sixties—all of them laughing and joking about overindulgence at New Year's.) Originally these garments were laced down the back and cinched tight by one's lady's maid. Mum's had hooks down the front—a long line of them so she could do the job herself. But what agony she must have felt, squeezing her small body into one of these after her carefree summer garb.

For everyday wear our clothing came from W. and J. Wilson's or David Spencer's department store. It would be of wool or cotton—of good cut and made to last. At Christmas the Aunts sent us all manner of garments, but these were often far too fussy for the west coast or not of the right size, so they went right into Mum's Peace River boxes. In theory, garments were handed down the line, but sometimes when things got to me they were worn out or didn't fit so, to my sisters' disgust, new stuff was bought.

Fashion was not *ordained* in Esquimalt, as it seemed to be in places like Oak Bay, where everyone tended to look alike in sweater sets and pearls, tweed suits and so on. The dress code was probably even stricter in the Uplands, where one was not allowed the necessities of life—like cats and dogs, chickens or horses and certainly not a clothesline! But then, you never saw anyone there at all. Were the inhabitants in a constant stupor—overcome by their newfound wealth? Or were they all off on grand tours? Whenever we drove through the Uplands we'd search for some sign of life. Once we saw a gardener slip away behind a bush. Perhaps there was a rule about gardens and gardeners too. Perfection, inside or out, was not to be disturbed. No, in Esquimalt one could wear or do whatever one chose. Life was simple, variety appreciated.

The men of our acquaintance wore the same sorts of things year-round—with fewer layers in summer. Dad may have had more outfits than some: his ancient tails and morning coat, his dinner jacket and riding gear, his plus-fours for golf and his beloved blazer and drill shorts. Compared to him, others looked pretty drab. But those relics of his, plus all our winter coats and greatcoats, had to be lugged down to the lawn to be aired and sunned on

Here is Dad, with his morning coat pressed, dressed for a special occasion. H.M.P. photo

a dry day in late spring. They'd be checked for moths; we'd turn the collars up and the pockets inside out, then brush them carefully. After that we'd lug them back to where they came from, their pockets stuffed with herbs, camphor or mothballs for safekeeping. In this way, woollen clothing lasted. It was a huge job—this spring checking. So if possible it would be done on a Saturday when there were many hands available. Otherwise Mum and I did it together.

As for the women we knew, some, like Alice Pooley, seemed to have kept on wearing clothing from the last century. They might appear in huge hats sprouting bouquets of flowers or feathers, their skirts to the ground, their jackets with tiny pleats and mutton-chop sleeves and bodices with many pockets and small buttons right down the front. Or fitted coats of corded silk, black of course, with sculpted buttons—some looking almost edible.

Many of my friend's mothers wore housedresses year-round—covered, sometimes, with a cardigan in winter. They were of cotton print, narrow in shape with short sleeves, rather puffed. In this way the *homemaker* had no need to roll up her sleeves. She was ready to plunge her arms into bread dough or a vat of hot sudsy water, to hang the laundry, do the ironing, race about the house with a carpet sweeper, broom and mop—or weed the garden. Intrigued by these garments that seemed so sensible, I urged Mum to get some. But she refused—said she wouldn't be seen dead in one and claimed they were a west coast invention. Maybe, or was it that she hadn't met any *homemakers* in the east? Nor would she use that term to describe herself. "I'm a wife and mother!" she'd say. "Isn't that good enough?"

Mum loved well-made clothes and enjoyed wearing beautiful things, like the floor-length silk-velvet opera cloak with its white fur collar that Dad bought her in a moment of madness, as he always had before *the Crash*, when times were flush. But she didn't *need* new things, as some women do. She managed with what she had.

There were many single women in Esquimalt, the *Spinsters of our Parish*—casualties of the Great War living on meagre incomes, who managed somehow to keep shod and find "coverings" of some sort to keep themselves warm, cool or dry. Some were cleverer than others at looking smart, but many had a pinched and desperate look about them, carrying on with only the dream of that lost love or the possibility that there had been someone for them somewhere—who died in that terrible war.

A glorious exception lived with her mother in a red house (that same deep brick red of many Esquimalt houses) just across the street on the corner of Greenwood and Lampson. Her name was Theo Paddon. She did what unmarried daughters were expected to do—looked after her elderly widowed mother. But there was nothing sad about her. She painted, and their house was full of bright interesting canvases that kept changing when Mum and I went there for tea. On those occasions I was allowed to explore their garden with its fishponds and little bridges and strange flowers—just across the road, but another world! Theo was a joyful woman, who used colour with dash and seemed to me both glamorous and exotic. She was older

Dad is dressed for the stables, while Mum is dressed for town.
H.V.P photo (1941)

than my brothers but came to our dances and tennis parties. When her mother died, she married her love and became Theo Bruce and was, by all accounts, extremely happy.

The cloche hat and long slender profile of the twenties suited Mum to perfection, and finding such clothing comfortable and adaptable, she kept wearing it. One could create a new outfit in a wink by adding some beads, a scarf, a belt or a hat of a different colour. There were, of course, many broad squat women who seemed about to burst in that style. I daren't hug them because of that and could see with half an eye their clothing would look much better on a thinner woman. Why didn't they just accept the lovely pouter pigeon shapes they were and be comfortable? With slender legs and arms, no one notices middles.

It was obvious that pretty arms and legs were essential. Why, then, had we, the five Piddington girls, inherited the heavy bones, the strong arms and legs of Dad's sisters along with the broad shoulders and narrow hips from Mum's side? Somehow we'd drawn the short end of the stick. Mum didn't make much of this, but she was obviously disappointed. And always, in the background, lurked Anna Cicely, her first and perfect daughter, who would surely have had the good sense to resemble all aspects of her mother.

Dad was much more accepting. We were beautiful to him. He loved and admired his sisters, after all, with their flashing Irish eyes, and he adored his mother. All of them were heavy boned, but hadn't his eldest sister, Florence Mignonette (Flossie to us), been a renowned beauty? For once, on a grand tour with her parents, some rich Americans had offered them a vast sum of money as they rode together to the top of the *Tour Eiffel*—if only they could adopt this lovely creature. They couldn't, of course. (*But what about the White Slave Trade?* we'd whisper to each other under our breath when Dad told this tale. Sometimes our parents seemed so unworldly!)

Dad wanted us strong and healthy—able to do all that our brothers could, yet looking and being as natural as possible. He didn't give a fig about heavy legs and arms if we were quick and active. We needed muscles to climb rocks and trees, to row boats or ride horses. And certainly Sylvia couldn't have been a whiz at polo if she'd had skinny ladylike arms.

Far more important to me than the size and shape of limbs was their adornment: a liberal sprinkling of bramble-scratches, scars and bruises was essential. And how I yearned for a cast cinching a broken bone. My friend Mary got a lot of attention when her limbs were in casts. But I had to make do with mending the limbs of dolls and found this so engrossing that, for a time, I considered being a surgeon.

As we grew, our ideas changed—so did our shapes. Pudgy small bodies stretched and became slender. Then changed again. Miracles happened then, as now. And once, in my twenties, when walking along an empty boulevard in the smartest part of Paris, on my way to see friends in the middle of the afternoon, an ambulance came roaring along—sirens wailing: *Pam pom—Pam pom—Pam pom— Pam pom—Pam pom!* It screeched to a stop beside me. The driver leaned out the window—whistled and said, *"Quelles jambes!"* Then went roaring off again. So they couldn't have been that bad.

Nowadays our daughter wears my dresses and my coats some- times—things I wore in Paris in the sixties, when I was her age. And I look with delight at her slender arms and legs—inherited from her father. Like him, she is strong. Stronger, even, than I was.

41. COOKING or THOSE MYSTIC RITES

In Mum's family, and Dad's too, as far back as anyone can remember there were servants, and the mistress of the house kept out of the kitchen—except on rare occasions to supervise certain dishes or to consult the cook. If inclined, she could make jellies, jams and fruit vinegars in season—but only on *Cook's Day Off.* Otherwise food was prepared by the kitchen staff and served at table—in the breakfast room, the dining room or the drawing room. Thus the daughters of each generation would appreciate good food but had no idea how to make it. Only after marriage would they control, to some extent, what was served in their own dining rooms. Until the Depression, it was like that in our house too.

Even for those not affected by the crash of 1929, things were changing. My sister Joanie remembers Sunday suppers with Aunt Phyl and Uncle Paul while nursing in Montreal in the mid-forties.

They had just moved from their big house to an apartment and felt they were camping—"playing house," with a cook as their only live-in servant. Sunday was her day off so she would leave the table set and simple meals prepared. They were to serve themselves and wash the dishes afterward. They did this together, feeling very modern, almost risqué. When she was there, Joanie helped but was surprised how long it took to wash so few dishes and to learn that glass *must* be washed in cold water. The first time Aunt Phyl and Uncle Paul accomplished this mystic rite, they were so thrilled they phoned both Mum and Auntie Bella long-distance to tell what they'd done.

Mum learned to cook in the south of France when she and her small boys were staying in a comfortable *pension* in Cannes. When conditions worsened, their *pension* was taken over by the military and they had to move into an apartment. In a panic she consulted the cook, who showed her how to roast things and to make soups and stews and other simple dishes. Mum went to the mayor about fuel for cooking. An ancient man, he sighed. There was none. But she could gather twigs and pine cones in the hills. Food was rationed by then, and amounts per person skimpy, so she gave the boys her butter, sugar and protein—while she ate fruit, vegetables and rice. Occasionally she bought a scrawny hen at the market and fattened it on their scraps. Once it was dispatched by the butcher, she would roast it for a special treat. She often fell asleep counting pine cones— but with them and those invaluable lessons from the cook, she was able to make simple meals and came to enjoy cooking.

Then, feeling faint, she consulted a doctor about a tonic. He was ancient too—all able-bodied men were at the Front. He saw with half an eye that she was starving. "Eat your rations!" he ordered. "You'll be no use to your boys if you collapse."

Like so many veterans of the Great War, Dad needed to do something positive—like work with the soil, grow food. So he studied horticulture at Macdonald College near Québec City, then ran a commercial apple orchard in the Eastern Townships. While there, Mum helped out as stopgap between cooks, but it was in Esquimalt, during the Depression, that she became full-time cook by necessity. Her twin, too, had to learn when widowed in 1924. Both became excellent cooks but would argue about whose sponge cake was better and whether their favourite cookbook should be called *Fannie Farmer* or *The Boston Cooking-School Cook Book*. How lucky we were to have such good examples.

Even so, most of my sisters didn't do much cooking until they left home. Occasionally they made fudge or candy or concocted something for special occasions, like Sylvia's delectable White Mountain Cake with Sea Foam Icing. Searching for that recipe just now, I found treasure. Tucked inside one of Mum's early editions of *The Boston Cook Book* (she had one for town and one for the Lake) was a recipe for "Mademoiselle T.'s Prune Cake" or plum cake. It is in French, in Mum's writing—a young and vigorous hand and obviously dictated by that helpful cook in the *pension* in Cannes.

My siblings who loved riding spent much of their after-school time mucking out stables, grooming any number of horses and exercising them. They found this fun, but there was little space in their days for anything else. I was supposed to ride too but was put on a horse at a very young age—then told to fall off. I looked down. Saw the distance, thought it ludicrous and refused. So I took refuge in the kitchen at an early age. It became a haven, and cooking my delight. When my friend Mary was staying with us at the Lake, we cooked together, cadging flour from the kitchen, turning it into bread, buns or cakes, adding lake water and salal juice for colour and flavour. Our kitchen tables were little seats nailed between pines and cedars just above the beach by earlier owners of Savira some fifty years before. For us, aged five to about eight, their height was perfect and we worked away completely engrossed—discussing, non-stop, the joys and complications of our world. When a batch seemed particularly delicious, we'd sell some to Dad or another big-hearted grownup until we had enough pennies to buy two five-cent all-day suckers at Shawnigan village.

In Esquimalt, we had both a wood stove and an electric stove in the kitchen. Mum preferred cooking on the Great Majestic with wood. This makes me wonder, now, who cleaned out the ash and cinders and laid the fireplaces throughout the house, then laid and lit the kitchen stove in the morning? And who brought in the wood or coal? I can't remember. When I was small, those chores seemed such an everyday thing they went unnoticed. I am ashamed of that now, for I know what an effort it is to keep wood stoves and heaters clean and functioning. So I marvel at what my parents managed to do so gracefully after 1929—things they had never done before. There is a huge difference between *having to do* and *doing occasionally*.

Later, when furnace oil became too expensive, both wood stove and furnace were converted to sawdust. Mum hated the pails of it sitting by the stove and the great pile of it outside. It was nasty stuff—heavy and awkward, and we all got fleas. But the promise was: "You can fill your hopper with your white gloves on!"

In the thirties and forties, decent females weren't seen outside without gloves. One wore spotless white cotton in warm

Mum preferred cooking on the Great Majestic, the woodstove brought up from Wychbury.
H.V.P. photo

weather, long white kid gloves—up over the elbow—for dances, and leather gloves or fur or woollen mitts in winter. The unclad hand was for ruffians—those who climbed trees, like us. Rubber gloves weren't part of our lives. Perhaps they hadn't been invented. But in our house, by the kitchen sink, there was always a cut lemon to whiten our hands—and a bottle of Hinds' Honey and Almond Cream. That name puzzled me. Shouldn't they have called it Hands' Honey and Almond Cream?

42. THE SORE EYE

When Phyllis was born, our Chinese cook told Mum her new baby was delicate. "I think you keep this baby warm. Keep hat on this baby's head." How prescient he was. All her life she has suffered from poor circulation. Though immensely strong, as that cook predicted, she is also delicate.

Because she was the tallest of his last three children, Dad called her "Hilltops," then shortened it to "Hilly," and most of us still call her that.

From an early age she suffered terribly from headaches. Each time they struck, she would have to lie down under the covers, wrap a mohair scarf around her head and cover her eyes with a cold compress. She might endure twenty-four hours of excruciating pain—during which she would vomit three times. Then she'd be fine—until the next one struck.

These headaches often came when she was asked to a party. For some reason her friends gave more parties than Michael's or mine. We were a bit jealous, even though she rarely, if ever, went to the parties she was invited to. A present would be bought, her best dress washed and pressed, shoes whitened or polished, and everything she needed readied. Then, at the last minute, just before Dad was to drive her across town, she would get what she called "a sore eye" and would have to lie down in a darkened room. This happened so often we came to expect it and so did she. Excitement and anticipation upset her so much they brought on a protective reaction, the sore eye. But it wasn't till years later anyone realized that what she had was migraine headaches.

As for the rest of us, if we were asked anywhere, we accepted with pleasure and we went. Only once was I thwarted. I'd been asked to a birthday party just a step down Lampson Street. I can't remember if that yellow house belonged to the Houghtons then or the Godfreys. At three or four years old I needed an afternoon nap, but, if woken I'd be bad-tempered. On that day I didn't wake until an hour after the party began. Then, as some strange lesson, I was walked up and down in front of the house. I could hear shouts and shrieks and see my friends playing and running about but couldn't join them *because I was late!* Curious, I thought then. And still do.

As for Hilly, migraines blighted her childhood and adult years, but after the birth of her third child these terrible headaches ceased entirely.

43. EARS

At some point during the fall of the year I turned six I started having earaches. I was enjoying Grade One at Lampson Street School and all the curious things we were asked to do, but what I remember best now was gazing up at the red leaves of a Virginia creeper that fluttered at the edges of windows above my head—then watching as each leaf was snatched by wind and floated away, out of sight. The Grade One desks faced south.

Well before Christmas my earaches got worse. They throbbed and ached or rumbled all day and at night erupted foul brown evil-smelling sticky stuff onto my pillow.

So I was kept home from school and moved from the southwest bedroom I shared with Mike and Hilly into Dad's dressing room. That made it easier for Mum to come when I cried or needed a fresh towel on my pillow.

This went on for months: the pounding and aching all day—the eruptions each night. I knew I should feel privileged sleeping there and being kept home, but I longed to go to school. At least I could spend time with Tim or be alone in the garden or the woods, be read to or play with treasures kept in my toys box.

It wasn't until spring that a doctor was summoned. He came one afternoon and examined me in the dining room. That seemed strange at the time but perhaps the light was better there. He had a hard black suitcase and lots of gadgets and tools and a machine with a light in it that he poked in my ears. Before he began, he tried to cajole me with a chocolate bar, a Nut Milk bar, the last sort I would have chosen in the whole world, so I had no confidence in him and wasn't a bit surprised when he said, "I see nothing wrong with her ears."

Gradually they got better on their own. But by that time I'd missed the rest of the school year.

While languishing there in Dad's dressing room, I remembered Mum's claim that he'd lost his business and clothes sense after leaving Québec, yet he always looked super to me—whether in riding breeches or drill shorts or slacks held up with his rope belt. He was carefree and casual—a bit windblown, a man of action who would go to town in summer in shorts and knee socks, an open-necked Viyella shirt under his old navy blue blazer with its regimental scarlet zig-zag trim, and still look smart and handsome. And he was splendid in his ancient dinner jacket, his morning coat and striped grey trousers or his evening dress and tails. But he looked best of all when dressed for polo, in his canary yellow woollen jersey and white breeches.

I thought about this as I lay in his dressing room recuperating. It was a smallish room and rather dark. On one wall was a painting of a Mum I didn't recognize, by their friend W.J. Copeman, her hair like a cloche cap on her head. There was a tall clothes horse with branching arms on which Dad hung garments he would change into, a comfortable chair, a window looking out onto the huge arbutus, and doors—into their bedroom, their bathroom, the upstairs hall, and a cupboard. One day, when I was supposed to be napping, I got up and peeked inside his mahogany chest of drawers with its inset brass handles. There, in the two top drawers, I found relics of his past. One held silk scarves, all of marvellous colours: cream, blue, mauve or green—some striped, some spotted, some zigzag, some paisley. On the right were his gloves. The ones I liked best were dove grey suede, thick and dense—of a quality I have never seen equalled. Tucked in amongst both drawers were bars of scented soap: Roger and Gallet's *Oeillet Mignardise*. Their scent thrilled me. Occasionally Dad would wear one of the scarves or a pair of those gloves. But most of these treasures were never used. They were indeed from another sort of life—an entirely different way of living.

But then my own cupboard, here in Sidney Bay, is full of

Dad occasionally wore his elegant scarves, each of marvellous colour and quality.
Knight photo (ca. 1944)

conundrums: elegant dresses and coats, silk blouses, even Mother's old floor-length opera cloak, all of them saved for who knows when—perhaps for our daughter, Arabella; perhaps for our granddaughter, Sophie—because there comes a time when good clothes become high style again. Just this summer Arabella went back to Vancouver with five or six pairs of my French, Italian and Spanish shoes—all scarcely worn but beautifully made and lined with fine leather. Recycling at its best.

And though Dad's scarves are frail and rotting, it pleases me to wear them—just as it would please him to see them worn. And I think of him when I open my drawers to the gorgeous scent of *Oeillet Mignardise* and whenever I bathe with that same luxurious soap.

44. LOLO

*D*uring my early years we had Lolo—living with us, then near us, or in our hearts. Now we have Lalo (the Chilean diminutive for Edward), our great-nephew, living in Toronto. Both were born on April 1. This piece is about Lolo.

Lolo or Lo was our name for Helen Roach. She came from Gloucestershire—or the West Country, as she called it. Her fiancé had died during the Great War, so she, like thousands of bereaved women, was left stranded in England without hope of finding a husband. Bright and enterprising, she made her way to Canada. Early in 1927 she came to live with us, hired to look after the new baby, Phyllis Angela. There were several other hearty, strapping girls, like Irish Eileen—governesses for the older children, who are remembered more or less by their charges, but they never achieved the status of Miss Roach. She was a family treasure.

Lolo was no more than five feet three inches but she carried herself well and looked imposing. When aggravated, or at a loss for words, she would tilt her long head slightly to the right, then gaze up to the left, as if for divine instruction. This made her seem wise and extraordinarily tall—especially to children. She had style, an attractive figure, was flirtatious and full of energy—the sort who stir the air when they enter a room. You could not ignore her. To *us*, the last three, she was magical. We adored her. But the letter R is not easy for small mouths. No one remembers who was the first to call her "Miss Loach"; then gradually she became Lo, Loie, or Lolo, and to this day, long after her death, she is still called one or other of those names by all who loved her.

When we ate upstairs in the nursery, Lolo would oversee our meals, and after supper she'd bathe and sing to us. Then Dad would appear and sing some more. We'd say our prayers with Mum and be

Lolo or Lo, on Roy at Wychbury, was a family treasure.

tucked in. She would check that our coverlets were folded at the foot of each bed and our raspberry-coloured eiderdowns were floating over our blankets. Then she'd kiss each one. And last, but not least, she would sing us a going-to-sleep song. It might be "Day is done, gone the sun, from the lake, from the hills, from the sky..." or "Now the day is over, night is drawing nigh, shadows of the evening steal across the sky..." Or her favourite, the Icelandic "On the wings of night declining sinks the westering sun to sleep..." Before she'd finished any of them, I'd be adrift in my steep-hulled boat-bed, floating over the wooden sea of our room, the others' two beds remote and distant—to be seen again next morning. These nightly sendoffs were the way of things in our house. But when I went away to stay with friends I was amazed to find other children ate with adults at every meal and weren't sung to—ever!

Lolo had a marvellous imagination. She made walks anywhere an adventure. In summer she often came with us to the Lake, and some of my favourite memories are of days too cold or too wet to go outside, when Lolo would take us to *a strange and distant land* we'd never seen before. We'd have a picnic there—all of us sitting inside on the floor. She was wonderfully appreciative of anything we made or did and praised us to the skies. We didn't get much of that at home. Our big brothers often thought us "idjits" or asinine and said so. But Lo's unstinting love tempered this—so those of us in her charge had a blissful childhood.

With the crash of '29, when our funds *went south*, most live-in help was let go. In the fall of 1933, when I was two, Lolo moved across the street to live in Fermoyle and teach at Royal Roads School, assistant to Miss Johnson. I was already Mum's charge, so it was Mike and Hilly who felt bereft for a day or two, until they found her again as their teacher. It was a wise move for Lolo, as at least five of us would be candidates for that school and others were sent there even from Victoria. Unable to pay for servants, some parents could still afford a little cash for school fees. So Royal Roads School flourished until 1941.

Wherever she was, I used to love sitting beside her as she prepared herself for the day or for a party. Mum let nothing but cold water touch her face. Lolo washed hers with whipping cream! She would dab at it with snatches of cream-drenched cotton wool and then, with a fingertip, take a little solid perfume from a beautifully carved small stone pot—rubbing it behind her ears and on the inside of each wrist. I wasn't the only one watching. Her lost love gazed at her from his silver frame on her dressing table, looking a bit stern. Was he wondering, as I was, if that cream would sour on her soft warm skin?

Miss Johnson, known always as Johnny, was a brittle, bird-like Englishwoman, a trained teacher who had come from a one-room school on the Prairies. I don't think she liked children much, though she was darling to us later, as adults. When we were small she seemed much more interested in her Scottie, Jock, her ancient car, Old Bill, and her Uncle Tim, who was rather smelly and lived upstairs at Fermoyle and would grump and clump about in plus-fours, a pipe clamped in his teeth. Johnny was brisk and rather scary and would never have thought of taking a child to her bosom, as Lolo would automatically. Once she ordered me into her office and demanded I not exaggerate or worry. No? I was eight years old. It was wartime. My favourite brother had just gone down with his ship (enough to give anyone nightmares). I felt I should worry a great deal more. Besides, I had switched from Lampson Street School, where we all went when money was short, and Johnny had put me into Grade Four—not Grade Three, where I belonged—so those first few months in 1939 were a challenge. It was Lolo who was the heart and soul of the school, responsible for all kindergarten classes and French, singing, dancing, drama, art, history and games. She arranged Sports Days, dance performances, Closings and Christmas Pageants—making most of the costumes herself.

In the summer of 1941, Johnny married and Royal Roads School was closed. I moved back to Lampson Street School, and Lolo opened another school in the southerly half of Bryden House, a huge and rather grand dwelling built on that wide triangle of land between Lampson Street School and Esquimalt High. She called it St. Kilda's and taught about thirty children—including our young cousin Pat Hamill. I remember it as rather an evil-smelling house with elaborate dark panelling and liver-coloured marble fixtures in the bathrooms. But the rooms were vast and high-ceilinged with huge windows, so they were bright and airy.

Michael remembers the day Bryden House burned down. He and Dad heard the alarm and raced up to help fight the fire, but it was no use. With her insurance money Lolo bought Fermoyle and began another school. By this time Hilly had graduated from high school and was hired as assistant teacher. Mum and Dad had already moved up to Shawnigan Lake to live year-round, so Hilly rented a room above the school.

After a while, Mum rented rooms there too. This meant we had a *pied-à-terre* in town—a place we could slip down to by train when we had to shop or do business. In 1948, the year I graduated from Strathcona Lodge School, we still had rooms there and I remember Mum saying, "This is the last time you can ever be late for school. I think you should stay in town for another day!" So I arrived in style, all alone in the train, the day *after* my last term began. Mum was full of surprises like that.

Lolo loved parties, and when she ran her school in Fermoyle she gave many of them. Food was still rationed but a party meant celebration: a lot of cooking, a lot of homebrew and a chance to play the piano, to sing and to dance. It was also an excuse for a new outfit. A clever dressmaker, she could design dresses for herself without patterns and would whip one up in a matter of days, basting and pinning the cloth together into a perfect fit. She wasn't strong on sewing seams, though, and many is the time her dresses gave way during her parties or she, or others, got pricked by stray pins. She would simply pirouette, dash into her room, pin it together again and re-emerge smiling.

She was an excellent cook. If ever there were a dull moment she'd say, "Let's make something better than nice!" And we would: a cake, fudge or something super-delicious. For years she came to us for Christmas, weddings and birthdays—an accepted and much-loved member of our family.

Once when Mum went to Québec for a month to be with her mother on l'île d'Orléans, Lolo stayed with us, although she was teaching at the same time. That made the separation far easier for all of us. And Granny arranged for a live-in cook while Mum was away.

Much later, when Mum and Johnny (then happily married and living in View Royal) became old-age pensioners, they decided they should warn Lolo about the initial paperwork required for such a thing. She was, of course, years younger but was getting a little forgetful. To their amazement they discovered she had been receiving her pension for about ten years. By then Dad had died and Mum had moved into the White House in Oak Bay. Lolo was staying with our former neighbours, the Murrays, in North Saanich and, as always, was totally involved with those she was with. Sadly, she never married.

The last time we met was in Eaton's. We hadn't seen each other for years as I had been living in France. She kept saying, "Helen, my dear, you've changed! You look so grown up!" But when I said, "Lolo, you've changed a bit too," she was astonished—"How have I changed? I can't have changed!"—and was upset.

Gradually her mind got as blurry as the face of her fiancé has become for me. But she lived to a great age in a comfortable home just off West Saanich Road—strong in health and body but a hazard to the staff, as she kept going out for strolls and would be found miles away, striding along in the wrong direction. Perhaps she was heading back to Esquimalt. Dear Lolo—were you singing? I bet you were.

Lolo died in the fall of 1993, aged 102. So she was only three years younger than Mum. Rona Murray Dexter gave a party in her honour. My siblings went—all except me. I wasn't invited. Considered, perhaps, too young to be included, as so often happened in the old days. Or just too far away? But I would love to have been there—to celebrate her life, to have wept with them all.

45. SHOPPING

I have always loved shopping, whether in Victoria, Esquimalt or at Cliffside Store—where we went for mail in summer. We'd row across, then trudge up that dusty road to the store on Shawnigan East Road. In theory we went for the mail—and sometimes heard the news as Mr. Valkard, the postmaster, handed us a postcard. He'd told Mum once: *It's too bad, Mrs. Piddington, but the So-and-So's can't come this weekend.* But the real reason was to see other kids, especially those we admired but scarcely knew. We'd sit on that dusty porch, trying to look nonchalant, sipping orange crush or grape soda—hoping for the courage to talk to or smile at someone, or be involved somehow in a conversation. After a bit we'd gather up the mail and whatever we came to buy and go back down that road, into the boat and home.

Once, in a fit of extraordinary courage, we decided to have a party and asked a lot of those kids to come to our place for a dance. And they came! The evening was a huge success until Dad decided we'd been dancing long enough and sent them all home. Just as well, as some of us had arranged to walk around the lake the next morning. Fifteen turned up for that hike. It took most of the day but was as much fun as the party—if not more.

Sometimes, when Mum and I felt in need of a little adventure, we'd row across the lake, climb the twisting path to the station and take the morning train north to "Duncans." That had been the original name of Duncan, and Mum liked to use it. Our train journey took about half an hour. That gave us almost four hours to explore the town, have lunch at the Black Cat Café and do a considerable amount of window-shopping. Then we'd catch the southbound train to Cliffside station and walk down the path to Cliffside Store and on down to the wharf where our rowboat awaited us. We'd row home again—arriving in time for a late cup of tea, feeling wild and cosmopolitan, our cheeks flushed, only to find nothing much had changed in our absence and the family had coped without us. They'd had three swims and were ravenous for supper.

In Esquimalt Mike and I went to Round the Corner in the village for one-cent candy, or I'd walk with Mum to Fulmer's Drug Store, to the butcher or the baker. Other days we'd go in the other direction, toward Head Street, to the other butcher or "dear Mr. Scott, the grocer." I loved those jaunts, for that's what they were. Everything could be ordered by telephone, in those days, and delivered in a matter of minutes.

When we went to town, Mum would wear her good coat of such a dark navy blue it seemed almost black, fitted at the waist then flaring out slightly with a cape around her shoulders. If it were cold she'd fling a fox-fur around her neck, if mild a silk scarf, but she always wore one of her tricorne felt hats with a veil over her eyes and nose, then tied behind to keep her very fine hair in place. Not to be outdone, I'd be in my going-to-town clothes: a double-breasted tweed coat and the essential felt hat (both from W. and J. Wilson's), the sort of hat that women wear in Ecuador. Both of us wore gloves—leather or wool in winter, cotton in summer—and off we'd go up Lampson Street to catch the Number 4 streetcar into Victoria. We loved those occasions. Away from the house, the family and her many chores, Mum was vivacious, chatty, funny—as if she had shed a good twenty years.

Mary (now Fran), Mum and Hilly go off to town in fine spring weather, 1941. H.V.P. photo

David Spencer's was one of our favourite spots, and I was often told how just a few years earlier it had been Angus Campbell's. Later it became Eaton's. Then, in another transformation, it became the Hudson's Bay Company. If we needed gloves we'd go to the glove counter and sit on high stools, our elbows on leather pads, our hands straight up in the air. While eyeing them, the saleswoman would ask about colour and style, then return with an assortment to try on. Each pair was wrapped in tissue paper and would appear brand new when taken from its box. Wooden tongs would be inserted in each finger and opened slightly, and the insides sprinkled with a little talcum powder. Only then would she slip the gloves onto our hands. The process would be repeated until something pleased us. This ritual took time and care. It made the buying of gloves, whether of expensive leather or cotton, a process as intricate and involved as Holy Communion to the uninitiated. It was a ceremony I loved.

Buying socks was much simpler. You chose a pair you liked the look of and wrapped one around your clenched fist. If it reached around easily, those socks would fit.

David Spencer's had a special device for fitting shoes. When you found a comfortable pair, you put both feet into an X-ray machine so you could see your feet inside the shoes and judge for yourself. We found this thrilling! No one knew or worried about after-effects.

Department stores and some large shops made free deliveries until well into the 1970s. You would see their trucks passing and repassing frequently and wonder if your friends and neighbours engaged in that urban trick: taking clothes home "on approval," wearing them once, then having them picked up and returned the next day—all without spending a cent! One shop that didn't deliver was the cobbler, Bob Hawkes, in Trounce Alley. We would take our shoes in to him because he did such a good job and was a nice and intelligent man with ideas of all sorts and an interest in politics. He made you feel better after a chat.

One of the marvels of the thirties and forties was just how much shopping you could do from home. There was an iceman who kept your icebox full with weekly deliveries. Cordwood arrived regularly for fireplace, stove or furnace, as did coal or, for the more modern, sacks of sawdust.

Often desperate people came knocking, looking for work or begging for food. Others made things and sold them door to door. I remember the day a pleasant-looking man arrived with a fistful of gadgets—half whisk, half spoon. He called them egg-lifters but their uses were many. They had nicely carved wooden handles and bowls of wire. Mum bought one—then wished she'd bought them all. She used hers till she died.

In the late 1960s, on $1.49 Day at Woodward's in West Vancouver, I was amazed to see a collection of such spoons. Their design was the same but much rougher—made perhaps by a very old man or by his son or grandson. Thinking of Mum, I bought them all and gave them to special people who, of course, thought I was mad. Unfortunately these egg-lifters came apart rather soon, so I was pleased to get the original one, that Mum bought, when she died. I use it often. It hangs by our wood stove.

In those days, anything ordered arrived almost immediately—especially from the village—for example, those delicious meat pies made by Durrant's Bakery would arrive piping hot, even when ordered at the last minute. Years later, after we left Esquimalt, Mum made a special trip back to the village to buy some of those meat pies for an occasion. Mr. Durrant was dead by then, but his son Ernie looked crestfallen and said, "Oh no! I'm so sorry Mrs. Piddington—we only ever made those pies for you."

From time to time a Watkins dealer came by. He sold flavours and essences—not things Mum wanted much. But the Fish Man came once a week. He looked as if he ate nothing but poached cod or sole, he was so thin and pale. Sometimes his daughter came with him. She was as thin and pallid as her father and about my age, but she never spoke. Poor things, I don't think either of them was well. Mum tried to buy as much as she could to cheer him up, and if ever I could persuade her to buy more than usual he would take a roll of paper from the dashboard and tear off a narrow strip for me. On it were round flat candies of no colour and no taste. Once the war started, the Fish Man didn't come any more. Did he go overseas or die of TB?

Sometimes a peddler came with a suitcase full of trinkets: scissors, needles, pincushions and small toys that might have come from Christmas crackers. Mum always tried to buy something but didn't need my help. And then there was the Fuller Brush Man. That was exciting! You never knew what marvels he'd bring or what samples he'd give us—like those tricky little bristle brushes that turned on a spindle, the best things I've ever found for washing combs.

My favourite of all was the Vegetable Man, Louie Wei. I waited eagerly for his weekly visits and always persuaded Mum to buy tons of fruit and vegetables. Even though we had a big orchard and vegetable garden, his produce was exotic and irresistible. At an early age Louie Wei christened me "the Shopper"—a name I loved. He came year-round, his truck laden with fruit and vegetables in season. At Christmas he brought wonderful wooden boxes of tangerines and mandarins, tied with bamboo rope, and dried lychee nuts and boxes of crystallized ginger. Of course we bought lots of all these, but he gave us more, plus a magnificent pot of chrysanthemums for Mum—larger and lovelier than I've ever seen since—and crystallized ginger in ceramic pots of dark green glaze or smooth and elegant blue and white. There would be Chinese candies for all of us and sometimes a doll for me. We always parted laughing and smiling—feeling so much the better for his visit. He seemed to love his job, but I wonder now, did he really feel jolly or was it just a façade for us?

I was fond of Mr. Smith too. Mum and I would go there more as an excuse for a row down the lake or a peaceful walk along Shawnigan West Road—a summer outing rather than a shopping spree. But he intrigued us both. Sometimes he said he had a niece or a nephew staying with him but mostly he seemed to be entirely alone, on a large piece of open grassy land that sloped gently down to the lake. His house sat among a cluster of buildings with an apple tree and a lone maple. Where were the fir and cedar that should have been there—the bog myrtle, the salal, the hardhack, the twisted bark, the red osier dogwood and the twinberry? Had he removed them all?

When we arrived at his wharf or walked down his driveway, we wouldn't see a soul. There was a gas pump tilting forlornly, and one of the buildings had *STORE* painted in large red faded letters on both sides of the roof. There was a dreamlike quality to Mr. Smith's place. It might have been lifted bodily from somewhere else, perhaps from another lake far away.

Inside the store we'd ring the bell on the counter. Eventually he'd appear—a tiny man in a crumpled brown suit and beige shirt buttoned to the neck with no tie, an ancient felt hat pulled down *plonk* on his head.

He would greet Mum with a faint smile and say, "Oh! You've brought the Shopper!" And we'd say what we always did: "Have you some Green Transparents today, by any chance, Mr. Smith?" And he'd reach behind the counter and fill a bag from the box he'd just picked. Sitting on the counter itself was a large glass jar full of peppermints, and sometimes Mum would buy me a tiny brown paper bag of these, too. There seemed to be nothing much else for sale: some cigarette papers, tins of tobacco, some A-1 oil and a few matches. He was a man of few words and fewer smiles. From the Prairies, Mum explained.

I can't imagine how he earned his living. We never saw other customers. He seemed to be there just for us—our own special treat. A treat repeated, without change. Something we could be sure of. And all three knew our lines to perfection.

46. MR. MANNERS

The first thing you saw, when you came in our front door, was a mahogany sideboard. On the middle of it was a round silver tray. This tray sat there, waiting for visiting cards. If someone wanted to meet Mum, they would appear at our house unannounced and hand their card to whoever opened the door. It would be left on that silver tray. If Mum were interested in meeting that person, she would leave her card at their house. Then invitations might be proffered, either way, by telephone or by a handwritten note. That was how you met people—unless you came upon them through friends or at parties. In that way, lots of cards were left at our house. So there was a constant stream of guests, with new people invited, mostly to afternoon tea.

As always, tea would be served in the drawing room and wheeled in on the wooden trolley. A large silver tray sat on top holding the cups and saucers—usually Mum's ribbon china with its side plates and slop bowl for tea leaves. It also held her silver tea set with its hot water jug, cream jug and sugar bowl and another jug of cold water to cool Dad's scalding tea. On the shelf below there'd be plates of thinly sliced bread and butter—both white and brown—scones or small crustless sandwiches for starters, with two or more cakes made for the occasion. If there was a cook there might be bikkies (Mum didn't make them). If any of us were around and old enough to be responsible, we would help pass the teacups and plates of bread or cake to the guests—keeping an eye out for empties. This was an honour and I loved doing it, watching to see if guests behaved correctly by taking the piece nearest them—or the biggest piece! There was no telling.

But one guest, though always invited, never appeared. This seemed awfully rude to me, but Mum insisted that he might arrive at any minute, and therefore slices of bread and butter or scones and some of each cake must be left for him. We didn't often have men, lone men, to tea. This one's name was *Mr. Manners*, and I couldn't understand why he should get such special treatment. Mum said we must never forget *Mr. Manners*—however aggravating he might seem.

But who ate those leftovers, a little dry around the edges after sitting about in the warm drawing room for hours? Was *Mr. Manners* in actual fact the older ones—my siblings who biked home from school starving but too late for tea? I suspected that but never actually caught them in the act. And I always forgot to ask.

47. ROYAL ROADS SCHOOL

After the scale and regimentation of Lampson Street School, Royal Roads seemed familiar—like being at home. For one thing it was held in Fermoyle (which always sounded to me like somebody gagging), a house built for a family. Classes were in rooms: the dining room, sitting room or study. Some had fireplaces, so if it were cold we'd have a fire in the grate. Upstairs there were bedrooms where two of the teachers slept, as did Miss Johnson's Uncle Tim and her Scottie, Jock. Outside in the garage was her car, Old Bill.

We did our lessons where our numbers fitted—so we moved around. There was no set room for Grade Four. I had been put there straight from Grade Two so was never taught long division or frac-

After the regimentation of Lampson Street School, Royal Roads School seemed familiar. It was held in a house built for a family.

tions, but that didn't seem to matter. Sometimes the whole school was together doing gym in the hall, or ballet or "Greek" dancing. And we sang together and acted in plays as a school. Lessons were not set in stone following a curriculum but were invented and changed depending on what our teachers read the night before or heard on the news. Apart from arithmetic, they seemed fresh and lively. For history we learnt a lot about early Britain, how people painted themselves blue with woad and the names and dates of all the kings and queens, including my favourite, Matilda Maud, the rightful queen who, when deposed, had to flee in a blizzard—south and west across England, with a shawl over her dress, her poor feet in soft slippers. Did anyone take her in, feed and warm her as she struggled to reach the ship that would sail her to France? All those history lessons came wonderfully alive thanks to our teachers and those long but narrow little books edited by the *Evening Standard* of London, England and beautifully illustrated by Mendoza—supplied to BC schools in 1937 by the Saint Lawrence Starch Co., to celebrate the coronation of King George VI. Extra copies were available for ten cents and two labels!

One morning we found a bowl of red leathery balls in our class-room. They were pomegranates—a fruit none of us had seen before. We held them, shook them, sniffed them, looked at the atlas to see where they grew—Southeast Asia and the Mediterranean. Then we painted them—both whole and cut in half—and ate them, pulling out each succulent seed and spitting out the pips. You don't forget lessons like that.

We were a mixed bag. Some lived very close, as we did—dashing across the street to get there; others had to be driven or come by bus. Some were extremely bright. Some couldn't manage regular school. But we were unaware of this. All we knew was that we all had weak-nesses and strengths. And everything was conducted in French or English, to the accompaniment of delicious homey smells from the kitchen: homemade bread, a newly baked cake, a stew or soup, or the sweet hops and malt smell of homebrewed beer.

Recess was called "Break" and took place in the garden. As long as we didn't enter Uncle Tim's kitchen garden or the flowerbeds, we could play almost anywhere and climb the trees. Sometimes we helped pick the cherries. Other times we'd have a "wounded solider," like my friend Mary, with her arm in a cast. Our favourite places were the woods behind the house and the open meadow that stretched the length of the property. We had lessons there sometimes, ran races, practised sports, explored and played all manner of games in that marvellous open space. At its lower end was a curious pit—rect-angular in shape and full of water. Why? And how? We spent a great deal of time observing this pit and were convinced that *little people* lived there. It was obvious! We could see their bubbles rising to the surface. This was a serious matter that we all discussed—an in-triguing puzzle—a secret we shared. We sensed that adults couldn't appreciate such a thing—nor could *the others* at the big school up the hill.

Then houses started springing up all over our meadow. We felt outraged but could do nothing. The Second War had started. People were pouring into Esquimalt. These weren't wartime housing—just comfortable houses for people who had found work there. That was the last year of Royal Roads School, for Miss Johnson had fallen in love and was about to marry and move to the Kootenays. Those had been wonderful years for me. My horizons had broadened in all directions. I loved each day there and would, had it been possible, have stayed on and on.

My one sad memory had nothing to do with the school. One day when classes were over, Mum came to see if I'd like to go for a walk. I said no, I'd rather go on playing with my friends. I hadn't known how much she needed company till she turned and walked away. So much is written on a back, and in the split second it took to read that message, I realized I'd chosen selfishly. But still I stayed.

It is hard for a parent—that rite of passage, the first time a child chooses others over them. But it is equally hard for children—to put them through it.

48. HAM and WONG

In Victoria's Chinatown in the thirties there was a broker who would arrange jobs, particularly the jobs of cooks. His name was Tim Kee. Over the years he and Mum came to like and admire each other. She would ask him to find us a good cook and he would choose whoever he thought would suit us best. Both the hired and the hiring paid a fee. Tim Kee was, therefore, a powerful and respected man.

Of all the Chinese cooks he sent us, my favourites were Ham and Wong. Actually several were named Wong—all gentle kind men who, like Ham, let me watch them cook. And let me experiment alongside them. They never laughed at my concoctions. Consequently I spent a lot of time with them and came to love them and cooking too.

At one point we had bantam hens that, in theory, spent their time pecking about near the stables. But sometimes the cocks got so fierce they ventured up onto the lawn and would intercept us on the way to the orchard or the vegetable garden to gather something for supper. Sometimes they were even down by the Riding Ring where the loganberries, blackberries and raspberries grew. So the cook and I would go together, carrying sticks—one looking ahead and sideways, the other behind to fend off attack en route or to keep guard while the other gathered fruit or vegetables.

Dad's sisters, the Aunts, were fascinated by royalty and sent each of us *all* the commemorative plates of the Royal Family as they were made—and sometimes beakers too. We didn't like them much at all, so to get them out of the way they were put on a high plate rack in the dining room, where they looked quite splendid against the dark green of the walls. Each one had a registration number on its back. Some of those Chinese cooks were as intrigued by royalty as the Aunts and memorized all those numbers so that when they took the plates down to be washed or dusted, they could put them back in exactly the same order. This wasn't something they were ever asked to do, but chose to do. We thought that marvellous.

They were wonderful cooks and made delicious meals for every day and also for grand occasions. Each morning they discussed menus with Mum and how many would be there for lunch and tea and supper. Then Mum would order the amount of food necessary from Louie Wei, the Vegetable Man, Mr. Scott, the grocer, and Mr. Lock or Mr. Young, the butchers. Those clever cooks could calculate down to the number of peas required for each person.

If we congratulated them for a certain dish or a particular birthday cake, it would reappear for each such occasion. But that didn't matter a bit. I don't remember anything those cooks made as being less than absolutely delicious. Or, as Dad would say, *scrumdigious!* I just wish they had made us Chinese food. How wonderful that would have been!

I always wondered what those cooks thought about our kitchen. We had an old-fashioned wooden kitchen cabinet painted light blue. It held flour and sugars, salt, baking powder and all the dry ingredients, spices and herbs. Its counter was zinc and all its bins and drawers were lined with zinc. You pulled a knob and out would flop a bin of flour or a bin of sugar. Another would reveal a pastry board, or you pulled out a drawer to find a breadbox. Inside the cabinet was a large funnel affair into which you put the dry ingredients for a cake. You turned another knob and everything was sifted. It was really quite convenient.

The kitchen walls were painted white, and all the doors and cupboard doors under the sink were a gorgeous ultramarine—deep blue, but with a lot of light in it. There was a wooden table against the west wall with chairs around it and a print overhead of Lord Louis Mountbatten—Mum's pin-up. The sink and drainboards and windows took up most of the north wall, the kitchen cabinet was against the east wall and the two stoves, wood (later converted to sawdust) and electric, along the south. In the centre of the room was a white enamel-topped table with blue trim and wooden legs of the same blue as the doors.

The pantry, between the kitchen and the dining room, held all the china and special glasses in closed cupboards, plus big tins of biscuits and cakes along the counters on each side, with lots of storage below. On the north wall was a sink with a tall curved spout designed for washing glasses and vases. On either side were special cupboards to hold them.

The door to the larder was just off the kitchen in the north wall. Beside it, another door led into the scullery, which held the tall cooler and another large sink for washing vegetables. Another led down to the basement and the cook's quarters. In the scullery an outside door took us to the icebox and the back steps. All told, the kitchen was a bright attractive room—a pleasant place to be, well organized for cooking, spacious yet convenient. And from the sink we could see lots of trees and all that passed along Wychbury Avenue, if we wanted to, and anyone coming to the house from that direction.

Of all the Chinese cooks we had, only two caused trouble. Once one of them was really rude to Mum while serving food in the dining room. Dad was still carving at that point, and when he heard what was said, he rose from the table and chased the fellow through the swing door, across the pantry, through the next swing door, across the kitchen and scullery and out the back door, telling him to "pack and go!" And he did, immediately. When Dad got back to his seat in the dining room he was stunned to see that he had both carving knife and fork in hand.

Another, called Jack, wasn't happy about anything. He scowled all day and was often rude. Eventually Mum had to phone Tim Kee and ask that he be replaced. A day or so later Tim Kee was shot—murdered. Mum felt terrible. Had her complaint caused his death? She grieved for him for years.

49. THE OLYMPICS

In Esquimalt the land rises from the southern shore up to a rocky ridge, then slopes slightly, flattens and rises again. Thus most of the inhabitants can see the Olympic Mountains, and many consider them *ours*. They stretch from east to west—right across the southern horizon: a curtain of glorious blue, pale and shimmering, so familiar they are part of our being. And they move! They grow slightly taller, rising before our eyes as the light changes, and then sink again to their usual height.

We could see the Olympics from Victoria too—all along the high ridge from Gonzales Beach to Ogden Point. But Victoria dips slightly to the north, flattens, and then rises unevenly in hills, so when we drove about the town, the Olympics popped into view unexpectedly, as a rare treat. Each time they did, Mum would say to us: *Look! There they are! Aren't they glorious?* And we couldn't help but agree. They were decidedly *our* mountains. I knew they were part of the United States yet could never quite accept that, and never have I heard an American even mention them. Perhaps they think of them as another pesky set of hills to go up and over. And they, poor things, must ferry across the Strait of Juan de Fuca to enjoy them.

I was told, early on, that there were towns and villages along that shore and on the foothills that rise up gradually. But that was awfully hard to accept when I could see with half an eye that they rose straight up out of the sea, those glimmering pale blue mountains—there for our pleasure. If we alone can see them, doesn't that prove them ours?

So to be sure, I wrote to my friend Paul McShane, who lives near them, across the waters in Port Townsend, Washington. And this is what he said:

> Yes, I can see the Olympics … from my living room. In answer to your questions, they look further away and smaller than I might have imagined. I'm not sure what that's about. I keep thinking the real and larger Olympics will show up some clear day.

Ha! I was right!

50. POLO

No one can remember when Dad began playing polo. Mike thinks it was in England while he was with the Royal Horse Artillery, but Dad told me he played polo as a young man in Québec City. Then, when he tried to play in England, he was told that as he was neither titled nor royalty, he had no right to play. He played anyway, but in those days, at the end of Queen Victoria's reign, polo was still considered the sport of kings. However, in Victoria in the 1930s, it was a game my father and brothers played, as did several of the fathers of our friends—like Colonel Greer and G.D. Tyson.

During our first few years in Esquimalt we had several horses and a pony. When Big Bar Ranch was abandoned in the early thirties, all the ranch horses were brought down too—some cayuses, some warmbloods, but most were Thoroughbreds. Those absurdly expensive horses, unsuitable for the ranch, made excellent polo ponies.

At fourteen, Sylvia surprised everyone with her skill at polo.
From then on, we had a family team.

At first our team consisted of Dad, my brothers Jamie and Peter, and a man called Dean Freeman. When he couldn't ride for some reason, Sylvia was allowed to play. She remembers Jamie complaining bitterly, "Surely we don't want a *girl* on our team!" But she surprised everyone by keeping up with the speed and manoeuvres, besides getting a really tricky goal. From then on, at the age of fourteen, she was accepted and we had a family team.

Dad treated polo like a military campaign. He moved that famous life-sized wooden rocking horse, built by naval carpenters in the Dockyard for a Garden Fête at our place in 1931, from the lawn to the stables and set it in the middle of a bowl-shaped wooden structure with walls that rose about five feet tall and were extended much higher with stout netting. On that obliging creature, players could practise their strokes for hours, sure that the ball would reappear somewhere within reach for another swipe. As well, Dad read books and studied strategy. He gathered his team in the library regularly and gave each player a number and a chit with that number on it; then on the Ping-Pong table they'd play polo—moving those papers around as if mounted, learning all the possible moves and naming each one. Thus during a game they could signal each other and react instantly. This gave them a distinct advantage.

Our white helmets and breeches, canary yellow woollen jerseys, polo sticks, balls and goal posts came from India, but Dad didn't find the sticks or their heads adequate. He had each player split his stick in half, then glue and splice it together again with linen thread. This gave extra flexibility. Then locally made heads of hard Canadian maple were added. Each team member was responsible for his own stick.

Many of the Vancouver Island polo players had large, slow, army-issue horses—still being issued all that time after the 1914–18 war. Ours could run rings around them. Sylvia remembers being charged by furious, swearing men spurring their huge horses straight at her. They expected her to swerve. But she didn't flinch. Kept galloping straight ahead. Or dodged around them. It wasn't long before we were the Island champions.

Vancouver teams, like that of Clarence Wallace and his three sons, were more of a challenge. They could afford spare riders and spare horses and transported them across to the Island in vans. We had no extras at all, and our horses had to be ridden to wherever the match was, be it across town or in Duncan, usually by family members—those not playing, if possible. Then Dad would bring all the gear, the uniforms (jerseys, breeches and riding boots), masses of oranges, emergency rations and thermoses of tea, plus Mum, the team and the youngest family members—all stuffed into the Packard. Joanie remembers how she and Mary would take the horses across town to the Willows—an open area of low, flat land in Oak Bay where there were exhibition grounds for polo matches, horse shows, horse racing and fairs, as well as a riding stable and the skating rink—or wherever the match was to be, each of them riding one and leading another. It was rather tricky crossing the Johnson Street Bridge, but luckily polo matches were usually on weekends so there wasn't much traffic. They were about twelve and thirteen. Michael did this too when he was even younger—once with a girl who was two years his junior. But often matches were close to home, up on the flat part of the golf links, in front of the Buxtons' house.

Everything in polo happens at such a fast pace, sometimes a chukka was over before I knew it. But I much preferred the breaks when all the players milled about without dismounting, sucking orange quarters and chatting gaily. Then I could see the players better and would roam among them, my eyes at stirrup level, perfect for checking their horses' sides. And whenever I saw savaged, bleeding flanks, I'd call out in a loud voice: *Blood…Blood…Blood!!* What a horror I must have been! Did I embarrass any of those responsible? I doubt it. But Dad would grin and mutter to no one in particular, "Out of the mouths of babes!" He hated spurs and only used them on rare occasions on a horse slow to gallop, but only after he'd removed the spiky part and inserted a ten-cent piece. That gave encouragement without cutting or hurting the horse.

Polo must be tremendous fun to play, and especially so as a family team. But when my brothers went off—first Jamie to join the Royal Air Force in 1935, then Peter in January 1937—others had to be found to take their places. Joanie has a letter Peter wrote to Jamie while he was training to be a midshipman in the Royal Navy. He'd been asked to spend the weekend at a large country house in the west of England. When his host apologized that polo would be the main entertainment, Peter expressed delight and, to everyone's astonishment, played as well as, if not better than, anyone else.

Joan and Mary would love to have played. Both were capable, but when Peter was killed right at the beginning of the war, and Jamie four years later, Dad had no heart for the game. Nor, I imagine, did Clarence Wallace. He lost two sons as well. So that glorious, carefree, polo-playing era came to an end.

Now Sylvia alone keeps vivid memories of that magical time. She could remake a decent polo stick today, if she had to, and she remembers all the team's signals, manoeuvres, and strategies. The rest of us remember delivering the horses, helping groom them, all the fuss and anticipation of the matches, the speed of each chukka, crowds of excited spectators, the passing of orange wedges between chukkas, cheering the players on from the sidelines or the observation of horse-blood shed. And Dad's excited play-by-play comments during those long drives home.

51. PETER

Peter Grosvenor Piddington was born on September 10, 1919, his middle name from the square where Dad's forebears lived before the family splintered in all directions. He was Mum's only child born in hospital, the dimpled darling, loved by all. From an early age he knew exactly where he was going and what he wanted to do with his life. Engines and the sea were his delight. He would sit at his desk for hours, designing some complicated structure in detailed diagrams, then construct a marvel that actually moved and worked. And he didn't mind that his baby sister sat on his bed, watching— quiet as a mouse.

There was no kindergarten in Esquimalt in the twenties, but Sylvia remembers when Peter started Grade One at Lampson Street School. She was a year and a half younger and his close companion so begged to be allowed to walk up to the school when Mum took him on his first day. When they arrived, his teacher asked if she would like to try school for the day. Yes, of course, she would! So, like all the

Peter was the darling of the family, beloved by all, and from an early age he knew exactly what he wanted to do with his life. T.A.P. photo

others in his class, she was given a handful of sticks and told to make a house. Everyone else made the façade of a house, but Sylvia, who often watched Mum designing her *dream house*, made a floor plan. That, she was told, was *wrong*. Insulted, she didn't mind staying home after that.

Peter stayed on, though, until the end of Grade Two. Then, because of a deviated septum, he caught so many colds a tutor was hired to teach him at home. Later, he and Sylvia went to Miss Harcourt's School for a while, up on Old Esquimalt Road.

In 1932 he was sent as a boarder to Shawnigan Lake School. Tom and Jamie had been there since January 1925. But after a year he complained that there was not enough mathematics and physics to suit him, so he asked to stay home and try Esquimalt High School, where he felt the teaching might be better—or what it lacked he could find elsewhere. And he longed to join the Sea Cadets. The trouble was their evening meetings were held at our suppertime, in Vic West—an awkward place to reach by public transport and too far to walk. He needed a bike but Dad couldn't afford one. So Peter entered every possible competition that offered cash prizes. His first win was five dollars for a sand castle. Then he won more for some sort of structure he built using Meccano. When he had fifty dollars he bought a Raleigh, and off he pedalled happily to Sea Cadets and all around town.

Besides his Sea Cadet projects and schoolwork, Peter was always inventing new ways to do things. For instance, one Easter he found chocolate clocks for sale in town. So that year, either 1935 or '36, we had an Easter Clock Hunt, and all manner of children raced about the garden searching for them. It was a huge success.

Peter was the sort of person who studied hard, worked hard, and made things run better and seem more amusing. While in his teens, Monopoly was all the rage, so he constructed a board using local businesses—Mc and Mc's Hardware, Scott and Peden's feed store, Diggon–Hibben's, the stationer, Angus Campbell's department store—and properties like Hatley Castle, the drydock, the Parliament Buildings, the Empress Hotel, Government House, the Royal Theatre, the York, the Dominion and the Capital (all movie theatres), and Terry's.

Terry's was a famous place in Victoria with a ballroom upstairs and a drugstore down with a long white marble counter where excellent ice-cream cones, milkshakes and sundaes were sold. It called itself *The Aristocracy of Soda Service*. We three youngest ones never managed more than a five-cent ice-cream cone, but Sylvia always chose their maple walnut sundae with two scoops of vanilla ice cream covered with caramel sauce, then whipping cream topped with a handful of walnuts—all for fifteen cents! Terry's most famous sundae was the Victoria Beauty—so huge and so rich that only affluent sailors or soldiers could risk or afford it. It cost fifty cents—way beyond our means. But if you finished it without being sick, you either got another one or your money back! Terry's also had a photographic studio.

But to return to Peter's Monopoly, it was much more fun playing when you knew exactly what you were buying or selling, rather than imagined properties in New York City.

By this time Peter was determined to join the Royal Navy but his nose still gave him trouble. If it were operated on, the Royal Navy would refuse him. So our parents found someone whose gentle massaging inside and out actually cured him.

At seventeen he went to Victoria College. I remember him crossing the back verandah to say goodbye—a kiss for Mum, a hug for me—then, flinging a scarf around his neck, grinning, waving and twirling his green umbrella, he'd hop on his bike and be gone. To me he was a grown man—my hero—and his presence, even fleetingly, made me feel wonderful. He lifted your heart and churned your vitals.

To my amazement, my brother Michael, two and a half years older than I, cannot remember much about him except for one magical day when, for some reason, just the two of them went off to find that year's Christmas tree. It must have been the winter of 1936, Peter's last Christmas at home. As they drove off in the grey Morris, the one with the rumble seat, he suggested they look for a tree in Colwood, about fifteen miles away. Apart from the pleasure of driving alone with his big brother, all Mike remembers now is that, at almost seven years old, he was fussed that it would be dark soon—too dark to see. Peter said, "Don't worry. The days are getting longer now!" But

Mike, always a stickler for detail, insisted then, and insists still, that two days after the equinox wouldn't make much difference.

This was the depth of the Depression. We had little or no money so could not afford the obvious—send Peter to university for five or six years of engineering. Canada had next to no navy at that time, but through the Sea Cadets he found a way to join the Royal Navy, get the training he yearned for and be paid a pittance as well. So in January 1937 he travelled alone to England to become a special-entry midshipman in His Majesty's Royal Navy. Henceforth he was considered British and required a local guardian. The perfect person was chosen: Cousin Amy Drury.

Peter loved everything about England, especially Cousin Amy, who was like a mother to him. She was a double cousin: a Scottish cousin and the widow of Granny's first cousin, Admiral Sir Charles Drury, RN, who had been in command of the Mediterranean Fleet. When making inspections he took his wife with him. Mum, as her favourite niece, received marvellous letters about their travels while she was at boarding school. One she found particularly fascinating gave a detailed description of Istanbul and the interior of the Sultan's Harem and all the women who lived there.

Cousin Amy was childless with a large and comfortable country house. She adored Peter and treated him like her son. As a *colonial*, who hadn't been at the Royal Naval College in Dartmouth since the age of ten, he didn't get the same treatment as direct-entry midshipmen and was not promoted in the same way, nor given all the perks. This didn't fuss him. His letters home were ecstatic. And at Christmas he sent us great boxes of presents. I still have what he gave me for 1937 and 1938 tucked away in this log cabin. One is a large, beautifully illustrated picture book called *Banjo the Puppy*. The other is an embossed china beer mug from Malta—perfect for a girl of seven.

As part of his studies, Peter cruised the Baltic Sea. While his classmates were promoted to sub-lieutenant or lieutenant, he remained a midshipman—part of the curious treatment of colonials, *those from far-flung parts of the Dominion*. Yet when his class cruised the Mediterranean, he was chosen to be the Admiral's Middy, a great honour. In his letters he sent watercolours of views he loved. It seemed that wherever he went he was comfortable and at ease—unlike the rest of us who are prone to be shy and somewhat awkward.

At the end of his course Peter ranked second in his entire class and was thus allowed to choose his ship. He chose HMS *Royal Oak*. Soon after that, war was declared and *Royal Oak* was anchored in the Orkneys at Scapa Flow, considered an impregnable harbour. A letter came saying he would be *down below* for a while, a term meaning "home" to our family, and perhaps hoping Mum would think that. But he meant "the engine room"—deep down, below decks—a place he loved and understood, but the worst place to be if a ship was in trouble. *No, she wasn't to worry, he'd he fine!*

On October 14, 1939, shortly after midnight, *Royal Oak* was torpedoed four times by a German U-boat. When the first torpedo struck, some twenty minutes before the last three, the captain and crew could not figure out what had happened, though they scurried about searching. The battleship was fuelled, ready to sail the next day. Some thought there'd been an explosion in the stores below decks; others that it was an aerial attack. Scapa Flow was secure! No submarine had ever passed its feeble defences, placed at most of the entrances to this eighty-square-mile harbour, so none was expected. The crew was ordered back to bed.

When the next three torpedoes struck, the boat sank in nine minutes. Before she did, she became a raging inferno with most of the crew stuck below decks. Though some 380 men survived, most of them were badly burned and covered in oil. Many more drowned in the icy water awaiting rescue. As a man called Owens swam away from the ship, he saw another man beckoning wildly—someone he didn't recognize, but obviously an officer as he was wearing pyjamas. When he turned and looked in the direction indicated—there was a conning tower close by! Owens survived to tell the tale, the only member of the crew to *see* the submarine. The other man vanished, presumed drowned.

Peter was always observant. He had grown up hearing Mum's tales about crossing the Atlantic in 1916 and how she had stayed out on deck to help the captain keep an eye out for U-boats. I like to think he was the man who gestured. It was the sort of thing he'd do.

A cable was sent to Cousin Amy, but she had no means of getting word to us quickly.

The night of the sinking, Sylvia was up late reading and was suddenly aware of Peter's voice calling her—calling and calling. Troubled by this, she couldn't sleep and was the first up the next morning. So she picked up the *Colonist*—sitting, as it always did, on the mat at the front door—but this time with a screaming headline: *ROYAL OAK SINKS!* And a large photo of Peter with the caption "Presumed dead." Weeks later Cousin Amy's letter came. Poor thing, she was heartbroken.

Mum and Dad were devastated. We all were. Condolences poured in from people who knew him, from strangers who had come upon this charming lad and been touched by him or bumped into him one day on the Number 4 streetcar or, for whatever reason, remembered meeting him. Letters kept coming and coming. Mum answered all of them.

Our parents tried to hide their grief. Publicly they showed pride: *He died for king and country.* Privately they were shattered—they had lost their favourite daughter in 1914 and now their favourite son in 1939. Neither of them ever got over it.

The Sea Cadets insisted an island be named after him, this lowly midshipman of the Royal Navy. So a good-sized island midway up the west coast of BC became Piddington Island, with Peter Bay its main feature. I've kept a map of that area with me ever since, but it was in 1971, on our way to the Queen Charlotte Islands, that Dane Campbell and I sailed there on *Atarax*, anchored in Peter Bay and explored the island—the first in the family to see it. Close by Peter's island is a group of tiny islets named after Canadian admirals. Even more curious, for us, is the fact that Piddington Island lies right alongside Campbell Island.

When Hilly and I met Cousin Amy, fourteen years after Peter's death, she spoke of him as if he'd just left the house and would return. We were studying in London—which wasn't a cheerful place seven years after the war. Londoners had been under such strain, and malnourished, for so long, they appeared haggard and grey and were apt to be rude or bad-tempered. It was a joy to get out of town. But always low on funds, and hating to spend most of the weekend changing trains that didn't take us anywhere near we wanted to go, we hitchhiked down to see her.

It was wonderful to be with someone who knew so much about our brother and wanted to talk about him. She had long since run out of anyone interested in hearing about her darling boy—even her devoted lady's maid, Miss Emeny, who'd known and loved him, had had enough. But we longed to hear about him. We three got along extraordinarily well, and each visit was sheer delight. She and Miss Emeny lived in an Elizabethan structure, all angles and slopes, where Good Queen Bess had spent a night—now the Hayes Farm Hotel.

Cousin Amy was in her mid-nineties when we met but was still full of life and eagerness. Each time we visited her she would rent a car and chauffeur to show us her favourite places. We loved her dearly and she liked us: our student garb—duffle coat and jeans—our mode of transport. She had done unusual things in her youth, too. She even designed special trousers for biking! She took us to see Homewood, her lovely old house, which had been commandeered and turned into a hospital soon after Peter's death—wanting us to see *his* room and the whole of her house where he spent so many happy days. We know little about his social life during his years in England, other than what he told us in his letters home and what happened during his stays with Cousin Amy. She assured us she had done what she could to introduce him to *suitable young things*. Though as a social animal, he had little need of help.

Much later, when I lived in West Vancouver, I saw a British film recommended by friends. Starring in it was a clone of my brother: his features, his dimples, his colouring, his physique and much of his charm. The actor's name was also Peter, and his birthdate could easily have been 1940.

Not long ago I met a friend and contemporary of Peter. We were attending a function for Old Girls of the first Strathcona Lodge School, held at Shawnigan Lake School. I remembered her name but we hadn't met since I was a child. She told me she was at a polo match at the Willows in October 1939 and remembers Mum's delight. She had just received a cheery letter from Peter. A day or two later a photo of his smiling face, and another of HMS *Royal Oak*, were on the front page of the *Colonist*. Its headline: "Allied Ship Sinks—Local Lad Lost!" Like us, she has never forgotten him.

52. LUCKY

For our daughter's first two years, Dane and I lived apart in winter. He was based in Sidney, on Vancouver Island, while Arabella and I stayed in my little house above Horseshoe Bay. Max, my large tabby cat, lived with us. He was a travelled fellow who'd spent three years cruising the coast and exploring the shore—up to and beyond Princess Royal Island. He was a cat of experience. When Arabella was born, he treated her as he would a kitten. Whether at sea or ashore he kept watch over her, awake or sleeping. When she crawled, then walked, he stayed close by. Once, when Sammy Lamont and Anne Clemence were staying with us, Max disapproved of Arabella's behaviour. He sat squat on his hindquarters, pulled himself up as high as he could and boxed her ears. He could have been her nanny.

Lucky Boy was mine. Born on Big Bar Ranch in a litter of unwanted pups—half collie, half English sheepdog—he was rescued from drowning by Mum and brought down to Esquimalt as a present for Peter, aged about ten. All the way down she held him on her knee and kept reassuring him, "You are a lucky boy—a really lucky boy."

That name stuck. Peter trained him and the two were inseparable, the best of friends. And Lucky Boy, or Lucky, as he came to be known, turned out to be charming, intelligent and handsome. His coat, long and thick, was such a dark brown it seemed almost black, with a ruff of white around his neck, a white bar down his muzzle and white on his belly.

We had had other dogs before my time. One came to a sticky end—a cautionary tale repeated by Dad. He was a Black and Tan who Dad adored, but the sort that eat whatever they come upon. One day someone forgot to close the feed-shed door. This dog got in and ate the horses' bran until he felt parched. Then he drank quantities of water to quench his thirst. The bran swelled. The dog burst. All I can remember is the sweet nutty smell of that shed—and the shut door.

Lucky had one small weakness. He loved cream—whipping cream. In those days our icebox sat out on the back porch, just outside the scullery, so the iceman could fill it without disturbing anyone. He came once a week and would drive his truck into the backyard—the gravel space between the two garages and the house. Then, depending on the season, he would bring us one, two or possibly three large blocks of ice. I loved watching him lift each block with a hook, then flip it deftly up onto his sack-covered shoulder, run up the back steps and flip it again into the ice side of the icebox. Lucky never touched bottles of cream, but if some was left over and stored in a particular white china jug, even if it were covered with one of those clever little cloth tops edged with elastic (the sort that are coming back into vogue now, though made of plastic), he could smell it through that heavy wooden door. He'd lean on the handle, remove the jug with his teeth and, without spilling a drop, carry it down that steep flight of steps, then down the garden path to the lawn, where he'd lap it all up.

He wasn't as clever at closing the icebox door. So whenever we found it ajar, a search party would set out to find the jug—clean, but intact, in a garden bed or on the lawn. Lucky never touched anything else.

By the time I was born, Peter was ready to go to boarding school. That meant Lucky had time to spare. He devoted it to me. By then he was full-grown—a large, solid-looking dog, not a creature anyone would argue with. Wherever Mum put me in my pram, he stayed right beside it. If she left me for a few minutes asleep on a rug on the lawn or in the meadow beyond the stables, he would sit beside me and keep watch. Mum appreciated his help. There was no one else to do this for her.

He couldn't push the pram when we went for a walk, but he came with us, heeling, and whenever we wanted to cross the street, he stopped oncoming traffic.

In summer he came with us to the Lake. But sometimes, if the car was full and Dad was driving back down the next day, he might be left outside. Once, by accident, he was left *in* the house. We realized this as soon as we reached the Lake, but in those days we had no electricity, no phone. There was nothing we could do. By chance Mum had to go back with Dad the next day. When they got there, Lucky was outside, wagging his tail—delighted to see them. It was obvious he'd checked all the ground-floor windows, but the only one open was in the downstairs lavatory. There he drank water from the toilet, stood on the seat and did his business into the toilet bowl, then scrambled up onto the high windowsill and jumped down a good four metres into the garden. The marks were clear. Mum gave him the best meal ever and lots of hugs and pats. And then he came with them up to the Lake—the local hero.

On two occasions Lucky had his lovely thick coat clipped short, either because it was hot weather or because his fur was full of burrs. He hated having this done, and the second time escaped from the vet before the clipping was finished and made his way home from town. Mike was in the stables when a strange, slender, rather grey, stubbly-looking shaggy dog ran in, wagging his tail and grinning. It was Lucky Boy.

When I no longer needed tending, Lucky began patrolling the neighbourhood—checking to see that everything was okay. From West Bay to the village, everyone knew him. Sometimes when we were out driving or biking we would see him trotting along. When he saw us, he might return with us or just wag his tail and continue on at a steady pace, as friendly and conscientious as the policeman in the village.

One foggy day in October 1939, just before his master, Peter, went down with his ship, Lucky was struck by a truck on Peters Street and killed.

53. MR. SCOTT, THE GROCER

For some unknown reason, Scott's Grocery on the northwest corner of Lampson and Head Street was always known to us as "Mr. Scott, the Grocer's," though he was called "dear Mr. Scott, the grocer" by Mum. The store was square with a high ceiling of embossed metal that made it seem endless. While Mr. Scott moved about briskly among the shelves and tables at floor level, Mrs. Scott sat, at least in my memory, raised slightly, enthroned in a little wood and glass structure in the middle of the west wall, where she took down orders or received payment. In my mind's eye, too, is a series of wires hanging from the ceiling, acting something like a toy train except that they shot a little shuttle about the store that carried notes and bills from one Scott to the other. The same sort of system was in place at

W. and J. Wilson's, that most elegant of shops in Victoria, where much of our clothing was acquired.

Mum bought all our basic groceries from "dear Mr. Scott," all of it going on account, rather like the shop in Beatrix Potter's *The Tale of Ginger and Pickles*. When Mum phoned to order what we needed, if they were out of whatever it was, Mr. Scott would say, "Oh, Mrs. Piddington, nobody wants *that* anymore! There's none of it in town!" And she would say, "My dear Mr. Scott—I want it! Please order some for me, now!" And of course he would. In a day or two it would arrive, by truck or bicycle, at the back door. This was a game they played—a sort of *recitative.*

Born during the Depression, I knew nothing but these anxious times, so everything that went on seemed perfectly normal. Yet there were signs, hints, clues of how our lives had changed and everyone else's too. And I asked myself, *Why is our house larger than those of my friends? We eat by candlelight in the dining room—use silver, good glass and china—while they sit comfortably in their kitchens—which seems much more fun. Everyone is struggling to stay warm and fed—yet, hard as they work, Mum and Dad seem to be enjoying themselves! Is this play to them—a dream they'll wake from one day?* But there was no escaping the suffering on many faces, especially of those men who kept coming to our door selling things or asking for handouts. They looked sad and dirty, their clothes and shoes worn thin—sometimes their "uppers" flapping or tied with string.

The answer, of course, went without saying: We were lucky. We had a comfortable house, an orchard and garden—we could grow fruit and vegetables and somehow have just enough to buy whatever else was needed—if we were careful. With a trickle of dividends coming in, whatever that meant, Mum said we could get by. Otherwise we'd be knocking on doors too.

But I knew there was something terribly wrong when "dear Mr. Scott, the grocer," almost sobbed when we brought Dad's monthly cheque, even when it was late. His face said it all. He knew it was hard for Dad to scrounge the money, but it was harder still for those in debt. This cheque would save him from financial ruin.

He gave us a present—always the same: a bag of opera creams, opaque pink, green, white and orange candies shaped like little jelly moulds, rough and dry on the tongue but soft inside and tasting of perfume—revolting candies, but candies nonetheless. No one ever refused to be the courier. Then we slipped back down Head Street on foot or on bikes, along Paradise Road to Lyall Street, turning left down Lampson to Wychbury and home—feeling very smug indeed and ready to share the loot.

54. JOHN

Until I was five, most of my friends were called John. The one I saw most of, and liked best, lived at the far end of Wychbury Avenue opposite our orchard and stables, his house high, square and dark brown, set well back from the road on land that edged the field where our horses grazed, and which stretched back almost to Lyall Street. In the space in front of their house, his father grew cut flowers for market. That was intriguing enough, but beside and behind the house were row upon row of greenhouses for potted plants—exotic things like *Salpiglossis* and many others. His parents were tall, quiet people who had at least two more extraordinarily handsome children besides my friend John. They played with my sisters.

John found our place wonderful and weird, particularly the way we set the table for supper in the dining room ("All those shiny glasses, and so many spoons and forks! How do you know what to use?"). I found his exotic in the extreme, and the jungle smell of those greenhouses lingers in my nose to this day. We were allowed to roam through them at will, as long as we didn't *touch*. Everything there was organized and calm. Not the rowdy chaos of our place. Even their house was different—rather dark, but simple and neat, with not much in it and oilcloth on the table instead of a tablecloth. I loved it. But John preferred playing at our place, in what he called our "yard." We made forts in the centre of Dad's Riding Ring. We knew the moment of ripeness of every vine and fruit tree and when the carrots were large enough to pull. We knew where the finest fairy slippers, peacocks and fawn lilies grew in our wild wood by the driveway. No, we never ran out of things to do. If it were raining we'd pore over the old copies of *Boy's Own Annuals, Chaps* and such like—

*John Maynard, Mike, Hilly and Helen pause between
broom forts and the golf links, 1938.*

stored on the bookshelves in the breakfast room—or we'd lie on the cork floor and play with games or puzzles. If we were feeling brave we'd go up to the attic and explore the box room, filled with ancient relics, cobwebs and dark corners. Or, braver still, we'd climb through one of those dormer windows and scramble up onto the roof!

Both of us preferred playing outside, and climbing trees was our big delight—so we went up every climbable tree there was. Once, at the tiptop of a high cedar between Wychbury Avenue and our garage, we thought we'd test flight. Surely if we jumped at that height we could fly—off and away like the children in *Peter Pan*! Then one of us thought of peanut butter, so we slithered down again and ran into the kitchen for a big crust of bread (from a Coburg loaf, of course) slathered in p.b.

We played together from the age of three or four until we were about eight, when we went to different schools. Or did they move away? Anyway, during those years we were allowed to go wherever we wanted—so we went in all directions.

One of our favourite places was the woods, or the Big Woods, that dark and glorious forest stretching from Wychbury Avenue to

Lampson, Munro and Fraser streets. At first we concentrated on the massive rock that edged the lower end of Lampson Street—the eastern boundary of those woods. We would climb up the mossy shelves to crevices where ferns and wild flowers grew. At the top were open grassy patches where one could lie unseen and watch the world go by on the street below or look out to ships at sea. There were trees thrusting through those rocks—lots of them—oak and fir and flowering currant bushes and lilies galore. We spent days exploring that rock face, building shelters and floating acorn boats in fern-edged pools—until it seemed a place for babies.

Far more intriguing were the deep woods. Apart from a couple of bridle paths curving through the trees—cut by Dad, with permission of the reeve and council, so he and others could ride or walk from Wychbury Avenue through to Fraser Street—these woods were untouched, primeval, the soil black from centuries of rotted vegetation. Growth was dense and deep with fir and cedar soaring upward, their canopies so thick we rarely saw the sky. And everywhere there were high banks of fruiting, flowering bushes: honeysuckle, twinberry, red huckleberry, salal and, my favourite, Indian plum, with its strange sweet/sour flowers—the first to bloom in spring. And somewhere deep in the wildest part was a *beaver pond*! We'd heard of it, dreamt of it, knew it was there. We even felt we'd seen it—but weren't quite sure—so we yearned to see it again. Determined, we'd push our way through those bushes, only to find more thickets of brambles, bracken or sword ferns. Sometimes we came upon bogs of skunk cabbage and soggy places edged with maple or black cottonwood—what my parents called Balm of Gilead, whose spring scent tickled our noses. They were fascinating too, but where was the beaver pond? Had anyone seen it?

Game trails were almost nonexistent in those woods, and the area was so large and lush it was hard to know where we were—or which way we were going—especially when we couldn't see the sun to get our bearings. So when we were hungry, we'd watch out for bright light glinting through trees and go toward it. That was south, we knew. But I was always mightily relieved when we could hear the rolling noises of the sea. That meant we were near Munro Street and Fleming's Beach—safety, home and lunch!

*

I lost touch with John early on, but I believe he spent his life managing grand hotels so would know, far better than I, which glass or knife and fork to use—and when!

55. THE CHRISTMAS PUDD

Today our house is redolent of Christmas cakes. I make at least six smallish ones each year—but if we have Christmas pudding, I usually buy it. It was the reverse for Mum. At Christmas, vast cakes would arrive from Maitland's in Montreal—sometimes two or three or more. The Aunts—Dad's sisters Flossie and Ethel—liked to send them to the males of the family, to their beloved "Arcie Grovie" (which was how he pronounced his own name as an toddler) and his four sons, thinking they might enjoy having a cake to take back to boarding school or off with them, wherever they were going. They weren't particularly good cakes but they looked impressive, they were a constant and, as Mum would say, "They filled the bill nicely." So she concentrated on Christmas puddings.

This meant a lot of preparation ahead. Fresh dried fruit would be ordered from "Mr. Scott, the Grocer's," and set to soak in brandy the day before the puddings were made. Suet would be ordered from one of the butchers and chopped up fine, and all the other ingredients measured and accounted for.

If by any chance she forgot about making her pudding, she was jolted into action on *Stir Up Sunday*—the Sunday before Advent—when the day's collect says: *Stir up, we beseech thee, O Lord, the wills of thy faithful people; that they, plenteously bringing forth the fruit of good works, may of thee be plenteously rewarded.* The message was obvious. Had anyone forgotten to make Christmas pudding? If so, get cracking, good women! Get a wiggle on!

It took about a week for Mum to assemble everything needed. Then, from some hidden corner, a huge white washbasin was produced—a bowl kept exclusively for this operation. And the job began.

I loved watching as she added all the ingredients: dried bread crumbs and flour, suet, brown sugar, salt, freshly ground nutmeg and mace, eggs galore, raisins, sultanas, currants, mixed peel, chopped raw apple, chopped almonds, grated rind and juice of a lemon, and sometimes grated raw carrot— and at the end, depending on how stiff the dough felt, a good big dollop of brandy to make the mixture of a "soft dropping consistency."

Then came the important part—the stirring! Each member of the family, and anyone living with us, took their turn, perforce, stirring this vast concoction—one stir for each year of their lives! This was not easy, I assure you, but it became *your* pudding, not just Mum's. And the outcome was all the more enjoyable for the effort expended. When the contents were well blended, the bowl was covered securely with a cloth and set in the larder overnight.

The next day three or more china pudding bowls were buttered carefully, filled with the mix and covered with cotton covers that could be secured tightly with cotton tapes around each bowl's rim. Then they were steamed for eight hours. When done and cooled, the cloth tops were removed and replaced with fresh covers. At this point the puddings could be stored until needed—even up to a year in a cool dry place.

On the day they were to be eaten, each pudding was steamed again for two hours, served piping hot—a sprig of fresh holly set on their tops—then flambéed with brandy. We always made two sorts of hard sauce to go with our puddings: one with brown sugar, the other with icing sugar. And the debate is ongoing as to which is better. This job was easy but time-consuming as one blends the sugar into the butter in tiny amounts. As with the pudding, it is the blending that makes the sauce. To be allowed to make hard sauce was a coveted rite of passage.

Dad, more than any of us, felt *plenteously rewarded!* He adored his Christmas pudding, and if any was left over he loved slices fried in butter for breakfast. We found the pudding too rich and too heavy, and though we always ate a little at Christmas dinner, for Mum's sake, we much preferred mince tarts with a good big dollop of hard sauce on top. Was it the memory of past dinners Dad liked, or the actual pudding?

*

At seventy-seven, Dad got back to Québec for the first time. When he knocked on his eldest sisters' door, they thought he was an imposter. They said their brother, Arcie Grovie, was young with fair hair—not white-headed with a beard! They wouldn't let him in.

56. MARY

My first playmates were boys. And almost all were named John: John Maynard, John Godfrey, John McNaughton, and so on. Then one magical day a girl appeared. I was outside playing croquet with Mike and Hilly when I saw Mum at the far end of the lawn. With her was a strange woman and a little girl. They came across the lawn toward us. Who in the world was this?

It was Mary Emmerton and her mother. Mary had large blue eyes and curly fair hair that hung to her shoulders. She wore boots, a flowered frock with smocking across her chest and a Kate Greenaway bonnet. Quite a contrast to my usual garb of shorts and T-shirts, my brother's castoffs, I had probably been put in a dress for the occasion—homemade by Mum, as always, of tiny floral print, with puffed sleeves and a smooth bodice and gathered skirt, edging around the neck and cuffs, and a sash in plain contrasting colour. Mum made these dresses to perfection—but only these. And she always made two—one for Hilly, one for me—no matter that there was a gap of almost five years between us. To her, we were *her little ones*.

Mum had mentioned one day how nice it would be if I had a girl to play with. I said I was perfectly happy with boys and thought she'd forgotten all about it, as I had. But here was Mary! I had never seen anyone so fragile, so dainty. She looked incredibly proper, but I soon found out she had a delightfully wicked chuckle. And she was game to climb trees and do all sorts of things. How had Mum found her?

We realize now that it was our mothers' mutual friend Renée Archibald who brought the two of them together and then the two of us.

Aileen Lutner, Mary's mother, sprang from the kings of Wales. She was a proud and capable woman who came to Canada in the twenties and fell in love with a gentle Englishman, Bill Emmerton, a man with no pretensions at all, who played the piano for silent films. When the talkies came in, he did what he could. Life was not easy for them. They lived simply, as comfortably as possible.

Mary Emmerton and Helen wear school uniforms of blue blazers and tams with grey tunics and socks, 1940.

But on that marvellous day the family, who were all in on this plan, vanished on cue into the house. And they stood, a whole gang of them, watching from the breakfast room windows. Mike says they held their breath and crossed their fingers, hoping we'd like each other. Even Hilly, who never approves of anything I do or say, says it was "so sweet." We stood facing each other for ages—two little girls just five years old, eye to eye, staring, deciding—she tall and slender, me chunky and slightly shorter.

Teenaged Mary and Helen go off to Victoria College, 1949.
H.M.P. photo

Then, having decided, we ran off to play. Friends—from that day on!

Mary came to stay often—both at Wychbury and the Lake. And I stayed with her on Rogers Avenue, behind Christmas Hill. I gained her steady insight and gentleness, different books, different toys, different approaches; while she, an only child, gained a large and noisy family.

We have shared so much it doesn't matter a whit if we don't see each other for years. We keep in touch by phone, by letter, by instinct. The bond is there. And when we meet we say, *Together again!* Over the years I gave her what seemed to me a more appropriate name: Maria Sofia. Our children call her Auntie Fia.

What touches me now is my family's interest in this matter: that they bothered to witness the event and felt excitement and delight that Mary and I bonded that day. And now, after all these years, that each of them has kept a clear memory of our meeting. Sylvia is sure there's a photo somewhere of the two of us running off together, hand in hand. But Hilly, who seemed at the time to have so many friends and endless parties to go to, says now, rather plaintively, "No one ever found a friend for me!"

57. STOKO

One day in the mid-thirties, Dad had an accident in the stables. Both his shoulders were crushed between a horse's flank and a loose-box wall. He was bedridden for weeks and still couldn't raise his arms. My older siblings did what they could—mucking out and grooming—but they couldn't replace Dad. So he phoned around asking if anyone knew of someone who might be able to lend a hand.

Thus one day Stoko came to tea. Afterward Dad took him down to see the stables. They had so much to talk about he stayed for supper and for the night. The next day he moved in.

The stables were like a small village about two hundred metres from the house, hidden by bushes and Douglas fir. Once through the gate off Wychbury Avenue and into the stable yard, one lane intersected another with buildings at each corner: the cowshed, stalls and loose-boxes for horses and the tack room on one corner, with a large feed shed opposite. On the third corner was the bowl-shaped wooden structure with netted walls and that life-sized wooden rocking horse in the centre. Opposite it was the chicken house and more storage. The stables had electric light, a toilet and running water. Stoko didn't have much baggage, which was lucky as the tack room, the place they chose for him to stay, was pretty full. The walls, of course, were covered with chaps, saddles, bridles and all the gear horses need. There was a cast iron heater in the centre of the

Stoko was in his fifties when he came to us, getting rather old for such a life, but his immense knowledge and love of horses were of great interest to Dad.
H.M.P. photo (1937)

room, a sink and a hot plate, yet room enough for a bed. Outside the door was a French cabbage rose, whose pale pink blossoms filled the air with sweet scent. Close by was a deep purple lilac bush and across the path a dark red peony. The view was across the orchard.

Usually Stoko ate with us, but he could, if he wished, be completely self-sufficient. In no time he became part of our family and, like "the Man Who Came to Dinner," he stayed with us for seven years.

Harold John Stokes was a gentle, soft-spoken person. Animals loved him and so did we. He came from a large well-to-do County family—grain merchants from the west of England. They were of the "huntin' shootin' fishin'" part of society that dropped their g's on purpose and felt small need, if any, to spend the Season in London. As the second son, Stoko was well-educated but had no prospect of inheriting either land or money and was untrained for any career other than the army or the church. In England his love of horses would not provide a livelihood, but if he left the country, his family could send him a small allowance.

So he made his way to Canada. For much of his life he rounded up wild horses in California and, once they were halter-broken, rode them en masse to Alberta. There he saddle-broke and sold them. The best were trained as polo ponies and shipped to England. He was in his fifties when he came to us, getting rather old for such a life, but his immense knowledge and love of horses were of great interest to Dad, as was the extra pair of hands.

Something happened the day Stoko came to tea that has bothered me ever since. My new friend Mary and I were five. Why or how we got hold of his hat I don't remember, but we did. It was very appealing—a soft brown round-topped fedora-ish hat, the sort Daddy Warbucks wore in *Little Orphan Annie*. Somehow, while he was having tea in the drawing room, we nabbed it and took it down to the lawn. Then we climbed a may tree, dropped his hat to the ground and jumped on it until it was flat. We knew we were being wicked but it was such fun. We were hooting with glee when we were found.

The family was shocked. But Stoko didn't mind a bit. He pushed his hat back into shape and grinned. But there was something incredibly sad about his eyes, even when smiling. Perhaps because, of the twelve children born to his parents, seven died in infancy and two brothers were killed in the Great War. That left just him, one sister and his older brother to reach adulthood. As well, we have since learned that he was a widower. Yet he never mentioned his wife to any of us. Perhaps she died in childbirth.

As I say, I've felt guilty about that squashed hat all these years—until our grandchildren, Sophie and Heydon, almost five and three and a bit, came to stay with us without their parents. At one point I had to leave them alone for a moment in the living room. When I came back they'd unhooked one of Dane's felt hats from the wall and were jumping on it—jumping and jumping—jumping and laughing, just as we'd done. Oh—that made me feel good! In the pleasure of that moment I felt my crime expunged.

Sometimes in winter, if it were empty and the weather really cold, Stoko moved into the cook's quarters in the basement of the house. Later on he moved up to the billiard room on the top floor. But all through that time, at least once a year, he took Hilly and Michael and me *out to dinner!* We'd go to the Poodle Dog Café or the Sussex Hotel and have grownup meals with all the trimmings—each of us choosing exactly what we wanted! During those dinners he would tell us about his mother, his childhood, his home. For all these years we thought those dinner parties were *our* special treat—ours alone. Not so. For he took Sylvia out to dinner too, and Joan and Mary, yet none of us knew about the others. He was the consummate host who made all of us feel that we, beyond any doubt at all, were his absolute favourites.

During the war, when men were desperately needed, Stoko took a job at the Sidney Roofing and Paper Company, whose yard was on the Esquimalt side of the Johnson Street Bridge, where the Ocean Pointe Hotel is now. One day a bale of shingles fell on a spade that had been left on the ground the wrong way up. Its handle struck poor Stoko with terrific force. He was badly hurt, his face bashed in. Doctors did what they could to rebuild him. But after that he never looked the same and could only walk slowly, with canes, and certainly not upstairs. And his poor sad eyes ran constantly.

We saw him often and dined out with him as before. But now we'd take the elevator up to the dining room of the Pacific Club, where he was staying. A place he could reach with ease, thanks to its lift.

After we moved to Shawnigan Lake and lived there year-round, we met on rare occasions. But he stayed on at his club, with its restaurant and services.

Dear Stoko, he was a warm and generous presence. The sort of uncle we longed for. A few years before he died, a niece and nephew, his brother's children, came out from England to be near him and brought him much joy.

Then, in the wonderful circular way of things, Mary Barlow, née Emmerton, who had jumped on his hat with me all those years ago, invited his niece, Jennifer, and Michael Hanna to dinner one evening when she and her husband were living in Esquimalt, on Nelson Street. Michael had been at Royal Roads for kindergarten with me and later on with Mary and me for Grade Four and then at Esquimalt High. He and Jennifer became good friends and married soon after they met. They were very happy together and had two sons. For a while, as newlyweds, they lived in his parents' house and then moved uphill a little, to the Drawing Room apartment at Wychbury.

And now, thanks to their elder son Christopher, who grew up in Esquimalt, I have been given a great deal of help with historical details for this book. How pleased and delighted Stoko would have been.

He and Dad died within five days of each other in March 1960. They had been friends for twenty-four years.

58. ROUND THE CORNER

Round the Corner was a shop on our side of Esquimalt village and perfectly named—for except for households on Lyall Street, everyone had to go around at least one corner to reach it. It was perfectly shaped too, with its small size, bay windows and central door, and could have appeared quite happily in Beatrix Potter's paintings. Just like her shop in *The Tale of Ginger and Pickles*, it sold almost everything one could want, and it was handy, for it was open six days a week and could, in dire necessity, be persuaded to open on Sunday too.

For children, it was a destination of choice because of its amazing variety of one-cent candy. We would go there clutching a few pennies and come out feeling rich as kings with an all-day sucker or a little bag of jawbreakers or one of those delectable flat bears made by Leclair—their hard pink innards coated in chocolate. They were my favourites.

The Coton family, who ran the shop, was perfect too. I have only a hazy recollection of Mr. Coton, but his wife and daughter, Marjorie, I remember clearly. They looked alike and were patient and kind. They didn't fuss but stood and smiled while we dithered over our choices and then seemed pleased to take in one cent, three, or possibly four.

Once, for some reason, Mum didn't want me to have candy. Instead she gave me a quarter to buy a nice big orange. I was to bring back the change. To be going there alone was exciting enough, but to have twenty-five cents was beyond my experience. I could scarcely believe my luck, so besides the orange I bought my first Oh Henry bar, for five cents and some one-cent candy. Then I set off for home, change jingling in my pocket. Once outside the shop door I realized how foolish and greedy I'd been. With no one to share my loot I'd have to eat it all myself, on the way home. So I trudged along, struggling to get it down. Jawbreakers take time to finish, and there was no pleasure in any of it.

I got home late and not a bit hungry. To my dismay, the entire family was seated in the dining room, waiting. I showed Mum my orange. She asked for her change and I handed over what was left. Everyone stared at me.

"And what did you buy?" asked Mum.

Crossing fingers I said, "Just an orange. I think they gave me the wrong change." No one asked me to swear on *Guide's Honour*. Or say *Spit to Die*. I was so obviously guilty—but no one said anything at all. How clever they were! I've fretted about this ever since. Silence is so effective.

The Cotons bought the store in 1931, when they moved to Esquimalt from Oak Bay. They called it Round the Corner after a popular song of that time: "Round the corner and under the tree, the Sergeant-major made love to me. He kissed me once, he kissed me twice, it wasn't the thing to do, but oh it was so nice." (Joanie says she remembers Dad singing this while exercising the horses.) Marjorie was twelve at the time of the move and was not altogether happy when asked to deliver flyers announcing the shop's opening—to everyone in Esquimalt.

For the Cotons, one-cent candy was infuriating. Children came one by one and might take ten minutes choosing what to buy. Each time the front door opened, a bell would ring. If the family was eating lunch, in the rooms behind the store, one of them would come down the three steps into the shop and wait while those momentous decisions were made. Then back to their lunch only to have the bell ring again and another little shopper appear clutching a penny. From our point of view they seemed perfectly at ease, without a hint of impatience, so none of us realized their annoyance. Yet Michael remembers one occasion when Mr. Coton asked some boys to clap their hands. It was not a self-serve shop but apparently quite a few helped themselves and slipped things in their pockets. Theft never occurred to me, though I was prepared, that once, to cheat my mother.

There was no central heating in that building. Both store and house were heated by the kitchen stove, which burned oil or sawdust. It heated their water too, so if the stove wasn't on there'd be no hot water. This may seem strange nowadays, but that is how it is in our house now. If we want hot water we keep wood in the stove. If we want a bath we feel the hot water tank. If it feels hot to the bottom we're in luck. When one of the Cotons wanted to wash they'd say, "I box the bath!" In our house we say, "I bags the bath!"

According to Marjorie Hawker, née Coton, no one was really aware of the Depression. It was just how things were. All were in the same boat. We looked after what we had. We adapted and compromised. If we needed something new, we chose carefully and made it last. These are hard habits to drop for all of us alive then. But then why should we? At home we saved paper bags and tins. As Mum would say, you never know when they'll come in handy.

Strange as it may sound with the general lack of money, Round the Corner flourished during the thirties. But during the war, when rationing began, life was difficult for the Coton family. Sugar, for example, came in one-hundred-pound sacks and was sold in pound bags. If the hundredth bag were short, they would have to cut into their own rations to make up the difference. And then there was the bother of clipping all the customers' coupons. Luckily for us, candy wasn't rationed.

Some claim now that our rationing was a farce—those who weren't alive then, or those not in Canada at the time—but I think it helped the war effort, if only by making people aware of shortages. Mum took it seriously and turned it into a math problem that she could enjoy—though it was always a nuisance. She, like everyone else, had to carry the family's ration books with her whenever she went shopping—then consider carefully what she could buy. When people came to stay, they were supposed to bring their ration books with them. Some did—some didn't.

But what happy memories that little shop gave all of us who grew up in Esquimalt—those lucky enough to have a cent or two for candy. Then to be treated like serious shoppers, as we always were at Round the Corner—that was really special!

59. THE ELEPHANT

One damp day in winter I went exploring down by the sea with my friend John. We were travelling west—somewhere past the beach called Africa and Macaulay Point—clambering over high dry rocks above the tide line and slipping and slithering along the greasy, seaweedy rocks below it, both of us having a lovely time. This was a place we knew well and went to often—alone, without grownups—not even older siblings. John was a little younger, a good and faithful friend.

We crossed over a grassy headland and came to another bay—and there, midway along the beach, was a massive brownish grey *creature*. Part of it was still in the water, but most of it was sprawled up and across the beach. We picked up sticks, in case, and crept closer. It didn't appear to be breathing but we couldn't be sure. Was it asleep?

Up close we were amazed by its size. Lying relaxed and limp on the sand, its girth was well up to our height and its length at least six metres. We felt Lilliputian beside it! What was this, with its leathery skin crinkled and cracked and full of ridges, with two sets of flippers and an extraordinary long curved snout—all pleats and cracks and crevices? It looked really old. We poked it gently with our sticks. It didn't budge. From its stillness and terrible smell, we were pretty sure it was dead. There was nothing for it. We circled it twice—then raced home to each of our houses—together. Who would believe a six- or seven-year-old who'd seen an elephant dead on the beach?

Nobody did, of course. They said we were talking through our hats! Then, when we went back with reinforcements a day or two day later, it wasn't there. Storms and high tides had sucked our elephant out to sea again. For ages the others jeered at me, and Mike would

*Ba and Mike explore "Africa"—
as the sea water roars in!*
H.M.P. photo (1937)

tell all comers: "Ba says she found an elephant, dead on the beach! Can you beat that?" But in fact we weren't so far wrong. I realize now it wasn't an elephant but an *elephant seal*—a huge one, a giant one— a creature rarely, if ever, seen in these waters. How lucky we were!

60. CHRISTMAS DAY

The very thought of Christmas makes me want to gasp. It is a feast for all the senses! A shudder of excitement runs through me. And there I am—in my little iron white-painted bed—longing for the day to begin so I can run downstairs and open my stocking. But it is pitch-dark and no one else is awake. I must wait.

Eventually the others stir. When everyone is washed and dressed (pyjamas and dressing gowns aren't encouraged downstairs) we rush down as a body to find our stockings bulging—each one in its place: mine near the telephone on the east side of the fireplace and Dad's at the far end, near the dining room door. There are presents too, piled all along the red leather bench in front! Everything looks marvellous, but we go straight to our stockings. There is a din of *oohs* and *aahs* and squeaks and squeals as these are emptied and the treasures laid out—mine on the bench of the nook nearby—the others' on a stair or a chair. These are tiny presents—what we call *tillies*—plus candies, nuts and a large navel orange at the toe. And pinned to each stocking is a "good-for" from Dad—a small amount of money to be collected later. Santa Claus, for us, is not a person but the act of giving, so all or any of us might give someone another little present from Santa.

Wrapping paper is saved in our house and kept in boxes in the box room under the eaves in the attic. Ribbon is saved too. Mum has a large lidded basket full of used ribbon, which is ironed, if necessary. But new paper and ribbons can be found in the armoire in the upstairs hall. Males in our family often wrap things in brown paper or newspaper and tie with raffia or string. Some things, too large to be wrapped, are just tagged. Lovely little stringed tags and Christmas stickers can be found at Woolworth's or Kresge's—good big envelopes of them, for ten cents. I do my important shopping there—like Mum's annual Evening in Paris eau de cologne—its bottle blue with a lovely silk tassel. It is my major purchase. And for Auntie Bella I buy a bar of rose geranium soap. It is her favourite and she is precious to me. But most of my presents are made by me—like scarlet knitted garters for Dad's knee socks, drawings of flowers for Tim or of fruit for Louie Wei. Sometimes I make collections of autumn leaves and gum them onto cards for relations in the east or the sad people I know, like Madame Stanner. A lot of *tillies* can be found at the church bazaar and Garden Fêtes. I have been squirrelling things away for months. It is fun choosing who gets what, then wrapping and tagging things!

When this orgy of opening is done, we have breakfast. The food is standard Sunday fare: hot buns, coffee and hot chocolate—plus a bowl of Mandarin oranges! The dining room is decorated with holly and cedar boughs. It looks and smells wonderful. A fire burns in the grate and candles twinkle—anticipation is in the air.

We set off for church—as many as can squeeze into the Packard, the rest walking. St. Paul's is beautifully decorated and bursting full. We wish everyone *Merry Christmas!* The air is sweet with the scent of fir and cedar boughs, and masses of poinsettias add to the rich colours of the little church. The sound of the organ is almost muffled by greetings and excited whispers.

Then the rector, splendid in his Christmas vestments, processes in with his server and assistant, followed by the choir. And the service begins, with its glorious liturgy and with Christmas carols—not heard till then—all of us singing our hearts out.

Lunch is simpler than usual: soup, cold meat and cheese with fruit to follow. Naps are suggested, then a long walk. There is no lolling in the drawing room, no curling up in a corner of the sofa with a book or stretching out full length on the muskox robes before the fire. That room has been out of bounds for days, the curtains pulled, the door locked. We pass it and shiver. Only the eldest have access.

There is no tea on Christmas Day—we nibble fruit and candies from our stockings, so by evening appetites are brisk. The dining room has been closed too. Sylvia is in there helping spread the best white damask tablecloth, setting the table with the green water goblets I find so difficult to grasp and the matching wine and liqueur glasses, the finger bowls, the silver spoons and forks, the silver salts and peppers, the silver candy bowls, the silver dishes for nuts and special raisins still on their vines, the silver candelabra and candlesticks—all polished and gleaming. A carving knife and fork are put at each end of the table—Dad to carve the turkey, Mum to carve the ham. Sylvia will fold the huge linen dinner napkins in her special way and put one to the left of each place. And above each dessert spoon and fork is a Christmas cracker. Then she'll arrange two bouquets of flowers to go on either side of the candelabra. Sylvia will do most of this alone. She is our expert—our perfectionist. Then serving spoons and forks will be set on the sideboard, behind Mum's chair, and mats for the hot plates and everything else to be whisked out of the kitchen, when needed.

We wear our best for dinner: Auntie Bella, Mum, Cousin Sara and Sylvia in evening gowns; Dad, Tom, Jamie, Peter and the two elder

Nixon cousins in dinner jackets; the rest of us in dresses or suits. And two by two and arm in arm we make our entry—Dad and Auntie Bella first, the rest of us following.

The dining room stuns us with its splendour. We eat here every night—yet it seems different—grander. Everything looks larger as all the leaves are in the table and extra chairs added. Place cards indicate where each person is to sit. The boys help Mum and Auntie Bella with their chairs and then the rest of us. When everyone is seated, Dad says grace and the meal begins.

First comes the oyster stew served in hot soup plates of Mum's favourite green dinner set. When finished, they are whisked into the kitchen, rinsed and set beside the kitchen sink. Thank heaven for the swing doors! In come hot green dinner plates, the steaming turkey stuffed at both ends, the whole ham, the bread sauce, the cranberry sauce, the gravy and all the silver vegetable dishes with boiling water in their lower compartments to keep things warm: one for sweet potatoes, others for mashed potatoes, creamed corn and bright green Brussels sprouts—cooked to perfection.

We little ones have been practising our manners for weeks and try to behave and to eat as the others do—but we are starving and everything tastes so good! At some point we all stand and drink a toast *To the King* and another *To Absent Friends*, which includes all our friends and relations, all of us clinking our glasses. Then we sit again. The table is cleared and in comes the Christmas pudding with a twig of holly stuck in its top, and a mountain of hot mince tarts and two kinds of hard sauce. The lights go out. A spoonful of brandy is heated with matches. The pudding is flambéed and blue flames dash all over it! We all have a small helping for Mum's sake but prefer the mince tarts with hard sauce. By this time we can hardly move, we are so full, but excitement mounts. Nuts and raisins are passed and nibbled at. Then come the chocolates, though nobody much wants them. We are waiting for the crackers!

At last we cross arms and, grasping the end of our own cracker and the end of our neighbour's, we pull like stink! With any luck there is a series of explosions—trifles, favours and hats burst in all directions and are retrieved. Then, hats on heads, trifles admired, the favours are read.

Hats on, we cross the front hall. The drawing room door is opened with a flourish and there, at last, is the TREE! Sparkling with tiny lights, huge glass balls of subtle oranges and pinks, and silver balls and ornaments, spun glass angels and twinkling tinsel. It is breathtakingly beautiful. This is the first time we see our tree. And it is worth the wait.

Then the eldest son is Santa Claus and hands out the presents. There are small gifts on the tree for friends and relations, but under the tree are mountains of boxes, the *real presents* and those from the Aunts. The huge box they shipped west has been emptied, yet each of the smaller boxes inside are wrapped as if to go to Africa, with each person's name and address in full—*Miss Helen Vivian Piddington, 441 Lampson Street, Esquimalt B.C., Canada*—and inside this box are several others, each with a card in an envelope with the above address, in full again. The Aunts don't go out anymore. Instead they hire a shopper. He is given a list and our ages and he guesses what we might like. Their joy is choosing, wrapping and addressing.

The Aunts send Dad and the boys their usual boxes of Maitland's chocolates, plus the special box of chocolate mice for Dad. Mike passes his around, but he thinks *one* chocolate a day is enough. Hilly and I don't agree. So we find his hiding place and push on the bottom of each one so we can be sure of choosing a hard centre next time. If he notices, he gets cross!

Sometimes curious garments arrive and even stranger jewellery. Whatever doesn't suit or fit us goes into the Peace River Box, but tomorrow we must write long and detailed thank-you letters to them, appreciating every single thing! Once, by chance, they sent me a beautiful taffeta dress of a gorgeous rich plum colour. It had crystal buttons down the front, a lace collar and a sash. For once it fitted me and I wore it with great pleasure as long as I possibly could. But a gold watch they sent when I was seven was smashed to smithereens the first day I wore it—playing baseball at school.

All this is a little overpowering for our cousins, who have no father. They are always blue at Christmas. They have their own festivities at home, then come to us for dinner and the tree. We try our best to cheer them and give them things we hope they'll like, but they don't cheer easily. Auntie Bella gives us small, intriguing, useful things.

When all the presents are opened, hot drinks, cognac and chocolates are passed around and we gather by the fireplace. Sometimes we sing carols around the piano and there is lots of talk and laughter. I try my best to stay awake. But sometimes I fall asleep and am carried up to bed.

Mountains of wrapping paper and ribbons greet us the next morning. This is Mike's birthday, poor guy! Two birthdays in a row seems too much. He will get more presents but everything seems a bit of a letdown. Mum and Dad try to invent a special treat for him, but we are weary and don't always feel up to a party. And there is a lot to be done—like sorting through the wrappings and saving the best and taking it all back up to the attic. And the ribbons must be gathered too. Sometimes in all the mess we find a toy we had lost or forgotten about. Now our presents must be taken to our rooms. I put mine in my toys box.

In the kitchen a massive washing-up is underway. For days we'll eat nothing but delicious leftovers—and Christmas cake. Plus, of course, the birthday cake for Mike.

There are so many things I regret not asking Mum, like how our Christmases at Wychbury compared with those she knew as a child. Were hers as magical as ours, as mysterious, as epic? Did she mind when her parents left them alone on the l'île d'Orléans in the care of Bessie Baine and took themselves off to Europe for the winter? I would have missed mine terribly at Christmas time, no matter who was in charge or how caring. Mum had ten siblings. Those in Canadian boarding schools would return home for Christmas, while the others overseas would go to relations or join their parents for the holidays.

For a long time I thought everyone's Christmas was as marvellous as ours. But where did these ideas come from? Was this the Irish way of celebrating Christmas, ceremonies passed down by Dad's mother's family? Or did they come from his father's side? Certainly they loved giving presents more than Mum's side of the family. Or did our parents, having had rather dull Christmases themselves, invent their own ceremonies out of thin air? The move to the west coast gave them the space and privacy to do things their own way, with no grandparents or great-aunts clucking: *Things weren't done like this in my day!* These questions, never asked, remain unanswered.

61. THE CAR KEYS

My eldest brother, Tom, was away studying at McGill for most of my early years. When he came home he seemed more like a visiting uncle than a brother. There were twenty years and two weeks between us.

Today, the 28th of June, is his birthday. He has been dead for many years, but on this day I always think of him. And what I remember best—or perhaps I should say, with the most pleasure—was what he did for me the year I turned seven.

Most of that year I had been kept home from school with aching and erupting ears. Because of them I got very little sleep at night. Perhaps I looked peaky. I was certainly rundown. In an attempt to build me up, Mum made my breakfasts after the others went to school: small servings of calves' liver or lamb's kidneys—treats like that. And for lunch she might give me a salmon steak with a knob of butter on top when everyone else was having soup and cheese. Like the breakfasts, I ate those meals alone. I couldn't understand why I was getting special treatment. Now, as a mum, I realize the Elephant's Child must have been really scrawny!

Well before my birthday, Mum asked which I'd prefer: a party or a day in Beacon Hill Park with her? Away from other children for ages, I chose the park.

On the day itself I came down to breakfast to find my *tillies* at my place on the dining room table. Among them was a set of keys. That was very odd. Then Tom explained. They were *his* car keys. He planned to drive us, and our picnic lunch, to the park—stopping in town to buy my present.

Our first stop was the pet shop, and there I was told to choose a turtle—whichever one I liked. He knew I was longing for one. In those days people painted flowers or scenes on turtles' backs, but I chose a beautiful plain one. Then the dilemma: would I carry him about all day in his little bag of water? No, Tom had already organized a turtle pool at home and would take him there.

Mum and I had a marvellous day, with time to cross all the bridges, visit the white Kermode bear and the other animals, inspect all the flower beds, climb up to the height of land where we'd watched fireworks from Royal Navy ships to celebrate the coronation of King George VI. And, most important of all, we had time to choose which of the many islands I would live on with the ducks. But I must say, like a mother whose child is with a babysitter for the first time, I longed to be with my turtle.

In the late afternoon, exhausted and happy, we caught the Number 4 streetcar home and marched down Lampson Street in gleeful anticipation. Those car keys were, without doubt, my most memorable birthday present. My childhood presents to Tom were very much duller. I gave him a bar of Neilson's dark chocolate. That was what he loved.

The last time I saw Tom he had what we think was Alzheimer's dementia. I took him a large bar of the best dark chocolate I could find. He had no idea who I was. My voice, my name, my nicknames, my chatter meant nothing at all—but he knew chocolate. He seized the bar from me and, like a greedy child, ate the whole thing in front of me. And when it was gone—he smiled.

As a small boy Tom was agile, quick on his feet, athletic. Then, when he was about twelve and at boarding school in Lennoxville, Québec, he was extremely ill. When he recovered he was slow, flat-footed, ungainly—not the same person at all. From then on, apart from tennis, he had little or no interest in sports and was not comfortable with young children, a self-absorbed man with a chip on his shoulder. He and Dad never saw eye to eye. And things got progressively worse between them over the years.

Nevertheless, Tom could be really good company and capable of kindness "beyond the call of duty," as we used to say. At one point Mum was told by the visiting dancing instructor at Royal Roads School that Joanie showed real promise. So despite our perennial lack of funds, she was given dancing lessons at the Royal Theatre in Victoria. And as she was too young to get there on her own, Tom was dragooned to drive her there and back. He didn't always stay the whole time but made it his business to listen to enough of the music used for each lesson so he could play it by ear for her practice sessions at home. Joan thought that was marvellous.

In July 1942, Tom married Kath Milne at the Anglican church in Metchosin, with the reception nearby at her family's house, Lamorna. I was their flower girl—awkward in a long and rather ugly yellow dress made by Mum. She had skimped on cloth because of the war.

Tom was already in the RCAF and not long after was sent to Wales to write the history of the war. Their marriage did not last, unfortunately, and Kath and their daughter, Helen Rosamund, went to live in Scotland. Eventually Kath married again and stayed there. We were very fond of her and remained close until her death. Helen,

While I was living in Paris in the 1960s, Tom came to visit and we explored the places he'd remembered from his student days.

who has two grown sons and lives with her husband in Scotland, keeps in touch by mail or phone, and she comes to Canada regularly to visit her many relations.

While I was living in Paris in the 1960s, Tom came to visit me. Perfectly fluent in French, we had a lovely few days together—exploring the city and visiting places and restaurants he'd known in his student days. There is a photo of the two of us eating in one of them. We are laughing, enjoying ourselves, and could be about the same age—just another couple dining out together.

62. SPORTS DAY

At Lampson Street School, Sports Day took place in Bullen Park on May 23, just before Queen Victoria's Birthday—an important holiday for us. (We used to sing a little ditty: "The 24th of May is the Queen's Birthday—If we don't get a Holiday we'll all run away!") Apart from softball played behind the school at recess or lunchtime, there were no sports at school, no warm-ups, no practising, no games at all. They were an extra—to develop on our own.

We loved to bike, play tennis and croquet, and were always running, so we were in good shape. At the Lake we swam, rowed the skiff in pairs or singly, paddled the canoes and kayaks, and hiked far into the hills, following streams to their sources. In town we practised the long jump on the croquet lawn until we were pretty good. We had special gear for the high jump and used the same bars for vaulting, though I don't remember these activities being part of municipal competitions. We practised for fun, and I remember the thrill of raising the bar higher and higher, then slipping scissor-legged over it—almost at my own height. So as a family we did pretty well on Sports Day and won a lot of races. I know I won the sack race regularly, but even coming first wasn't enough for Dad. We should have been faster or more graceful. He wanted at least one of us to be Olympic material. We weren't. No matter, it was still fun—a thrilling day, one of the best of the year.

At Royal Roads we had Sports Day too, held on a suitable warm dry day in June. Here there was much more variety, with special races for juniors, aged about three to seven, and more complicated races for the seniors—those slightly older. As these were much smaller events, there was a lot of cheering from kids and parents. Whoever won the most races was awarded a silver vase, donated by our father. It would be engraved with the school's name, your name and the date. I used to look longingly at the vases won by Joan and Mary. But when at last I earned a vase, it was wartime. Dad's donation was a thing of the past. He could not be persuaded.

During more affluent years, when my sisters went across town to St. Margaret's School, Mum, Dad and I always attended their Sports Day, and I won the Visitors Race. Those big St. Margaret's girls impressed me enormously. I longed to go there too. Somehow I absorbed the names of their contemporaries better than I did my own. But, exciting as all these Sports Days were, practising sports at home was more fun. Poor Dad, his Olympian dreams never came true.

63. STREETCARS

Montreal and Toronto had horse-drawn streetcars for years before they were electrified. But in Victoria the National Electric and Tramway Company plunged right in, laying tracks for electric streetcars exactly where they wished them, so by February 1890 two streetcar lines were functioning—the first in Western Canada. Tracks were laid to Esquimalt that October, and by 1891 two more lines went to Fernwood and to Oak Bay. Our line was the Number 4—its route was from the village along Esquimalt Road, through Vic West, across the Silver Spring Brewery land, past Victoria West Park and over the Point Ellice Bridge, then up Bay Street, turning right on Douglas Street and into town. It came back along Government Street to Bay, and over the bridge again to Esquimalt.

The cars weren't particularly comfortable as their seats were of wooden slats or woven wicker, either hard or somewhat prickly, but they were dependable, easy to maintain, cheap and frequent. Their usual pace was slow and sedate. We had time to look about and enjoy the ride. However some conductors drove them wildly, either to make up time or for their own amusement, so cars would rattle and wobble as they careened along. This terrified some, but we loved it. Our stop was at the corner of Lampson Street and Esquimalt Road— a short uphill walk when going to town and an easy downhill jaunt when coming home weary, our arms full.

The brilliant economist and urban planner Jane Jacobs discusses streetcars versus busses in her book *Dark Age Ahead*, arguing that electric streetcars were and still are more economical from the point of view of maintenance and far more durable than busses. She claims they vanished in North America not because they were impractical, but because corporations selling gas, oil, rubber tires and internal combustion engines wanted the business. So the modest non-polluting streetcar was vilified, jeered at and eventually scrapped. What a pity!

I wish I'd known when small that Grandpapa Porteous and his associate, Sir James Ross, bought out the horse-drawn streetcar companies in Toronto and Montreal in the 1890s, re-laid the tracks and electrified them. For years the Porteous family had its own private streetcar or "tram," as Mum called them. But feeling this ostentatious, most of them preferred travelling in public trams, with everyone else.

Now streetcars have become the *modern* thing—the perfect way to lessen our carbon footprint. It sounds as if they may be reintroduced. But in Toronto those old cars are still in use. Bravo!

64. WORDS

They say I walked before I talked so was expected to keep up with my elders and betters when we strode out together. This was not easy on short stubby legs, so words burst out of me: *Cally me! Cally me! Please!* And they worked. Strong arms would always hoist me up. After that I chattered like a magpie—words had power!

As a family, we talked constantly. Words were treasures, they belonged to us and we used them carefully. Some weren't used by the people around us, coming, as they did, straight from our Irish granny: *idjit, hidjis* ("hideous"), *lashings* (meaning "lots") and, my favourite, *tilly*—the measure the milkman used in Québec City. You would ask for a certain number of scoops and then good customers got an extra one free. That was the *tilly*. For us it meant the little extra present given on birthdays and at Christmas. Stoko gave us another word—his own: *luxurous*. And if food was particularly delicious, Dad called it *scrummy* or *scrumdigious*. If we'd eaten too much and had a stomachache we had *a pain in our pinny*. *Guttersnipe* was a word I liked as it sounded like what I thought it meant. We would never say *given a chance* but always *given half a chance I'd...* But I can't remember if anyone else said that outside our family. We kids would say *the honest truth*—not just *the truth*. We'd be *worried sick*, not just worried. And if someone told a fib it was a *taradiddle*.

We weren't given to swearing, though I'm sure my brothers did—when provoked and out of earshot. And Dad would have hollered something like *damnation* when his horse crushed him against that loose-box wall. But we had to be content with *drat, stench* or *botheration*. That was it. Once, when I was about four, a new word popped out of my mouth unbidden. I said *Golly!* My sisters seemed shocked.

Mum was fluent in French and Dad could speak well enough, so a number of French words and phrases snuck into our lingo: *Mange, mon enfant, mange mange! Calme toi, cherie! Soit sage! Voyez vous? Allez vite! Oop là!*

It was the size and shape of words in the mouth, the feel of them on the tongue, that I liked—though some were really difficult to form. Perhaps our doctor was weary the night I was born, or a little drunk. He didn't notice I was tongue-tied, my toes webbed. "You were born imperfect," my siblings would jeer. "He should have gone *fit, fit, fit* with a sharp knife and made you right!" To this day I have trouble saying *thr* or *f*—must scrunch up my courage and concentrate to get them out at all. But I can swim!

What I loved was the different ways of speaking, even within our family. How some could be explicit in a few words while others had to rattle on and on. And the stresses on words—how slight changes in Dad's stories, repeated sometimes ad nauseam, could make them come alive or die. My elder siblings said "chuldren" for "children" and "enathing" for "anything"; Dad said "tha ra" for "thorough," and on and on.

And all the different ways of reading out loud! I loved being read to, so refused to learn to read and actually decided I never would learn. My brother Michael, always patient and kind, would read me the funny papers, giving all the different characters their own accents—L'il Abner, Dick Tracy, Tillie the Toiler, Olive Oyl, Prince Valiant, Popeye the Sailor, even the Katzenjammer Kids. Reading for me was listening. In the same vein I became a trained seal for my older siblings, who would ask me to sing my favourite songs as I heard them. The only one I can remember was "Oh Susannah," which I insisted went "For I come from Alabama with a Band-Aid on my knee!"

Then one day, while sitting on the throne in the bathroom by the night nursery, I began to read despite myself. A box of soap flakes sat on the pipes across from me—beside the hairbrush used for spankings. It had been there as long as I could remember. I knew the brand name. I knew the letters. Suddenly both melded together into my first read word: *CHIPSO!* Then there was no stopping me—but, joy oh joy, Mum went on reading to me, and some of the others did too, because they loved doing it.

Speech has changed so much since then. When we *bit* an apple, we took a *bite* out of it. It was then *bitten*. A hen *laid* an egg. We might *lay* the table to be helpful, but we would *lie* down on our beds. It was a subtle but essential distinction: one an intransitive verb, the other transitive. And we dangled modifiers to avoid the dreaded *split infinitive*. We were taught a few basic rules—of number, gender, tense—so as to have the means of achieving clarity in speech and written word. We did our best to follow those rules.

Nowadays ignorance of grammar and spelling is considered democratic—one's right. Nothing is taught. Children must rely on spell-checkers devised for another country's lingo. People use too many prepositions. They put verbs at the ends of their sentences and adverbs wherever they wish and add the letter "s" where it's not needed: *anyways, a long ways away*. Speech comes out all weak and wobbly—uncertain. Even the CBC uses slogans like *Canada lives here!* Whatever that means. Clarity has vanished. Can it ever be retrieved?

I think it can. People seem keen to learn. They latch onto the latest error in no time. Like starting a sentence with "again" when nothing has been stated—or using the possessive "myself" instead of "I" or "me," saying "incidences" when they mean "incidents." Now these are standard fare—begun in error and then suddenly acceptable. Perhaps if we repeat *Lie Down—Lie Down* often enough, it will seem curious and new and become fashionable.

65. EMILY CARR

My friend Mary told me long ago that when I was *older* I would remember something we experienced together, something bizarre—which is to say something that puzzled us both when we were small. I have an inkling of what that memory will be but want to reach the point of clarity myself—not see it through her eyes.

The strange thing is, when I mentioned this event I was to remember and now do, she had forgotten it entirely. "Ah," says she. "Now that you remind me, I can build on that again." Then she produced another occasion we experienced together—one she had never mentioned before. Both these memories involve Emily Carr.

Miss Carr's reputation crackled around the town as a feisty, obstreperous, scornful woman. A good friend to some, she let nothing or no one cross her when she needed to paint. To most she was someone to avoid. Few appreciated her talent as an artist, as a writer, but Mum did. She loved her drawings and her paintings of trees with a passion—but loathed what she called *those plasticine poles*! But then, she couldn't *see* totem poles at all. They weren't part of her, as they are of us. And Mum was probably a little jealous. She had a twenty-four-hour job looking after all of us when, most of the time, she yearned to paint.

Now my own memories: On one of Granny's visits to the coast in the late 1930s, Aunt Fran, who always came with her, announced she wanted to go to Emily Carr's studio. She had heard about her work through the Group of Seven and was intrigued. Would Mum arrange it? Grandpapa Porteous, their father, had been a part-time painter, a collector and a patron of young Canadian artists whose work he admired. He dearly wished that one of his children would become a painter too. But, of them all, he felt only Mum had talent. So it grieved him when she married young instead of devoting herself to art. When his youngest daughter came down with polio in her teens, there wasn't much she could do, sitting in her wheelchair. She wasn't interested in writing or sewing or photography, so a lot of money was spent training her to draw and paint. Ultimately she made friends with artists like A.Y. Jackson and did some lovely work.

On the day of their visit, Miss Carr's studio was jammed full—with paintings on the walls, hanging from the ceiling and stacked in corners. Granny said, "Now, my dears, I want you each to choose a painting—anything you like." Both Mum and Aunt Fran preferred the freedom of her oils on paper. The price for these was forty dollars. Aunt Fran, for whom money was of no account, chose a lovely study of a Douglas fir. But Mum, who would have loved one, said, "Oh! No thank you, Mum. I couldn't accept such a present. I could feed my family for a month on that amount!" And that was the end of it.

Some years later, Aunt Fran died, then Granny. Mum and her surviving siblings met at their family home on l'île d'Orléans and each chose what they wanted from the estate. The first thing Mum picked was Emily Carr's *Tree*, that painting chosen by Aunt Fran all those years ago. Its value had risen a great deal, but at that point she could afford it.

Fast-forward another twenty years. Dane Campbell, a professional photographer in Victoria, was commissioned by the Vancouver Art Gallery to photograph all of Emily Carr's work in private collections in Victoria. At that point Mum was living in the White House in Oak Bay. When he arrived, there was a terrific din coming from her apartment. Mum was frantic. She'd just bought a new radio and couldn't find the volume control. He solved the problem instantly. She was so thankful she called him *Sir Dane*.

A few years later, when Dane Campbell and I were deciding whether or not we'd sail to the Charlottes together, we arranged to meet, for the first time, at Mum's apartment. When he stepped inside to be introduced, to my astonishment Mum said, "Oh! It's Sir Dane! What a pleasure!"

For many years Mum had Emily Carr's *Tree* hanging in her drawing room and enjoyed it enormously. When she died she left it to me for as long as I liked—on the strict understanding that it become part of the Carr collection at the Art Gallery of Greater Victoria. It is there now.

And those other memories? One is rather mundane—that's the one Mary just remembered. She and I are in town, walking along the street with our mothers, when Mum stops us and says, "Did you notice that woman we just passed? It was Emily Carr."

The other, the hazy one that is clear to me now, is more intriguing: Mary and I are six or seven. We are alone, for some reason, on Constance Avenue, going toward Saxe Point Park. On the opposite side of the road a woman approaches in a cart pulled by dogs. As she passes a group of small children, some reach out and pat the dogs. Miss Carr cracks her whip and strikes them. The children cry out in pain. She and her dogs trot on. All of us gasp. There are no adults present. I wish now that I'd checked her expression as she passed us. Was it smug or contrite? But my eyes were on those sobbing children.

I was brought up to revere Emily Carr as a special person—for her paintings, her drawings, her pottery and, later, her writing—but never had I witnessed such needless cruelty. Is that why I *forgot* this episode?

66. DISCOVERY ISLAND

$\mathcal{D}$iscovery Island has about the same landmass as Esquimalt, from south of Lyall Street, minus the Dockyard. It sits off Oak Bay—the largest in a group of small islands. In fair weather you can see it clearly, a low, rather featureless island. Closer to, it is covered with clumps of thick growth: bushes and stooped firs, their backs to the wind, their branches leeward.

Once or twice a year we'd leave Esquimalt early in the morning and sail there—to that magical *never-never land*. We'd muster at the Royal Victoria Yacht Club, as many of us as were eager to go. We knew Captain Beaumont well, but his other guests were usually strangers—people we'd not met before and never saw again. Occasionally there would be a group of young officers from the Royal Navy, but mostly there were families with young children, like us. We would wear comfortable summer gear: shorts or simple cotton dresses, windbreakers, running shoes and sun hats. But some of the other children wore winter city clothes: grey flannel trousers, woollen pullovers or weird knitted woollen dresses and leather-soled shoes—garb we thought totally unacceptable for hot summer days and scrambling over rocks. Yet this only added to the otherworldliness of those occasions.

Our hosts, Captain and Mrs. Beaumont, were gracious and welcoming and obviously enjoyed a mixed bag of people. Weather permitting, we'd board *Discovery Isle* and putter across to Discovery Island in about forty minutes. Once there we'd anchor in a bay and row ashore, then spend the entire day island-bound.

As far as I know, the Beaumonts owned the whole island but for a lighthouse and a small Indian reserve. The shore was edged with a high flange of sea-smoothed rocks, interspersed with coves and tiny pebble beaches. The interior was fairly flat with spinneys of thick fir forest and bushy thickets and lots of open grassy spaces. Hidden amongst all this was a sprinkling of deer and wild sheep. To the west you could see Victoria, a spot in the distance. To the east, and even farther away, was vast San Juan Island—part of the United States. Yes, we were in a thrilling and utterly different world!

Captain and Mrs. Beaumont were English, not Canadian at all. They came to BC long before we met them yet sounded as if they'd just stepped off the boat. So did most of their friends. Their house, designed in part by Samuel Maclure in 1922, was a fair distance from shore and tucked well back behind trees, so was protected from westerly winds. We walked to it along a raised wooden track that ran between high bushes, but for supplies and heavy things there was some sort of mechanized cart. Mrs. Beaumont had studied landscape gardening and grew magnificent flowers and vegetables—her garden was walled to keep out the deer—and for a while she inspired our Frances Mary to do the same thing.

The Beaumonts had no children of their own, but they enjoyed us—that was obvious—and we were free to do whatever we wished. Sometimes Captain Beaumont took us for walks along the rocky shore, and on rare occasions he let us put our fingers through a hole between the bones in his calf—a bullet wound, he said, from the Boer War? Its provenance kept changing. And he had been in the navy, for heaven's sakes!

We'd leave Esquimalt early in the morning and sail to Discovery Island, that magical never-never land, and run wild with the wind and the sheep.

Mostly we'd go exploring by ourselves—running wild with the wind and the sheep, sometimes glimpsing startled deer as we raced through dark and twisted firs and across those tufted open spaces. It was my dream to walk around the island's circumference without stepping off the rocks, but invariably we would only be partway around when it was time for lunch or tea, and we'd have to hightail it overland—straight across the island. There was so much room. I loved it there!

At noon we were served a fabulous lunch of rich and delicious things: slices of Melton Mowbray pie, cold chicken, roast beef, various chutneys, salads of all sorts (none of them quivering), delicious breads and cheeses with special crackers and quantities of fruit. Then at teatime they'd produce endless exquisite *petits fours* from the Bon Ton—all iced in pale subtle colours. We were used to good food at home, but theirs seemed fabulous.

Their house sat low on the ground with large comfortable rooms leading one from the other, jammed full of treasures from around the world: fine paintings, carvings, spears, shields, daggers and lots and lots of books. In the front hall was a long wooden chest. We were warned never to get inside it, because when the top was shut it would lock and we might be stuck there—forever. The inference was that someone had died in it. We weren't children who helped ourselves to other people's things without invitation, but I must say that chest was awfully tempting.

Once when young RN officers came to the island with us, we took them exploring. I was about six and perfectly at ease, and thinking they needed entertaining, I chattered to them all the way. At one point one of them asked Hilly why in the world she called me *Ba*. Now Hilly was shy and prone to silence, but on occasion she could be extraordinarily brave. She looked at them in astonishment, pulled herself up to her full height and said, "Because that's her name!" I was so proud of her.

I wonder, now, how on earth the Beaumonts managed to entertain so lavishly and as often as they did. Was Mrs. Beaumont really as well-to-do as Mum claimed? Dad insisted Captain Beaumont hadn't a bean. Those jaunts must have been a huge expense for them. Perhaps they knew what an enormous treat they were for all of us. I just hope they enjoyed them too.

From time to time the Beaumonts came to lunch at Wychbury and sometimes stayed on for tea. But when they did, they seemed anxious—conscious, always, of their need to get back to the island before dark.

During the war, two British evacuees, a boy and a girl, came to stay with them. They were young schoolchildren, relations, I think—city children. An idyllic situation, I thought. But they weren't much fun and didn't seem at all happy on the island, so they were sent off somewhere else. Later on, when Mrs. Beaumont fell ill, Hilly visited her in hospital as often as she could. She was the only one of us living in town at the time. When Mrs. Beaumont died, Hilly had been teaching for a while and wasn't sure what to do next—so Captain Beaumont asked if she'd like to come to the island and be his housekeeper. Thinking of the hole in his leg and that wooden chest, she declined.

Many of our friends and contemporaries were never invited to Discovery Island. Others were not allowed to go there, even with friends. The trip across was considered too dangerous—or Captain Beaumont's seamanship was deemed inadequate. Or was that just sour grapes? Whatever their situation, *we* waited eagerly for our annual invitations to the island and were never ever disappointed by any of it.

67. PICNICS

Mum's family home, near the village of Sainte-Pétronille on l'île d'Orléans in Québec, sat high above the St. Lawrence, looking south. One of their summer treats was picnics on the beach below, with the eleven children, relations, guests, parents, nannies and servants all carrying down what was needed—food, drink, rugs, bathing suits, towels, sun hats, parasols—all of it down, down those steep and endless steps. It was such a long way down they tended to drop their burdens without much care the minute they reached the beach—so inevitably there'd be sand in the food. Or the salt or the drinks were forgotten so someone would have to troop up and down again. Mum loathed those picnics and that beach that never co-operated—the tide always too low or too high. For her, picnics were to be avoided at all costs. As was swimming in the sea.

"No thanks," she'd say. "I'm a lake person. There'll be no more gritty meals for me—if I have anything to say about it!"

Most of us disagreed on both counts, but when it came to meals—the where and the how—she ruled the roost. So picnics at Wychbury were rare—little more than Tim sharing his lunch with me. Or, when I was considerably older, feasts of fruit or whatever else we could cadge from the kitchen to carry up to the roof, *en cachette*, with friends. As young kids and adolescents we felt brave as lions. We had to be. The only way there was through one of the attic dormer windows—then a steep scramble up to the flatter parts. The view was fantastic but the route, there and back, gives me the shivers now, just thinking of it.

Otherwise, the closest we came to family picnics were Sunday lunches on the lawn in warm weather—all of us seated on the green wooden bench that stretched along the dip between the croquet lawn and the tennis court. We sat there feasting on cold meat or chicken, bread and butter, cheese, fruit and those delectable meat pies from Durrant's Bakery—watching tennis, the players coming or going as matches ended.

Mother's twin sister, Arabella Cicely (Aunt Ara to most, but to me Auntie Bella), was an almost identical twin but with very different tastes and ideas. She loved both picnics and the sea. Fearless and independent, she drove a brown Studebaker, then a pale yellow car called Primrose, and often swam in the sea alone. Sometimes she took us with her—to exotic places like Esquimalt Lagoon in front of Hatley Park, to Botanical Beach beyond Sooke, or even to Cowichan Bay. As soon as we got there we'd rush into the icy sea—in and out again. Then we'd sit about in what she called "wet suitings" (something not encouraged at home) while devouring her *emergency rations*—so unlike our food. With her we felt like wild adventurers and came home exhilarated.

Once, though, Mum couldn't avoid a picnic by the sea. It was when Towner Bay Park was being developed. The man in charge, A.E. Scott, tried to get a number of friends interested in investing. Dad was intrigued and insisted we go to a meeting-cum-picnic on the beach. Mum hated the idea of sharing land but couldn't get out of the picnic. Perhaps that was why she forgot my bathing suit. Everyone else rushed into the sea. But at three or four I refused to swim in the nude. So I stood on that pebbly beach, feeling righteous and pouty, while they enjoyed the lovely warm water.

No wonder. Just a few days before, I woke from my nap earlier than usual and went down to the back verandah to swing in the hammock. It was a very hot day. I lay across the hammock, swinging, for quite a long time—rocking higher and higher—until I became aware of Dad. He was sunbathing below me in the nude, just beyond the hammock and out of sight of anyone but me. I was astounded. There he was—with his penis standing straight up to heaven. I'd never seen anything like it! So I stared and stared—until my staring woke him. Surprised and embarrassed, he roared, making me feel I had done something wicked. Of course I wouldn't swim in my bare skin after that! I'd have to shout, as Dad had shouted at me! And give them nightmares too!

Against Mum's wishes, Dad became a charter member of the Towner Bay Country Club and bought one of those lots. Some of my older siblings camped there occasionally, but when money was really short, the lot was sold.

Later, when I was five and quite grown up, I met the Emmertons, Mary and her mother, and went on outings with them. They loved picnics and often included me. One of their favourite spots was our own Fleming's Beach, a place I knew well because that's where we swam, when not at the Lake, and where we explored often, in every season. Its crystal clear water was coldish but bracing, and the view across to the Olympics was glorious. It was all so familiar, yet with them it was different, for we went far to the left-hand side of the bay, where the beach tucked into a curve by the bank and faced west. After lovely long swims we'd eat an exotic lunch of hard-boiled eggs, brown bread and butter, and large cold broad beans, followed by chocolate potato cake, tea or lemonade—all homemade. They took me to other places, too, and it was always fun.

Recently I went exploring in some of my childhood haunts, including a pilgrimage to Fleming's Beach. What a disappointment! There

Sylvia, Irish Eileen (the nanny), Mum, Helen, Mary, Mike, Hilly and Joanie get ready to swim at Fleming's Beach, 1932.

is an organized parking lot where our sledding hill used to be, a boat launch and a paved path between the base of the rock cliff and the sand. Everything seems organized and worn out. Worst of all, a breakwater stretches across the mouth of the bay, almost closing it. Thus, what was once moving water—crystal clear and cold—is now a still and stagnant pond. Obviously this was done for the convenience of boaters, but what a criminal shame! It has wrecked the beach for swimming and for picnics. Even in April the water stank and was filled with lumps of slimy growth. What must it be like in summer?

I used to wonder why the "Ems" came to Esquimalt so often, apart from coming to see us. But Bill and Aileen were married at St. Paul's Church in 1930, with their wedding reception at a friend's house on Constance Avenue. Later, after we left Esquimalt, they bought the Sismans' house at 1024 Munro. Then, not long after their daughter married, they switched houses with Mary and their son-in-law and lived on Nelson Street.

But to get back to picnics—sometimes at the Lake, Mum would relent and we'd make a fire in a cleft of those sloping rocks between the old pine on the point and the beach. Then we'd all troop across from Savira's kitchen, carrying whatever was needed. Well away from sand we'd roast wieners or sausages, crunch on apples, toasted marshmallows and homemade buns. Then we'd heat milk and water for cocoa and tea.

As night deepened around us we would stay put, sitting on cushions or warm rocks, till it got really dark—smelling the woodsmoke, sweet gale and wild mint; listening to loons and lapping water; watching sparks fly. We'd tell stories and sing our favourite songs: "Ranzo Boys" and "Moscow's Burning" and "Row, Row, Row Your Boat"—in rounds. There was just the dark around us, and our own voices. We might have been hundreds of miles from our house—and from everyone else's, for that matter. For all of us, even for Mum, those picnics were sublime.

That point, and the beach beside it, has belonged to me for a long time now. I have held on to it all these years because of those picnics—but some day soon I must sell.

68. RUSSIA

One day in the mid-thirties, Dad announced that we were moving—all of us together, in a body—to Russia, just as we'd come from Québec. Mum was amazed. She hadn't heard a thing about this and asked "Why?" Dad said he'd had his ear to the ground and was impressed by Stalin's clever reforms, and we would be better off there. I think he liked the idea that everything would be provided by the state. But Mum said she had her ear to the ground too and had quite a different view of life in Russia. Perhaps she'd heard of the *planned famine* in Ukraine and the five million dead because of it. And how Stalin's "favourites" were sent to the gulags in Siberia, "disappeared" along with anyone who opposed his cause.

"No!" she said. "Go, if you must, but we'll stay!"

And we did and so did he. So we never did turn up in those extraordinary photos the Soviets took of everyone they sent to Siberia. What beauty, courage and acceptance there is in those faces of the doomed—most of them to die from cold and starvation or unbearably hard labour. But some survived their twenty-five-year sentences and lived to tell the tale.

There was a powerful and heart-rending program about this on TV recently. Peter King, a contemporary British photographer/archivist, fascinated by the survivors of Stalin's régime, went to Moscow and managed to find hundreds of those old photos from the thirties and forties of all the people sent to Siberia—many of them taken by the famous Russian photographer Alexander Mikhailovich Rodchenko. Later Rodchenko and all the other photographers were forced to black out the faces of those who were shot—or who died from the effects of the gulags—as if by taking those photos, they too were implicated.

In 1931 a Mongolian family made the long journey to meet their glorious leader. Stalin picked up their pretty little daughter and held her in his arms, and the two of them were photographed grinning at each other. Someone made a sculpture from that photo and cast it in bronze. Stalin was so delighted he had a great many copies made—to be displayed around the country. Then suddenly all those sculptures were destroyed—as were the girl's parents, the sculptor and that photographer. But somehow the girl survived.

Could Dad have withstood a régime as quixotic? Surely he would have complained at some point and been shot. Or, at least, been sent to the gulags with all of us, to appear in the records as *that ridiculous Canadian family*—shown, perhaps, in those saved photos, our faces all blacked out.

Thank goodness Mum was there, to counterbalance his enthusiasms.

69. RIBBON

Each fall Mum and I made a special trip to Victoria to visit the Notions Department at David Spencer's. Our purpose was to choose ribbons for the lavender sachets she sent to relations in the east, or gave to her sister in Saanich and local friends. Mum had some fifty cousins on her side. Dad had four sisters. Most of these were on her list.

Mum could have found ribbon in the village, but she wanted special ribbon of interesting patterns: zigzags, stripes, spots or flowers, embossed or embroidered. Sometimes she chose plain ribbon of special or subtle colours. She had already bought metres of coloured organza, also from the Notions Department, which she cut into squares of about twenty-five centimetres that were laid one over the other to make a star shape—perhaps of the same colour repeated or combinations of colours. The ribbon would enhance each individual sachet and was chosen with care.

David Spencer's was famous for its long, comfortable benches where the weary could rest their bones, just inside the doors on the ground floor. The store also had "islands" for special things like gloves or ribbons—where nothing else was sold. I think they were round, but they may have been hexagonal. The ribbon saleswomen would be inside those islands, and we would sit on high stools around the periphery, just as we did when buying gloves.

The choosing took hours, so on these occasions we would leave home by ten and take the streetcar to be in town by eleven. Mum would survey the situation with her favourite saleswoman and have things put aside. Then, around one o'clock, we would take the lift up to the top floor and have a hot lunch in the restaurant—a place that smelled delicious and served really good food. This was a special treat. Mum would have reserved a table by the window so we could look out over the rooftops of the town below us, and across the harbour to glimpses of Esquimalt and the Sooke Hills. Sometimes gulls would land at our window and sit chatting on the ledge beside us. Both of us expected and needed afternoon naps, but on these occasions good food and excitement sustained us.

After lunch we would descend and Mum would make her final decisions and purchases. For a small person this choosing seemed to last forever. It was difficult sitting still. So I would turn on my stool from side to side and practise Dad's foot exercises for Olympic figure skaters, twirling my ankles inward and outward, or in alternating directions. But the fun of that didn't last long so I'd turn my back on the proceedings and watch the other shoppers and the passersby. I was obliged to stay there and sat with mounting excitement—because at the end of it all, short snippets of my favourite ribbons would be bought to adorn my pigtails or be made into hair bands when my hair was worn loose. Eventually, when Mum finished choosing and all our shopping was done, we'd leave. Excited and weary, our arms full of packages, we'd take the Number 4 streetcar home again.

Mum grew quantities of lavender in great round bushes in a long row between her standard roses, which edged the path between the house and the croquet lawn. She would clip her lavender in sunlight, just after the full moon, when the flowers were at their best and their scent glorious. Then she would spread it on trays in shallow layers, covered with muslin, and leave it to dry—out of the sun. The back verandah was a perfect spot for this, as long as it didn't rain. When they were properly dried, I was allowed to help pull the flowers from the stalks. That was hard on the hands but the sweet scent was worth it. Once it was all sorted and picked over, Mum put a handful of lavender in the centre of each star of organza and cinched it up with ribbon. The results were stunning and gave her great pleasure, making a direct link to the south of France. But then more choices had to be made: Who got which and how many?

All these sachets would be boxed in nests of tissue paper. Then each box was wrapped and tied with ribbon, wrapped again with brown paper, secured with twine, labelled and sent east, which meant Québec in our house —the exception being Toronto, where her school friend Marian Osler lived.

I've always wondered how those sachets were received. Did recipients groan: *Oh no—not again!* Or were they pleased? Had they any idea of the effort involved in making them? Mum would have loved to send costly gifts but these sachets were the best she could do, with both time and money so short. And they were what she would have liked to have been given—but wasn't, of course. In fact, I don't think anyone sent her anything other than cards or little notes, the occasional cheque or hand-me-downs.

It was Dad's side of the family that gave—those same people who developed *hates* for each other, and sometimes feuds. How they loved giving presents!

70. EVERYDAY MANNERS

Manners, Mum insisted, were the grease that makes the world run smoothly. Neglect them and trouble begins. So we tried our best to be considerate, to share, to be thankful: those were the basic premises from which our manners sprang.

When we came down for breakfast, we kissed Mum and Dad and said *Good mornings* all round. At breakfast, as at all meals, grace was said by Dad, but we didn't have to wait and sit down together, as we did in the dining room. And we could race off to school without ceremony.

In the dining room our food was served at table: meat and desserts by Mum and vegetables by one of the older ones. Only at high tea on Sunday evening were cold cuts and salads passed around. Preferably you didn't ask for things but waited until something was offered. In despair you could say, *Please may I have…?* But you didn't interrupt or butt in. You always said *Please* and *Thank you* and you were expected to finish everything on your plate. But if someone loathed something, he or she was given just a tiny bit: *un tout petit soupçon*, Mum would say.

Salt was in saltcellars—never shakers. Using the tiny spoon provided, you put a small amount of salt at the edge of your plate and dipped your food into it. Butter, if needed, was put on the edge of one's dinner plate or side plate, with the butter knife. You never buttered a slice of bread or a bun but broke off small pieces and buttered them. When we had chicken or meat on the bone, we could pick it up and eat with our fingers if we said, *The King, God Bless Him!* When we had corn on the cob or asparagus, it was always eaten in the fingers. That was the way one did things—the way one *could* do things anywhere. And if we were giving a dinner party, a finger bowl was set at each place. Meals were fun. There was talk and laughter and there were Dad's stories—familiar maybe, but always with a new twist. Unless you were helping to clear the table between courses, you didn't get up until the meal was over, except for emergencies, and then you asked to be excused.

In the street Dad inclined his head, made a tiny bow and tipped his hat to women, those he knew or admired. He did the same thing when he entered a shop or an office. And last thing in the evening, following Granny's example, Mum taught us to tidy toys, books, magazines and newspapers—but especially to plump the cushions in the drawing room, when we went to bed, so the room would look pleasant for the servants in the morning—even if there weren't any.

In theory, children didn't speak until spoken to. Then, when introduced to adults, we said: *How do you do, Mrs. So-and-So?* And she answered: *Very well, thank you, my dear, and how are you?* And we answered: *Very well, thank you.* However we felt!

But there was a different code when we spoke to other kids. One could be honest, enthusiastic and, at times, brutal. You used a different vocabulary and said what you thought, though you tried not to hurt other people's feelings if you could manage it. And if you saw you had, you said you were sorry and made amends.

71. EARLY MORNING TEA

*C*ach morning, once Dad had dressed and gone down to feed and water the horses, Mum would fill her kettle with fresh water from the bathroom and put it on the hot plate by her bed. When the kettle sang she'd scald the teapot, empty it, add tea and fill it with boiling water. While it steeped she'd snuggle back under the covers for a few moments of peace and quiet. If she hadn't done so already she'd read the daily lesson or the gospel or whatever book she was reading. She wasn't alone, but her companion, Winston the Pooh, or Pooh for short, didn't say much. He'd have woken her, as he always did, with a gentle paw on her cheek—his signal: *I really think it's time for our tea, Madame!* When it was ready she'd fill his bowl with milk, then add a little tea. (This was known as Cambric Tea—a special drink for children and cats.) She'd put his bowl on a mat on the floor by her bed. For her the reverse: a little milk in her cup, then a lot of tea. This was their private indulgence—a ceremony the two of them enjoyed alone. And each might have several cups.

No one can remember, now, where that jug of milk was kept. My guess is on the windowsill. As a family we slept in cool bedrooms with windows wide open, wind or cool breezes caressing our cheeks—quite enough to keep milk sweet overnight. But we all liked warm bathrooms.

Had Mum done this always, with all her cats, I wonder? Or was this a special treat she shared with Pooh—a moment of calm before their busy days began?

72. THE WASHING OF WIGS

In our family we didn't talk about washing our hair. It was our "wigs" we dealt with. Though my elder sisters preferred bought shampoos, Mum used Castille soap for Hilly and me. It came in long golden bars, and whenever hair was to be washed she'd shave a handful of soap into a small pot she kept for this purpose. Then water was added and the mixture warmed on the same hot plate she used for her morning tea. When creamy and translucent, it was ready for use.

For convenience, Mum washed our heads while we were in the bath so she could sit on the edge and proceed using a handheld showerhead. There were no showers in those days—not in our house anyway. This worked very well, except that since becoming chief cook and bottle washer, instead of lady of leisure, Mum's hands had become less sensitive to heat, and sometimes the water she used on us was far too hot. It was said that everyone for miles around knew exactly when my wig was being washed because my shrieks went far and wide! How I dreaded those scaldings.

Then came the final touch. Mum would take some chamomile powder from a blue and green envelope and mix it with warm water. This was her special rinse for fair hair. When chamomile wasn't available (it had to be ordered from far away) fresh lemon juice and water did a good job. She, Hilly and I were blonde, while the others had begun as blondes but soon became brunettes. They might use a henna rinse. Mum had yearned for an auburn-headed child like her great- and great-great-grandmammas on her father's side. Aunt Evie, her sister, was carrot-topped, but unfortunately Dad did not share the necessary gene for red hair. A little henna would have to do.

Apart from the rigours of those early hair-washings, which often meant a scorched scalp and shoulders, I loved the feeling of a clean wig—especially when my hair was long. Then I could swish its silky smoothness and feel the air rush through.

When I was small, my hair was curly—short curls around my head or long curls to my shoulders. Then Mum thought it would be fun to try pigtails. So she plaited my hair and almost immediately it went straight. Only on rare occasions—when the moon is right and the atmosphere just so—are there waves or *almost* curls. But no amount of wishing will make them stay. Instead it is the males of the family who have curly hair: Dad, my brothers—Jamie and Michael— my son, Adam, and his son, Heydon.

73. BIKES

After Peter bought his bike, Dad saw how practical they were and bought one for each of his daughters when they were old enough to manage an adult bike. After that the three eldest rode them across town each morning to St. Margaret's School and home again at night. Or they biked to Esquimalt High. On weekends they explored our world—zooming about in all directions. Not long after, Hilly was given one too and joined them. Then Mike got his. I waited breathlessly for mine.

By the time my legs were long enough to ride a big bike, my sisters were driving cars and taking busses or had left home. So there was always a spare bike and sometimes two or three to choose from and Dad saw no sense in buying another for me. All our bikes had foot brakes and no gears and were quite heavy, but to us they were sheer delight. We rode, wind or rain in our faces, hair streaming out behind us. Helmets did not exist.

We loved zipping down hills. One of our favourites was at the lower end of Lampson Street, where there is a steep stretch—with enough room to slow down at Munro, the cross street. Once Joanie was sailing down that hill. Showing off with a group of friends and coasting at top speed, she stood—with no hands. The cloth of her pant leg caught in the chain and over she went—chin first onto asphalt! She was not a pretty sight: slightly concussed with her chin split open. She needed stitches and her wound took a long time to heal. The next time Jamie came home he asked, "Why has Joanie a dirty chin?"

On bikes we explored Esquimalt, Victoria, Oak Bay and out into Saanich. We thought nothing of riding up the Malahat to Shawnigan Lake, and we tried to stay on the whole way without getting off. In the steepest parts we'd stand up and keep pedalling. Only if exhausted would we dismount and push. There was always the Cut-off to look forward to, winding down to Shawnigan West Road, and then almost flat ground the three miles on to Savira. Dad always honked his horn to announce his approach—two longs, two shorts, repeated—so we did too, with our bells—no matter that no one heard them.

The summer of 1936, when Joanie and Mary turned thirteen and twelve, they went to Guide Camp on the Sooke Flats. When they got back to Savira they longed for more adventure and begged to be allowed to bike up-Island by themselves. Mum and Dad were agreeable. They gave them five dollars each and a blanket and wished them Godspeed. Their only advice: sleep in cow barns, as horses won't eat hay that's been slept on.

All along their route, people were really kind. Their first night was at that wonderful valley-bottom farm on the highway, just north of

Cobble Hill Road. Five nights later they reached their destination—family friends who lived north of Parksville. They kept horses so allowed the girls to sleep on their verandah—a huge treat for those hardbitten travellers.

I'm not sure if they slept in the same barns on the way home but, as always, the return trip took far less time than their journey up the Island.

Riding a bike without a helmet is even more magical than sailing because you are free. You can change direction in a second, stop or spin around. You can see everything, hear everything, smell everything and feel the wind against your body. And you are in control.

I gather the only place one can do this now is in the Florida Keys, where people still use

Joanie and Mary went to Guide Camp on the Sooke Flats, and returned tanned and tough.

bikes with foot brakes—those lovely old steady bikes that you can ride with your feet on the handlebars, if you wish, and your lunch and whatever you find en route in your basket—wicker of course! The next best thing is sitting in a rumble seat. But there you are at the whim of the driver.

Meanwhile, I have not given up. Some day soon there'll be a bike with my name on it under the Christmas tree—or leaning up against the breakfast table on my birthday. A bike with foot brakes, a bell and a basket! I believe in dreams.

74. RAIN

Mum says we live on the "Raincoast" and it is rain that makes our trees so vast, our wild flowers and bushes plentiful, and our fruit and vegetables so delicious. Rivers and streams rushing down into the sea, because of the rain, bring food to the fish and all sea creatures. Over the years those same streams carve great valleys in our hills and mountains. Yet rain falling on your face feels so gentle. I love it, being out in it, running through it, getting soaking wet, hearing it pattering on the ground or thundering on rooftops—the way it slips down pavement in great tongues and forms puddles we can jump in. I can't tell Mum, though, but if I had to choose, I much prefer the rain to snow.

My brother Michael has a theory that rain falling on beaches doesn't wet you as it does on land. Be that as it may, in Esquimalt rain is standard fare year-round, especially in winter. So we wore gumboots, slickers and sou'westers for the worst storms. For gentler showers a series of navy blue Burberrys is handed on down the line. With them go rubbers that slip on over our shoes, their tongues covering the vamp. For *soft* days we wear stout oxfords. Mine have "anti-scuff shark's skin toes" and don't mind going through puddles a bit. I love these shoes and the little plastic shark's tooth on a bright silk ribbon that comes with them to prove their authenticity.

Adding comfort to our protective gear is the cloakroom just inside the door off the back verandah. It has hooks for coats on each side of the steps that lead down to a sink. Above those hooks are wire-mesh shelves where we put damp mittens, gloves and berets. We each have our own spots—the youngest near the top steps, on down to the eldest at the bottom. The basement door is left open so heat rising from the furnace dries our clothes overnight, leaving them warm and ready for the next day's shower.

One year I have my very own raincoat of brown and white houndstooth rubberized cloth, from whose pockets furred cough drops might emerge months after they'd been proffered by Mum on the way in to church—in case. That coat has an odd smell, but to have one's own new garment in a big family is a rare delight during the Depression, just as it is to have *new shoes*!

75. SKATING

𝒟ad loved to skate. Before moving west, he took part in ice-dance competitions in Québec and New England and often won. But Mum, even as his fiancée, didn't skate well enough to be his partner so had to be content with the cast-off husbands of good skaters. In those days women wore nothing but black for skating, with long sleeves and skirts all the way down to the ankle. Mum thought these outfits both dull and cumbersome. "They make us look like crows!" she said. So when Dad was to compete in Boston, she had her dressmaker design a long-sleeved scarlet outfit with a full skirt to mid-calf. When she appeared in this outlandish garb, people were aghast. But a member of the royal family was there and remarked to his neighbour in a loud voice: "Who is that woman in red? Isn't she stunning! I say, what a good idea!" Ever since, most women skate in skimpy and twinkly coloured costumes. But if anyone dares wear something simple, long or black, they are thought elegant or eccentric.

Dad loved to skate, waltzing and twirling around the ice with Mum in Québec City.

When there were skating rinks or arenas in Victoria (which sounds almost as rare and wonderful as *When there were bears in Denmark*), we would be there, all of us, part of the crowd, struggling to keep upright, practising our basic figures, with a little grace, if possible, while Dad cut capers around us or waltzed and twirled with Mrs. Homer-Dixon or any of the other good skaters. Everyone else went round and round the arena, singly or in pairs. Those rinks would last a year or two—then burn down. So our progress was slow, and before the next one was up and ready we would need larger skates. Luckily we had a big collection of all sizes stashed in a huge wooden throne in the front hall. When its seat was lifted, there they all were. It was just a question of choosing the right pair. But all of them were figure skates. No hockey or bob skates allowed.

As clearly as I hear the canned music of those arenas, the scuffling sounds of skates on ice and the excited cries and thumps of the fallen, I see the *getting there*—the long, slow journeys from Esquimalt across town to that *terra incognita*—otherwise known as the Willows—where the ice rinks were, driving almost always in fog, with one of us walking ahead with a flashlight—leading the Packard. But

We would go to Thetis Lake, and zoom after Dad on frosted wings.

whenever Jamie was home on leave, there was no fog at all. He would pilot the Packard, airborne—a foot or two above the road!

And then there were those magical years when it froze, then snowed, and Mum would be out before breakfast, pummelling the night's collection from her precious cypress tree—her treasure from Provence. We would go skating on Swan Lake or to the Izards' on Admirals Road and launch ourselves from their wharf out and across the frozen waters of Portage Inlet. Or, better still, we'd go to Thetis Lake, where we might rendezvous with the Murray family. We'd go for the day and, when hungry, sit on the snowy banks and have hot chocolate and *pain au chocolat*—though really just lumps of baking chocolate in chunks of Coburg loaves, but delicious anyway.

Then that marvellous sensation: setting off on ice so fresh and firm you'd hear it crack and crinkle—bending a little underfoot, then swelling up again as you raised your skate. "Don't worry," Dad would say, "that means the ice is strong!" Then in ones or twos or threes we'd zoom off after him on frosted wings—into the distance and around that ring of lake—each stroke a small arpeggio of sound.

Who could forget that?

76. SLEDDING

In the distant past, glaciers ground Esquimalt's rocky surface, so any slabs that thrust themselves up through the soil seem wrinkled as elephant's skin, cracked maybe, or hollowed—but basically smooth. Whether along the shore near the sea, in the middle of meadows or deep in the forest, such rock is there, and it begs you to run along it—to race along it, barefoot.

One rocky hillock down by Fleming's Beach became a quarry for road building. It was also our tobogganing hill. And while Mum and Dad waited for what they called "decent weather"—deep dry snow and low temperatures—so they could dash about in their horse-drawn sleigh or zoom off on snowshoes, as they had done in Québec, the rest of us were content with just enough snow for toboggans and sleds.

We could practise on the front lawn with very little snow, but the best place by far was the gravel quarry as we could swoop down at tremendous speed, almost to the beach. In our day there was still a lot of that hill left, so a great many could zip down it together and still leave space for others to scurry back up to the top. I loved that mix of friends and strangers, all enjoying this rare treat together—the shrieks and roars, the laughter and giggles and the cries of those inadvertently bumped into. Some were rasher than others or poor judges of distance as they crashed often. And others acted in a madcap manner on purpose, like our sister Mary, who would steer sharp left near the bottom of the hill, trying her best to reach the beach—if not the sea.

As that hill was bitten away by the quarrymen, sledding became treacherous. And nowadays no one would guess it had ever been possible, for all that remains is a cliff above and a parking lot below.

In my mind we are always careening down that hill or clambering up again for another turn. We are never sledding down Lampson Street, as we always did on the way there, or lugging our sleds and toboggans back again afterward—uphill, going home. No. We are *there*, on that hill, in bright sunshine, in the midst of all that gaiety: going down—going up—going down—on and on—on that marvellous rocky slope that is nothing more, now, than air.

77. THE FRONT HALL

Wychbury's front staircase swept down in a three-quarter turn—right down into the huge front hall. Halls like ours were a feature of Samuel Maclure's large houses, with rooms leading from them in all directions. A rounded banister edged the staircase with a square wooden pillar at each turn—the most important, a supporting beam, rising from the floor of the front hall right up to the ceiling of the upstairs hall, so the last stretch of banister was perfect for zooming down. Your back would slam into the beam if you went backward. Or if you were rash enough to go forward, you could catch it yourself with your hands. Those who'd given up travelling by banister could make an elegant descent without looking down, as these steps were designed with deep treads and shallow rises. We young ones often came down on our bottoms, *bump bump bump*. That way you missed nothing going on in the hall below and made what seemed to us a rather grand entrance. We girls wore stout underpants—often of the same stuff as our dresses—and the boys were well protected by their shorts.

At the bottom of the stairs was a portrait of Grandpapa—or so I thought. I would commune with him often. I knew Mum loved him dearly so considered him my friend. It was a shock to discover it was someone else entirely—a French officer my parents admired during the Great War: Monsieur le Maréchal Foch. So he became my friend by proxy, and eventually the print of him, in its good frame, was given to me. I have him hanging to this day in my studio, as a sort of "familiar"-cum-guardian. From time to time visitors recognize him and greet him appropriately.

The front hall was the heart of our house, and a lot happened there. Almost the size of the drawing room, it had a large brick fireplace in the centre of the north wall. A wrought iron seat, some ten or twelve feet long, stretched beyond the hearth on both sides—stuffed with horsehair and covered with deep plum morocco leather. It came from a military mess, and was bought by Dad at auction. I often lay full-length along that seat, whether or not the fire was lit, dreaming—perhaps of that extraordinary Christmas when, to my absolute delight, I had *two* stockings: the usual woollen one and a *bought* stocking of red mesh that came stuffed with cheap but utterly entrancing toys—one of them a small bag full of tin cooking pots just large enough for mice! I'm sure it came from my big sister Sylvia, who always seemed to know exactly what I yearned for.

Another treasure in the front hall was the old grandfather clock that stood to the left of the library door. We can't remember if it came from Québec or was bought at auction in Victoria. It was a handsome piece of dark carved wood. We all enjoyed the sounds of the ticking and melodic chiming. Eventually it stopped, so Dad took it to town to be mended. We were to be phoned when it was ready. When there was no word for months, Dad called and was told a part was on order. More months passed, and more. Eventually Dad dropped around to see what was happening. He found that the owner of the shop had died and everything in it had gone to his heirs. Undaunted, Mum painted a clock face on paper to replace it. One could rely on the time of day that way.

There were two large leather chairs on the left-hand side of the fireplace: one black and smooth and glossy, whose back you could slide down; the other deep red and soft with lots of button eyes. Two or three small people could sit in them together quite comfortably. When we had dances, these chairs would be pushed into the library so the overflow of dancers from the drawing room could use the front hall. This was perfect for us as we could peek over the banisters from the upstairs hall and watch the goings-on or, if really brave, creep partway down the stairs in our pyjamas and peer through the railings without being seen. We saw a lot more than we were supposed to—dancers who chose the hall for privacy to hug, dance cheek-to-cheek or give the occasional kiss! Sometimes guests would catch sight of us and wave or chat. I loved watching these swirling figures, the beautiful dresses, the tails or the dinner jackets. Everyone seemed so happy. I yearned for the day when I could join them. But by then war was raging and all of us were busy—"doing our bit." Big house parties were becoming a thing of the past. There were dances, but in public places. Any extra funds went to Victory Bonds—not for dresses, booze, music or special food. That era had ended.

But Christmas stockings and *tillies* continue to this day, wherever we are, for every single member of the family—plus guests!

78. HORSES

It wasn't that I didn't like horses. I loved them! But I didn't want them bridled and saddled with a person on their backs, especially if I were that person. I wanted them running free. One of my favourite things was to go with Dad to the horse pasture across the road from the stables. As soon as they saw him, their heads rose, jaws still munching. Then to his "Hola! Hola!" they would run in a body toward us—like dogs whistled for a walk, their heads held high, excitement on their faces. And up the field they'd canter, manes and tails flying in the wind. So beautiful! That to me was sublime—horses free and moving as they wished.

Then we gave each one a treat: an apple from the orchard or a carrot—sometimes a sugar lump. And Dad would say, "Now, remember

I didn't want the horses bridled and saddled with a person on their backs. I wanted them running free! H.M.P. photo

your thumb! Cup your hand and keep your thumb well down. And don't be nervous!" And those huge beasts would nuzzle our hands so gently—they might have been giving us kisses. That's how I liked them best.

I saw no sense in the world in getting up on their backs and bobbing about. But had it been possible to run with them, to run amongst them and keep up with them—that would have been a dream come true!

I kept that in mind and ran as much as I could so that some day we might run together.

*

Children are running on that land now, at least I hope they are, for that field and the Maynards' property next door to it have become the site of Macaulay Elementary School. Do any of those children dream about running with horses?

*

When Mum and Dad left Wychbury and moved up to live in Savira at Shawnigan Lake, Dad found homes for all his horses but three:

Tess, Goldcrest and her full-grown colt Titus. Fran and Michael rode them up to Shawnigan to summer at Uncle Charlie Armstrong's—a temporary measure while the move took place. But after it, Dad was out of commission: exhausted, dispirited, aching in every limb. It had been really hard for him, leaving Wychbury.

The horses were homesick too, and one day they leapt the fence, cantered down Shawnigan West Road and up the Cut-off to the highway. There they turned right—then galloped full tilt down the Malahat, through Langford, View Royal and Esquimalt—going home! Poor darlings, they expected to be greeted, patted, praised, watered, fed. But no one was there.

Someone we knew saw them racing along and came to Savira to tell us. Mike went to the rescue, but it was dangerous for one rider to lead two horses up the highway. He needed help. Frances was fishing and could not be reached. Hilly was busy and I was away sailing. So he went to a house near the stables where young Alice Proteau lived. She loved horses and had been helping Dad in exchange for lessons for quite a while—a small slender person but willing and capable. Her parents gave their permission, so the two set off the next morning: a lad of sixteen and a girl of eleven.

This time the horses were left at the Elfords' farm, where Shawnigan West Road starts—closer to our place and with better fencing. And there they stayed until Fran took possession of them that fall and began a lifetime career: schooling horses and teaching riding.

How I would love to have seen those three careening down the Malahat! Then Mike and Alice riding them up again! How gutsy they were—all of them!

79. VISITING and VISITORS

In my exalted position as the Depression Baby, with that sizeable gap between Michael and me, I spent much more time with our mother than any of my siblings. This wasn't her choice, but necessity. I was heavy on hand—her companion, whether she liked it or not. To her credit she never made me feel *de trop*, though it must have been aggravating, having me tagging along wherever she went.

Thus it was I attended all manner of adult affairs: church meetings, lectures, concerts, gatherings and tea parties. Sometimes I went to elegant luncheons (or "nuncheons" as Mum preferred to call them) at the Empress, where children weren't really expected. Once I spent two or three hours outside, alone in the hotel's sunken garden, exploring—waiting till her lecture ended. It was fun at first, but I was really glad when she came out to collect me.

What seemed normal to us—a middle-aged mum with a young child in tow—was a shock for some adults.

Most of the time I enjoyed trailing about with her, sometimes the only child present. And I liked going to the houses of her friends. Some had children my age to play with, but most had children grown up and long since gone. Some of these women were pleasant and made me feel at home. Others ignored me utterly and that was fine. Mum wasn't one of those aggravating parents who'd praise their children in front of others and say ridiculous things like: *Isn't she the loveliest thing you ever saw?* Dad maybe, but not Mum. She was apt to apologize. But some of her friends, who'd probably had both nannies and nursemaids and therefore very little hands-on experience with children, would discuss me as if I were inanimate, an object or some sort of garment to be altered—a sweater (what we called a "jersey") to be undone and knitted again in a better shape. The worst offender was a huge woman my parents were very fond of—whose name was never mentioned without a "dear." Whenever she came to our place, or we to hers, in short order she'd swing the conversation to my person—especially my legs. She called them "her strong understandings." Every time we saw her, some such comment was made. And Mum, who would have loved it if we'd all been dainty like her, would say, "The pity of it is my girls have Jimmie's sisters' legs—not mine." (Mum always called Dad "Jimmie" after the picture on Sunny Jim Cereal.) Then, realizing she was in dangerous territory as her friend's legs were much heavier than ours, she'd change course and say something like: *Well anyway, Ba has really small ears.*

Strangely, it wasn't the slender pretty women or the elegant ones who made these comments, but invariably the large plain ones—with lumpen daughters to match. Mum couldn't understand why I wasn't as fond of these *good women* as she was, and why I would try to vanish when they arrived—or beforehand, if possible.

Though urged constantly to "act like a grownup," it seemed to me there was very little difference between children and adults. Some behave well and are kind. Others are horrid! But the worst of those unfortunate women had a sweet daughter whose son became my friend later on. So there's always hope.

80. IN TOWN WITH DAD

I never knew where we'd end up when I went to town with Dad. We might spend all morning in the Provincial Museum, which was part of the Parliament Buildings then, and a place I loved. Sometimes he left me there for an hour or two, as he knew I'd be both safe and happy—engrossed in all the treasures displayed in the glass cases. There was so much to see. My favourite things were the Indian carvings: wooden masks and rattles, ancient stone bowls and beautifully made tools. We didn't see much of the Indians in Esquimalt. Sometimes they'd be walking along Admirals Road or hanging about near the beer parlours—but they didn't take part in things, which was a pity, I thought. So I decided early on that when I grew up I would learn all I could about these people. One day the curator spoke to me, and when I told him my plans, he said it was Anthropology I should study—West Coast Anthropology.

Other days we'd go to Diggon-Hibben, the stationer. Or we might go to Mc and Mc's, the huge hardware store on Government Street. Dad loved hardware and would spend hours choosing tools—always of the best quality. "You gain nothing by buying cheap tools," he'd say. And to prove his point, when I was the ripe old age of seven, he bought me an expensive hammer. It was a beauty! But I was shocked at its price. So we took it back and I bought a much cheaper one and a lot of little trifles and felt quite smug for a while. I've regretted that silliness ever since but seem doomed to repeat it as I am drawn to bargains.

One of our favourite stops was at Scott and Peden's, the wholesale feed store. We'd go there for vegetable seed, curry combs, dog brushes, chicken feed, salt blocks, bran and oats for the horses, bales of hay for them and the cows, and straw for their stalls and loose-boxes. The smell of the place was wonderful—a blend of feed and rich, fermented molasses. One day he bought me a beautiful Chinese vegetable basket with two handles—probably much more expensive there than it would have been up the street in Chinatown. But I admired it, so he bought it for me. I have it still and keep raw wool in it, to be spun and used whenever there's time or need. When we finished shopping, we'd fill the Packard's trunk, put the overflow inside and go home hungry and satisfied.

Sometimes we didn't shop at all. Dad had business to do and would ask if I'd like to come inside to the office waiting room or stay in the car. He knew my answer. I always chose the car. It was one of my favourite things—sitting watching the world go by. I'd be happy there for hours, observing all the people coming along the sidewalk: how they moved, what shoes they wore, their expressions and what they carried. I never tired of watching them. Eventually Dad would come back with some amusing tale and I'd tell him what I'd seen. We both enjoyed these shopping jaunts and trips to town and all the

The CPR express and ticket office in the harbour was a beautiful building that looked like a Greek temple to me.

special things we did together that made up, I like to think, for my refusal to ride and reluctance to work in the stables.

Another favourite place was the CPR express and ticket office, that Greek temple down on the harbour where the CPR ships docked. I never saw anything arrive as vast or exciting as *The Red Canoe* must have seemed, but all the parcels were thrilling and it was such a beautiful building. At Christmas we sent masses of boxes to that mysterious place "the East." They'd go overnight by boat to Vancouver, then travel right across Canada by train, and once in Québec they'd find their way to our various relations.

On the way home we might stop in Chinatown for some Keemun tea for Mum, or crystallized ginger in those pretty coloured cardboard boxes, exactly the same to this day. Our parents had enormous respect for the Chinese of Victoria. If ever we were in town on Saturday, Dad would drive us past their school and say, "Look! They built that school at their own expense and they are teaching all their children Chinese. Isn't that splendid!" I wanted to learn it too. And still do.

81. PIPES

Our pipes weren't Irish or Northumbrian, unfortunately, but the hot-water heating pipes that kept our whole house cosy. They sat in all the hallways and in every room and kept the temperature constant and comfortable. It was rather like having a cow, or several of them, bedded down in corners but with no mooing or chewing or swishing of tails. And certainly none of the huffing and puffing of forced air that rushes up at you at intervals when a hot-air furnace remembers why it is there and comes to life, with its churning and belching, in the middle of the night—jolting you, startling you. No, hot-water heat was far better, practically silent, a civilized delight.

It was our furnace that heated the water, and that heat forced the water up, around and through the house and into all the pipes. On occasion, if the water got terribly hot because of an airlock, the pipes rumbled and shuddered until some brave soul opened the valves a tiny bit—to let off steam. This was considered dangerous. We children were forbidden to do it, though we knew how.

Otherwise those pipes were wonderfully well behaved—as quiet and soundless as some wished we were! And in a pinch one could dry things on them—things like wet mittens or clothing that needed just a touch more warmth.

They were like our streetcars—such a good idea but almost lost now to humankind because they make no money for the greedy.

82. BOOKS

Our house was jam-packed with books. The library was full of them—even if there was a Ping-Pong table in the middle of it, there were books all around its edges. And every other room had bookshelves or cupboards full of them, too. Even the front hall—that light and airy room—had inglenooks on each side of the fireplace with leaded glass cupboards stuffed with the classics. Under the seats below the cupboards were magazines like *Blackwood's*, *Holly Leaves* and special celebration copies of *Illustrated London News* or *The Tatler*—too good to throw away. And of course old copies of *The Beaver* and *Maclean's*.

With so many books and magazines, we had no need whatever to go to the public library. And each Christmas and birthday we were given more books—usually beautifully illustrated in colour or black and white. The coloured books were gorgeous or subtle or both, like the tales of Beatrix Potter. One of our favourites was folded up and pleated so that you opened it out like a snake and had a story one way. When you turned it around where the spine might have been, another illustrated story unfolded. It was called *The Children at the Pole* by Willy Pogany.

Probably my favourite book of all had been bought for Tom before the Great War. It had no words, just pictures of elaborate picnics for animals with tables of food set in the woods by streams—everything ready for a party to begin—yet someone or something had already tasted a slice of each cake. What a good idea! Another favourite was *The Wonder Clock*, a present to Mum in 1898—when she was ten.

We were taught to care for books early on: to wash our hands before reading, to leave their jacket covers on to keep them clean, to turn pages at their corners and to do so carefully. And *never ever* lick a finger when turning pages! Or crack the spines! Because of this early training we had no compunction about sharing our books amongst ourselves. Once, however, I drew on the inside covers of my copy of *The Tale of Mrs. Tiggy-Winkle* as some sort of protest. Nothing was said. It wasn't necessary. I knew I'd been silly and was ashamed.

There were so many children's annuals in our house, spanning many years, like the *Girl's Own* and *Boy's Own* and *Chatterbox*, which had appeared each year in the twenties, filled with stories, serials and poems. *Rupert* and *Tiger Tim* had hard covers and were inches thick, filled with comics (that we called "funnies"), riddles and puzzles with lots of pictures and characters that would reappear each year. Bonzo was one of them. I loved all these—especially the boys' annuals—and am haunted still by a series of stories about Ninepins that were causing havoc in London. Hordes of them would appear suddenly out of the mist or fog, long lines of them marching behind people—keeping up with them and all of them human-sized!

And then there were my beloved E. Nesbit books, *The Wind in the Willows,* Christopher Robin and Peter Pan, right on down to the Big Little Books—cheap and small but fun. There weren't many Canadian books in those days, but one I loved was called *The Good Companion.* It was about a blind man and his dog. Not much happened but it struck a chord, and I think about those simple black-and-white drawings still.

Books were an important part of my life—I lived in them. Before I could read I spent hours poring over them, imagining the stories, lying on the muskox robes in front of the fireplace in the drawing room after tea with late afternoon sunlight slanting in the windows.

Almost everyone in the family read to me at some point, but my favourite reader was Mum. Every day after lunch the two us or, when I was really small, three or four of us would snuggle together on the *chaise longue* in the drawing room and she would read until she got drowsy and fell asleep. You knew this was coming when her tempo slowed—a phrase was repeated—then a word—and she'd be off—sound asleep. The others would slip away but often I dozed with her, fascinated by the churning and gurgling—the rumbles of her innards—her "plumbing," as she called it. Mum read so easily she sounded as if she were talking. Sometimes I complained: "Mum, you're speaking again—please read!"

Lolo, too, made what she was reading come alive. While she stayed with us she read to us a lot. Then at Royal Roads School she read to the whole school, both poetry and prose. Whenever I read "The Lady of Shalott," "The Highwayman," "The Poplar Field" or "Kubla Khan," I hear them in her somewhat theatrical, thrilling voice. What a difference a voice makes!

83. TENNIS

We expected dry grass in summer, and tawny lawns. You had the choice: keep lawns well watered or use them dry. For croquet, we chose the latter. But for tennis, much of our time and effort went to preparing the court—far more time than we spent playing the game.

The grass had to be kept green, cut and in good trim, then flattened by a heavy iron roller with a diameter of about seventy centimetres. Then the shape of the court was marked with a clever device. Its handle, rather like that of a manual lawn mower, pushed a metal bowl on two wheels, fore and aft. This bowl was kept full of a thick lime solution, and as you pushed the thing along, rubber strapping ran through the lime, then onto the grass, leaving a clear white line. Pegs set in the ground marked the dimensions of the court, but you needed a good eye and a steady pace to do the job well. We all helped as we could, but until we were a fair size, we younger ones were more useful as ball boys. Though there was high wire netting supported by stout uprights at each end of the court, tennis balls had a way of escaping in all directions and it was up to us to scamper after them.

At one point Peter decided Bingo might be the perfect solution for that roller. He made sacking booties and attached them to her hooves. She obliged by pulling the wretched thing over the whole area. However, those booties didn't work very well, and her hooves made dints all over the grass—only compounding the problem. Actually the roller wasn't enormously heavy. I was able to pull it by the age of ten, but my favourite job was marking the court.

A pyramid of cousins (Peter on top, then Eck and Pat Nixon supported by Tom and Jamie) horse about on the tennis court. H.M.P. photo

People came from far and wide to play on our grass court, and tennis parties were held often. The trouble was no one could play until the grass was dry of dew. Then, by about four o'clock, the damp onshore breeze off the Strait of Juan de Fuca softened gut, making tennis rackets unusable. So even in good weather there were only about five optimum hours per day for tennis, and the rule *Never leave your racket on the grass* made sense anytime.

When conditions were right, those keen to play did so until their match was over. No one would stop to go in for lunch—whether family or guests. So lunch was brought outside and eaten all along the green wooden bench that marked the divide between the croquet lawn and the tennis court, where the land dipped some forty centimetres. Then everyone was happy. Players could play to their heart's content and spectators could watch as long as they liked. Or play croquet.

84. JAMIE

Jamie, or "J" as Mum called him—or "J, my darling"—was really good-looking with an air of quiet authority. He could be charming and amusing but was shy with children and made scant effort to be warm or pleasant to us. We admired him from afar, as a godlike figure.

My earliest memory of him was at the Lake. Our cottage was bought furnished. Many of its contents dated from the 1880s, when it was a hunting lodge and then a small hotel. The rooms were jammed full of Victoriana, including an ancient gramophone and records from the turn of the century. The day I remember, everyone was there—certainly Peter and Jamie and masses of others. We were on the verandah listening to records. Peter was fishing catfish over the railing, hauling them in. It was very gay and noisy. I can almost hear the voices calling and laughing—everyone moving and jumping about. I asked for my favourite again, a brown liver-coloured record called "The Yama Yama Man." Apart from the chorus, which repeated over and over—"the Yama, Yama, Yama Man..."—the lyrics were squeaky and weird. They would suddenly speed up, then slow down again. I found it entrancing. Perhaps Jamie wanted something current, like "The Continental"—who knows, but he grabbed my choice and flung it, spinning, far out over the lake. It skipped several times, shattered on the surface and sank. There were old books at Savira, too. One I despised was called *Elsie Dinsmore*. Every page—if not every paragraph—ended with: *And Elsie Dinsmore cried and cried!* I felt just like Elsie that day.

Jamie did fairly well at school and very well at sports: rugby, sailing, rowing, but particularly rugby. He was a fine horseman too, an important member of our polo team. But when he graduated from Shawnigan Lake School, prospects were dim for young men in Canada. His godfather, George Macdonald, was CEO of a chartered accountancy firm in Montreal. He offered to train him and, if he liked the work, make him a junior partner. Once again Esquimalt High came to the rescue, and Jamie spent a year there taking extra French and mathematics. But though he loved playing rugby with the Wanderers, he loathed accountancy.

His dream had been to join the Indian Army. He felt life in India would suit him well, with the chance to play polo and all. But he lacked the facility for learning languages quickly and easily, so was not accepted.

In the mid-thirties there were rumblings of war. Canada's armed forces were in chaos and it wasn't much better in Britain. But an Englishman in Victoria, Henry Seymour-Biggs, made a business of connecting bright young men with the Royal Air Force. Through him, Jamie was accepted on a two-year short service commission. This was extended in 1938. He had always yearned to fly. So there he was, a pilot officer, following his bliss.

He became a bomber pilot, a squadron leader and, by the time he was twenty-eight, a Wing Commander. After a great many missions he was sent back to Canada to train pilots from the Commonwealth, Norway and Poland as part of the Commonwealth Air Training Plan, first in Calgary, then at Pat Bay. He was unofficially engaged to an English girl and in love with another, or so she thought. But back in Victoria he re-met Phyllis Maude Heath Parkes—an old pal of Peter's—now a grown woman, a nursing sister planning to go overseas.

One keeps hearing, nowadays, that life began in the 1960s: no one ever made love or even thought of it until then—the inference being that all who predate that era were conceived by immaculate conception. Be that as it may, a lot of tennis was played at Wychbury during the spring and summer of 1942, but Jamie and Big Phyll, as we called her to distinguish her from Hilly, though keen tennis players, weren't much interested. Instead they spent hours rummaging about, on and under rugs, chortling and giggling, on the sidelines. Carrying on in a way Jamie would have called "asinine" had we been doing it. And we ate Sunday lunch *inside* that season, which was puzzling. And, stranger still, Phyll and Jamie didn't seem to need lunch at all. By July they were engaged.

"Doing it" was making babies. I knew that, but just before I went to Guide Camp that summer I learned a new word—"fuck." I had no notion what it meant but liked the sound of it, especially when sung as a sort of jingle: *Fuctety fuckety fuck fuck fuck!* Some of the big guides looked askance but didn't explain. They must have been relieved when I had to leave camp early to be a flower girl again, for Jamie's wedding at St. Paul's. Did anyone hear my little song, still fresh and new, on my lips? Ba, all innocence, clutching a posy and smiling sweetly in a white silk smock—bought this time—chanting under her breath. Though I didn't realize it at the time, this was the right word for the occasion certainly, as their baby was born in jig time!

I was all innocence, clutching a posy and smiling sweetly in a white silk smock at Jamie's wedding. Knight photo

After Jamie rejoined his squadron, Dad, despite his best intentions, got all caught up again in the *glory* of war. One day, while saying goodbye to his daughter-in-law on the back verandah, he tried to cheer her with a hearty "Be proud and pleased, my dear. He's over there fighting for king and country!" But Big Phyll snapped back, "No! He's fighting for me!" Then, patting her swelling belly, "For us!"

Jamie would have agreed. His many letters to his wife were full of tender advice about rest, diet and all the latest ideas on childbirth from Britain. When she was born, he named their child Pamela Anne.

At three months, she and her mother set off to join him in England. They would live in the country, somewhere safe, yet near enough to see him often. While they were pausing en route with Granny at l'île d'Orléans, the message reached them: Jamie and his crew had been shot down over Hamburg. He was missing, presumed

*The Lost Boys: Peter and Jamie together at Shawnigan Lake,
just before Jamie left to join the RAF. In those days it
was not unusual to lose two sons.* H.M.P. photo

dead. For us his death was as shattering as Peter's—but it was far worse for Big Phyll. And worse again for Pam, who grew up with a grieving mother and no father. By then so many terrible things had happened, with so much grief and destruction in all directions, that one more death didn't strike the world at large with anything like the force it had in the fall of 1939.

When hit by enemy fire, Jamie kept flying so some of his crew could bail out. There were two survivors—but Jamie lies buried in a small town near Hamburg in a beautifully kept park-like cemetery, a crew member on either side of him. Recently his daughter, Pam, and her son, Joseph James Clancy, made a pilgrimage there.

Both Jamie's and Peter's names are engraved on the cenotaph in Esquimalt's Memorial Park and also on the one in Duncan. We were glad Mum was never asked to be the Silver Threads Mother, those who lay wreaths at cenotaphs on Armistice Day in memory of the dead. But in those days it was not at all unusual to lose two sons.

85. PAT

There were two Pats in my childhood. One was a first cousin, Charles Patrick Nixon, the second son of Mum's twin sister, Arabella. On his eightieth birthday in 1997, I wrote him a poem:

My earliest memories, dearest cuz, are always at Savira
When you would sit beside young Ba
At lunch on the verandah—
With merry gests and sparkling eyes
You squashed the wasps on meat and pies
And won my heart forever.
And always in the evening dim
You'd wow us with a concert of your *Merry Widow* hymn.
Where are they now, those summer days
When cousins played together?
And twinly mums would each bake cakes
And swear hers were the better!
For you were always there for me

> Though I was small and pudgy
> You seventeen and me but three
> Both loving chocolate fudgy!
> Now you are grown and very wise
> You write me lovely letters
> About our ancestors and such,
> Our elders and our betters.
> Oh hero of my childhood days—oft *copain* when in Paris
> We'd dine and walk along the Seine
> And trudge about the *Marais*.
> You've made my life a happier one with family trees and jolly chat.
> May many more birthdays come your way
> My dearest cousin Pat!

After a stint at Victoria College, Pat joined the Royal Canadian Navy and trained with the Royal Navy, as Canada had no naval college in the 1930s. Part of this training took place in South America. On the way there, when his ship stopped in Nassau, he went ashore to see Grandpapa's splendid winter residence, called Carmacoup House after the Porteous family seat in Scotland. When Grandpapa was getting on and beginning to find his usual grand tours in Europe a bit taxing, he decided it would take far less energy to spend winters in the lush warmth of Nassau. So all through the Great War, special Italian stone was brought across in the holds of empty freighters. With this his house was built. By the time Pat got there, Grandpapa was dead and Granny went there rarely, as she found the view dull and the land flat.

On his way up to see Carmacoup House, a woman stopped him in the street, gazed into his handsome young face and said two words: "Mother's Joy!" Which of course he was as he wrote to her faithfully, every week, until she died. The next time he was in Nassau the house had been sold, but a maid called Martha, who'd been there since it was built, answered the door and said, quick as a wink, "You must be a son of one of the twins!" She had never met either of them but had heard about them and seen their photos.

I met Pat again in London when he was married, with two small children. Hilly and I were there, studying theology and art. Both Pat and Henny were very good to us, but at that time those fourteen years' age difference seemed a lifetime. There was a gulf between us.

*

The second Pat, his niece Patricia, was born in Toronto and lived there until she was seven, at which point she was brought west to Victoria and left, unceremoniously, with her Granny at Hill Farm on Wilkinson Road—so her mum and dad could join the Royal Canadian Air Force. This was a nasty shock for her and a jolt for Auntie Bella, who didn't want a child on her hands at all. They never warmed to each other, which was a great pity. I liked them both, very much.

Patricia was younger but often stayed with us—in town and at the Lake. Or I would go to Hill Farm and stay with her. Auntie Bella expected us to behave like adults. When we didn't, she let us know but she also gave us a great deal of freedom, sending us off for the day on bikes, with emergency rations—her grape juice and sandwiches—dangling from the handlebars. Sometimes we set off exploring into the unknown, or she'd suggest destinations like Beaver or Thetis Lake—each surrounded by deep woods where the last of the hoboes lived, the unemployed from the Great Depression who were too old or frail to join up or be hired. There they could go about barefoot in summer—saving the remains of their shoes for winter—wash themselves and their clothes in the lake; eat berries, wild greens, fish and wild fowl; and be better off by far than in town. They didn't bother us at all, and if they called out as we biked past, we'd say "Hi" or wave. To us, their life seemed idyllic.

Sometimes we'd go off on jaunts with Auntie Bella. Ned Boydell, her second husband, didn't come with us. Gruff but kind, his delight was growing iris of every shape and colour. He had been in the merchant marine, and when he was called up, well past middle age, during the Second War, he went off again and did his bit in Ottawa as a consulting engineer, testing the engines of new ships on the eastern seaboard. We loved him and so did Auntie Bella.

Once, at breakfast, Pat and I were served black currant jam dated 1918. I presume it was made from fruit grown in Auntie Bella's garden at Admiral's House, on Admirals Road in Esquimalt, where she'd lived from 1918 to 1922 with her first husband, Commander E.A.E. Nixon. He had been the first commander in charge of the Royal Naval College of Canada in Halifax—until the explosion in 1917—and then in Kingston and at Dockyard. For her, this jam was precious and was offered as a *treat*—but unaware of its significance, we found it gritty and dull, and in 1942 it seemed straight out of the ark.

At thirteen, Pat seemed more like sixteen. So while I was at boarding school, wearing a tunic and blazer and long black stockings, she was going to formals in proper evening gowns. When her parents returned from eastern Canada they decided to stay in Victoria. They rented an apartment in Wychbury for a while, then bought several acres near Cadboro Bay with their veterans' land grants and lived there for about thirty years. Now Patricia is in Ottawa—a granny with seven grandchildren.

For years I lost contact with both of them but came upon Pat, the elder, when I went to Ottawa after my studies in England. I had developed a yearning to go to the Arctic, and my old friend Mary, who was working there, in Ottawa knew this. So when she met Bent Sivertz, the head of the Arctic Division of Northern Affairs and Natural Resources, at a party, she told him about my dream. "Tell her to come and see me when she gets here," he said. So I did and he hired me on the spot. Then, when he asked where I was staying, I discovered that Pat was not only his friend but had been a fellow officer in the Royal Canadian Navy.

During the seven years I lived in France in the sixties, whenever Patrick came to Paris we spent whole days exploring. With his love for, and grasp of, French history he taught me a great deal about places I thought I knew already. The two of us tramped about, our eyes glowing with the beauty of the city, imagining how and where our ancestors had lived, both at Versailles and in Paris, before the Revolution and marvelling at their escape during it.

Patricio, as I call him, is getting a little shaky now. Which is not surprising as he turned ninety in 2007. But he phoned yesterday, from Ottawa, sounding about twenty. He has been awarded the *Légion d'Honneur* for his help to France during the war. For example, at twenty-six, as captain of HMCS *Chaudière* during the battle of

Normandy, he provided an anti-submarine screen on the flanks of the assault area.

*

Patricio died in Ottawa when he was ninety-one. Patricia lives there still and I look forward to seeing her again.

86. TROUSSEAUX

We slept well last night, our heads on clean, beautifully hemstitched linen pillowcases made from my mother's trousseau sheets. Mine has an extravagant *P* embroidered on it—obviously a gift from Dad's family. They liked elaborate design whereas Mum's family preferred simplicity. Anyway, they would have insisted her initials be *HMP*, small, discreet and elegant—but muttering the while, as they ordered, then wrapped, these presents: *Change the name and not the letter—change for worse and not for better.*

On her wedding day, with Auntie Bella on the left and Aunt Fran on the right, Mum looks straight ahead into the future.

Given my druthers I would use nothing but linen sheets except in cold weather, when cotton flannelette seems a must. Somehow, after Mum died, I acquired four linen sheets—two from each family. Those from Dad's side have hemstitching at both ends. All date from 1910 so it isn't surprising that only one is still intact. To keep it in good trim we use it several times each summer. Old linen has a tendency to rot, especially if not used. The middles of sheets give way, but their sides and ends make good pillowcases.

Most of Mum's trousseau went up in smoke, along with most of her wedding presents, when their house burned down in the Eastern Townships of Québec in 1924. She was saddened by this loss, of course, but it gave her the chance to replace things with simpler designs that suited her better.

Dane's parents were married in 1941 while the Battle of Britain was raging. Clothing and cloth were rationed, yet his mother managed a long white wedding dress and a going-away outfit of finest Yorkshire wool. I believe it hangs in state, to this day, in a cupboard in North Saanich. They got a lot of handsome presents too, but I'm not sure about bedding, sheets and towels.

It's a really nice idea to send brides off with new clothing, bedding and towels, but does anyone have trousseaux these days?

87. DANCES

It seems amazing, now, how lavish our parties were all through the Great Depression. Dances in private houses were common events, to which men wore dinner jackets or tails and women evening gowns—their arms covered in long white kid gloves that went up beyond the elbow. While women wore high-heeled pumps, sometimes of cloth to match their dresses, men wore pumps too, of black patent leather with flat grosgrain bows at the vamp. I didn't notice at the time how threadbare many of these garments were—or how demoded. To me they looked glorious!

Those long kid gloves were pesky, though. You didn't take them off at the door when you arrived, as one normally does with gloves. Instead, you undid the little pearl buttons at the inside of each wrist, then pulled off the finger part, curled it into a little ball and tucked it up inside the arm section on the outside of your wrist. This sounds quite a performance but it becomes second nature after you've done it once or twice. I know, because I had to wear those gloves too, in my teens and twenties when I went to parties in evening gowns.

Some people hired orchestras for their dances. Others used wind-up or electric gramophones, playing hard rubber records with thorn or steel needles. Sometimes Tom played the piano for our dances. He could play by the hour—whatever was wanted.

Beforehand, the house would be cleaned, *stem to gudgeon*, and the drawing room emptied—with only a few chairs left around the edges and rugs rolled up. The floor would be vacuumed and then one of us pushed a waxing machine with a long handle, carefully, all over the surface. Talc was sprinkled over the floor, and to make it really slippery we rubbed the talc in a bit, with our feet. The same thing happened in the front hall, as some liked to dance there. One of us would dust all surfaces while someone else filled all the cigarette boxes and made sure there were enough clean ashtrays dotted about for our guests' convenience. Mum was the only smoker in our family and she only smoked outside, if wasps were troubling us during a meal. But you had to be prepared for guests.

Two sorts of punch would be made: one alcoholic, the other not. Durrant's Bakery supplied sausage rolls, meat pies and Parker House rolls—all three smaller than usual. *Petits fours* would come from the Bon Ton, in Victoria.

Dad loved dancing and dances but might grumble about the expense. Then Mum would insist it was our responsibility to hold dances when others couldn't—because of space and all. "Others be damned!" Dad might say—forgetting himself. Then he'd have a glorious time dancing with all the best dancers, while Mum made do, once again, with the duds. But she knew what to expect and how much these occasions meant to Dad and to all our guests. "Well worth scrimping a bit," she'd say.

We three young ones would watch as guests arrived, peering through the railings of the upstairs hall. Then fall asleep to the din of music and laughter.

Such dances continued through and after the war in some houses, but not ours. And there were formal dances at Royal Roads when it became a naval college. They took place at Christmas and in the spring and were splendid affairs, with lots of young cadets needing partners. It helped having a brother there, of course. For all such dances, girls wore evening gowns, which we called "formals," and the lads donned dinner jackets or their uniforms. Only one dress was bought for me—there were so many gorgeous hand-me-downs available in our house. My favourite of them all had been Sylvia's. It was pale grey-blue chiffon, the bodice close-fitting with tiny shoulder straps, the skirt layer upon layer of swirling tulle studded with sequins and tiny beads. It was a dress of dreams! Boys were expected to buy a corsage, which was sweet. *I hope you like orchids*, they'd say, handing you carnations or daisies.

I did Grade Nine at Esquimalt High in 1944–45. I don't remember learning much at that school, but the music and dancing were sensational—just as they are at Esquimalt High now. Why, I don't know. Are musicians, like the Jickling brothers of my day, still attracted to that school? Or does the school transform ordinary students into talented musicians? When I was there, music seemed to seep along the halls and through the doors. We were transformed by it. At lunchtime, after school, at the rare evening dances in that terrible last year of the war, we, all of us, became graceful whirling dervishes—dancing in ecstasy! It was a magical year for me. And dress was of no consequence. We all walked or biked to school dances so it was a question of short skirts or dresses for girls and casual clothes for the boys.

What a brutal blow to be sent to boarding school. At Strathcona Lodge School on Shawnigan Lake, things were quite different. It might have been a nunnery. There seemed nothing lovely there except books and the landscape. Just an imposed sense of duty to what the school *had been*—but wasn't now, because *we* were there. That was the inference. And when we had dances with the boys from Shawnigan Lake School, either in our gym or theirs, there was no live music—just records—and the boys, though often charming in themselves, danced like wooden marionettes: their arms pumping, their feet squashing ours. We waltzed or foxtrotted. No jitterbugging at all. It felt like the Dark Ages.

Once acclimatized, I found the lessons, especially history, English lit, maths and Latin, fascinating, and I gained lifelong friends. As for the Shawnigan boys, love letters zipped back and forth between the schools, there were sailing parties and skating—when the lake froze—but there was no more joy in dancing for me and probably not for them either.

Perhaps dancing is like skating, driving or riding a bike—once accomplished, never forgotten. I hope so yet have never again achieved that joyful abandon of my Grade Nine year at Esquimalt High. I long to lose myself in dance again, just as I long to borrow one of my sisters' bikes and go careening off down old logging roads.

But now, when music makes my feet start moving, I dance—all by myself. And have a lovely time!

88. LAMPSON STREET SCHOOL

Mr. Creelman was the principal of Lampson Street School when I was there. He was perfect for the job: a neat and dapper man who moved smoothly. Everything about him was restrained and strong. He was, without doubt, the captain of our ship. And it was glorious—something between a castle and a palace. The rooms were huge and high-ceilinged, the halls endless. We felt privileged to be there, to be part of it.

One day he called the entire school into the assembly hall. Somebody had borrowed, broken or stolen something. He stood in front of us and looked us straight in the eye and, walking up and down the front of the hall, called out, "Did you do it? Did you do it? Did you do it?" His eyes pierced into ours. When they met mine I felt so guilty I nearly raised my hand.

During class, if you heard your name on the loudspeaker—*Will so-and-so go to the principal's office now!*—you quailed. It meant *the strap*! So when my name was called one day, I went in fear and trembling. What had I done?

Jamie was missing in action. Mr. Creelman wanted to comfort me. He was gentle and kind, and I believe he gave me a hug.

The first time I went to Lampson Street School I was six and glad Mum was with me. Then one of my classmates asked why my granny had brought me. I didn't want Mum hearing that, so the next day I said I could manage alone. And I could. Unless you were really late there were always lots of children hurrying up the hill, running, walking or riding their bikes. I felt sorry for kids with young parents. Mum and Dad made mistakes sometimes, but they'd had years to sort things out—twenty years. And how could anyone manage without older siblings?

The two-storey school was built of brick with some stone. Two elegant stone staircases led to the front door—but were not to be used by children. For us there were two other entrances: one for boys, one for girls. Before the bell rang in the morning, after recess or after lunch we lined up with our classmates in rows, waiting. No one was allowed inside the school before the bell rang. If you were found inside, it meant the inevitable!

The classrooms smelled of oiled wood, Dustbane, chalk, graphite, ink and that indefinable odour of anxious children herded together. Each classroom had a cloakroom, its walls studded with brass hooks for coats and lunches. There were offices, an infirmary and an auditorium with a stage. The toilets were in the basement, and the gym was in a separate building behind the school. I don't remember going there. The playground was bare earth with a few oak trees spotted about and some large rocks for clambering over. You had to invent your own fun and we did.

One day my right index finger intercepted a hardball. It is still twisted and bumpy. If only I'd gone straight to Miss Morrison, she would have done the right thing. She always did. How I wish I had known then that she'd been a nursing sister during the Great War and, like Dad, was in Salonika. She must have had terrible experiences too. But for us she was efficient, gentle and kind. A number of girls chose nursing because of her.

As a rule, we went home for lunch—running down the hill, then up again, to make it within the hour. Once we had spaghetti and I swallowed mine so quickly it didn't digest. Mum was off somewhere that afternoon, so after school, feeling a bit odd, I went down to the stables to see Dad. Before I got there all that spaghetti came up in a rush—splat on the path, intact. I was fascinated and appalled. It was the first time I'd vomited. It happened to a girl in our class once.

She tried to reach an open window but missed and was made to clean up the mess herself—all of us watching. I thought that cruel.

Our Grade One teacher, Miss Walker, was pretty and kind. She dressed in attractive brown outfits with pleated silk collars. Most of the time schoolwork was fun. Still, I couldn't imagine spending twelve whole years at a desk. But earaches rescued me. After Christmas I was kept at home.

The next year I was put straight into Grade Two. Grade Two teachers were always *dragons*, and there were two of them at Lampson Street—I suppose to toughen us up. Schoolwork wasn't a problem, but once in art class I disgraced myself by colouring mountains blue, like the Olympics and the Sooke Hills. Our dragon held up my offending work and hissed, "Everyone knows mountains are either green or purple!" Because of that, Mum put me back into Royal Roads School the next fall.

When I went back to Lampson Street School for Grade Six, we had Mr. Jones—an energetic man with a scar across his face. Had he been demobbed? A splendid teacher, he kept us on our toes with spelling bees and lots of tests, and once a month he lined us up around the room, first to last. For those who loved tests this was fun—for others, agony. There were about forty in our room. One lad was eighteen and still there. It was so sad. Most of us had fun, passing notes, putting fawn lilies in inkwells to see their vein structure, yet learning all the time. Ours was the best elementary school in western Canada; we had to consider that!

Home economics should have been fun as I loved cooking and sewing, but everything was done by the book and took hours. Sometimes our teacher held up her own work as a good example, calling out, "See gulls! See gulls!" That was worth the tedium.

I remember Mr. Downard fondly and loved mathematics and choir with Mr. Bigsby. We had no instruments but we sang a lot and acted in plays. And once, in a Christmas pageant, I had to annunciate, "On the first day of the twelfth month, when they had gathered in all the fruit...," struggling to pronounce all those awkward *ffs*.

Fire drills were standard fare and so were air raid drills. With practice, the school could be emptied—with everyone across the road and up in the Transfer Woods—in three minutes.

It is curious how one remembers some things and not others. The faces of some classmates, Miss Morrison and Mr. Creelman, some of the teachers, even a janitor—the kind one—are perfectly clear: their expressions, their smiles, the colour of their clothing. And one exuberant girl with rosy cheeks and long black hair who broke the dress code of the day by wearing scarlet and maroon together. On her they looked terrific. Many of us were shabby in our siblings' hand-me-downs. Mum insisted we wear old things to school and save our best for home—but it was the reverse for most. One spoilt only child wore cashmere sweaters and kilts, made for her.

In Grade Eight I was sick at New Year's. When I came back my class was divided into *brighties* and *dummies*. They had forgotten me. And popped me in with the *dummies*. Terribly ashamed, I did not do well.

But all in all the teaching was good and the beauty of the building swept us along like a great ship, making us feel privileged and special. And the days and months ran smoothly, thanks in large part to our skipper, Mr. Creelman.

89. GEOGRAPHY

Geography: The surface of the earth, its form and physical features, natural and political divisions, climate, products and population. That, in essence, is the definition given in the *New Shorter Oxford English Dictionary* of 1993—a rather bleak assessment of the world.

My geography begins in our garden, our house and all I can see from its roof with my far-sighted eyes. It takes in the heat of summer, the scent of the air, the feel of wind, rain and snow, especially the snow of April that surprises us so often it becomes expected, for an hour or two at least. It includes all the native plants and flowers in the woods and fields, as well as those in our garden, and the songs of quail and pheasant and all the other birds who call it home. The rainforest of trees—the huge ones and those we climb—the rocky outcroppings we know and love, the deep woods, the beaches and the sea edge we explore, the paths and routes we take to go our divers ways on foot, on horseback, by bicycle or car, for fun or duty—all this became part of us. By contrast, Mum and Dad are centred in Québec. Only in old age do they admit their hearts and minds have grown to BC's scale—that they are indeed people of the west coast.

With each family outing my world expands. I take in what we pass, observe differences and move, in my mind's eye, into houses, rearrange gardens, imagine peoples' lives. Some of our routes are repeated, known by heart—like the way to Shawnigan Lake. We drive through Esquimalt village, dip down along Admirals Road, pass the Songhees Land, turn left at Craigflower Road, then uphill past the Four Mile House to View Royal, past the Six Mile House (another handy pub) and through tidy Colwood, followed by Langford, always rather sad to me, and on to Langford Lake. Then down the hill to the chill mystery of Goldstream with the Rock of Gibraltar nestled in trees to the right of the road—always greeted by us in passing. By degrees we pull ourselves up the Malahat—all of us tightening our knees, as if on horseback—urging the old car on. Wherever possible we catch the view eastward through the trees, especially when passing the two coffee shops—Scenic View and the Malahat Lookout—both in a state of flux—about to sell, go broke, burn down or be rebuilt. We never stop. Our goal is to reach Savira, empty the car and hop in the lake!

Sometimes we take new routes—past Mount Douglas Park or around tiny Prospect Lake or along that incredibly straight and narrow road, the Interurban—once, if you can believe it, a railway line that ran from Victoria all the way to Sidney. In my day, alas, it peters out where it jags into West Saanich Road, just past the Dominion Astrophysical Observatory. Gradually this area becomes less foreign but retains an aura of *terra incognita*. Some East Saanich roads make me uneasy to this day—as if at any moment they might slip off into the sea.

Once, when I was four or five, Mum and I drove up-Island with her friend Mrs. Spurgeon and her son, Robin, who was my age. We stayed for a week or so at Qualicum in a hotel, all meals in the dining room and all day out—way out on the sand flats gathering sand dollars. It was intriguing for a day or two, then tedious as the sea was so far out—and when it licked its way back in again was still too shallow for swimming. I was glad to get home to familiar Fleming's Beach where there were pebbles, rocks, great logs and deep and pounding sea.

Slowly my knowledge of the world expands from Esquimalt to Victoria with its wide streets, large department stores and the Royal Theatre, where artists like Anna Pavlova and Isadora Duncan once danced, Paderewski played, Stephen Leacock read his stories and many other famous artists perform willingly. Sarah Bernhardt acted there years ago, and her performances are still discussed in the late thirties. The Empress, our huge hotel, faces the Inner Harbour, as does the Parliament Buildings, just down the street and around the corner, its shape and windows outlined at night with yellow lights that twinkle like fairyland. Nearby my beloved Beacon Hill Park stretches south to Dallas Road with its sidewalk edging cliffs that fall far below to rocks and the sea. Farther along is Ross Bay Cemetery, where the famous are buried. One can walk or drive along that route all the way to Oak Bay—even to the Uplands.

There are so many different sorts of people in Esquimalt. Where do they all come from? I ask. Mum says: *People have always moved around—settling and resettling in the same spots. Sometimes they come in peace and blend in. Or they "do everyone in" and take over.* Why are we all so different? *Ah,* she says, *we seem different and special to those who love us—but the joke is we are exactly the same under the skin. For we all came from Africa eons ago. Every single one of us. And we've been moving about ever since.* Did we all have dark skins long ago? *We did. And depending where we chose to stay, our skin colour changed or bleached.* So we are all related? *We are indeed. You'll learn more about this when you study anthropology.* She makes it seem so simple. Millennia in a few short words.

As for us, the inhabitants of Esquimalt and surrounding districts like Victoria and Saanich, many of us may sound English, but we are fiercely Canadian and sing "The Maple Leaf Forever" and "O Canada" with gusto. Yet some of Victoria's merchants insist on decorating their shop-fronts with half-timbering and put up signs calling themselves Ye Olde English this or that to attract American tourists and increase sales. This is phony and we hate it. And there are still signs around, where men are hired, saying, *Englishmen need not apply.* So many have suffered from sweet but ineffectual remittance men—some of them fit, they say, only as markers—to plough toward. Some people take their eiderdowns across the country by train, then by sea to England every few years to be recovered, or send their children to British schools and universities—just as Rhodes scholars are often chosen from Vancouver Island, but that doesn't make them English.

At home we despair of Dad's accent, picked up, Mum says, in his early twenties from brother officers in the Royal Horse Artillery, who'd made fun of his Québec City English—clear, quick and clipped, as we speak it. But some of his words seem ridiculous, and we complain about them—like *tha ra* for "thorough," which we pronounce with lots of *rrrrs*. A friend, whose family has been in Canada almost as long as Mum's, spent a year with her at a boarding school in England, where her accent was ridiculed. Years later, when they met again in Victoria, the strength of her English accent astonished Mum. Apparently accents even more pronounced can be found in Vancouver.

No, on Vancouver Island we are a mixed bag, polyglots who come from far and wide: Aboriginal people; the Chinese, who reached these shores long ago; the Japanese; Indians, like the Kapoor family; Québecers, like us; people from the Prairies, from Ontario and the Maritimes, from Wales, Ireland, Scotland, England, Holland, Poland, Russia, from Italy, France and Germany. Some came because of the gold rush of 1858. A considerable number were here already—well before Vancouver Island joined BC—and, loving the place, they stayed. Our first governor, Sir James Douglas, was part Scottish, part African and part West Indian. And Amelia Douglas, his wife, was half Irish and half Cree from the Central Plains. Their offspring became high society. Their descendents still are.

As I grow among this blend of people, I begin to see beyond my ken. On, to those dream places, to the world at large: the Sooke Hills, the Olympics, those islands eastward from Discovery Island—those looming, mountainous spaces where there be dragons! Then south and east, to Mount Baker—that vast triangle of ice and snow, a mountain off our map, yet one that follows us around wherever we go, bobbing into view like some large adoring puppy when we turn a corner or pass a clearing: *Here I am again! Admire me please!*

And then, of course, the rest of Canada—stretching eastward over the mountains, the Prairies, the Great Lakes to Québec and beyond to the Atlantic coast, the way to Europe, to Russia and China, all the way to the Pacific Ocean again. And north over forest, lakes and tundra to the glittering Arctic—frozen solid in winter, yet full of sunlight, life and birdsong in summer, I'm told, as so many birds go there to breed in amongst the northern animals. We see them flying overhead each spring and fall. Or south to the United States, Central and South America and the South Pole—all frozen too, plus penguins! Then on again, westward to New Zealand and Australia, to India and Africa and all the countries in between. How close they look on our globe. How small our world. How much of it will I see?

90. THE SATURDAY MARKET

Whenever we could we went uptown on Saturday morning for the Victoria Public Market. When I was still quite small, I gathered that while some people went "downtown," others went "up," and one shouldn't confuse the two. We always went uptown, which made sense, because to reach Esquimalt Road, which took us directly into Victoria, we had to go up Lampson Street or up Head Street. (Later I realized the terms "uptown" and "downtown" referred explicitly to New York City, and where you lived there determined whether you went up or down.)

Dad often gave riding lessons on Saturday mornings, so it was a treat when he was free and willing to go to the market. Mum loved it—no matter that there was very little to buy there and even fewer customers. It was in danger of closing if it wasn't used. Sometimes we all went, but often it was the three youngest or Mum, Dad and me.

As in all markets you felt a sense of excitement, and those who went were faithful. You could count on seeing "Hail Columbia," as we called our bishop, Harold Sexton, the bishop of Columbia. Because of him, we enjoyed attending services at the Cathedral, especially if we sat in the gallery, where we could peer down at all the people processing below yet be at eye level with the robin—immortalized by a stonemason because it insisted on nesting, exactly where it sits to this day, during all the noise and confusion as the nave was built. Bishop Sexton would greet us with delight at the market and the Cathedral—as if our presence was important. He was famous for telling people things like: *I don't mind what you wear in church. Come in your pyjamas if you like. Just come!* He was large and imposing. I thought he was wonderful but my friend Mary was convinced he was God. She and her mum would drive all the way from Rogers Avenue for the market and would also go to the Cathedral on Sundays.

Often we'd see John and Jock Grant and their daughter, Nancy—from Oak Bay or the Molsons from Rockland Avenue with their dear little daughters—one brown-headed, the other blonde. All of us shoppers went about with a basket on one arm, trying to fill it.

The Market Building must have known grander days, when there were fewer shops and more market gardens, for it was large and roomy with high, echoing, pigeon-filled ceilings and open sides, in the manner of nineteenth-century French covered markets of metal and glass. When we went there were big gaps around the stalls and none of the crowded bustle of markets I've known since—like those in Vancouver, Toronto, Ottawa, Kitchener, London or Paris. And Mum remembered the crowded markets of Québec City, Montreal, Nice and Cannes. But in ours there seemed to be more ghosts than people.

As for the stalls, they didn't hold much either: a rabbit, perhaps, or a scrawny hen, strings of garlic or sausages, bedding plants, a Christmas cactus, some head cheese, jars of jam and honey, a few dozen eggs, perhaps some buns or loaves of bread, and the odd pound cake. That was about it. What gaiety there was came from customers greeting old friends or from Mrs. Butler, who always had a cheery word. She sold butter: fat rounds of sweet butter the size of tobacco tins with the image of a cow munching grass stamped on top. We always bought four or five pounds, whether we needed them or not, because she and her butter were special.

I don't think anyone went there to provision themselves but more to uphold a cherished institution that had seen better days—that, and to see their friends. Despite its lack of provender, we left our market feeling happier and nourished, if not in body, then in the soul.

91. HALLOWE'EN

In Esquimalt, trick-or-treating happened in small groups or bands—just kids, no parents. Having your parents accompany you would have been a disgrace. If you were too young to go out after dark, you stayed home and had the fun of receiving others at your door, all costumed in marvellous disguises. Sometimes we went to private parties or gave our own. Otherwise it was trick-or-treating—quite a bit of tricking, but nothing too desperate. You might find your garbage can in a strange place, things like that. We much preferred the treats.

I was lucky because I had siblings to go with, but once, when I was about eight, Mum insisted I stay home. That seemed to me a bally shame as it was the first time Joan and Mary would let me join them. So I risked it and went out anyway. Hilly, Michael and the Maynard kids were with us. We had a glorious time roaming far and wide, gathering lots of loot, sometimes from houses I didn't know—and had never even seen! One such house was set a long way back from the road and surrounded by trees and high bushes. A narrow path went straight across the lawn to the front door. As we approached, a dim light showed from inside. None of us knew this house, but feeling courageous we marched to the door en masse and knocked. No one came for a time. Then there was a faint rustling sound, a moaning and a sighing, and a high voice began to squeak—then moan. We ran all the way home. I was so terrified I let Mum see me. That was not a good idea. I was kept home from school the next day—*and not given a note!* That meant a lecture on my return and a scolding from Miss Johnson, the headmistress of Royal Roads School.

The main thing about Hallowe'en was dressing up. Mum was clever at making costumes. Her famous *piece drawer* held an extraordinary collection of material of all sorts, and during the year she saved anything that looked intriguing or might have potential as a costume. The armoire in the upstairs hall was full of such bits and pieces, too. And in the attic box room there was a collection of old costumes that could be the basis of something new, plus masks that could be refurbished or changed. Once a beautiful black woollen dress of Mum's, with a circle of bright embroidery around the cuffs, shoulders and chest, was attacked by moths, so she cut it up and made a costume for Hilly, who won a prize as a Hungarian girl. Some enterprising siblings made their own costumes. Peter sewed leaves all over his clothing one year to be Peter Pan. Sometimes we gathered Old Man's Beard in the woods and made mustachios or even beards or gummed it onto masks for hair. Perhaps some people bought masks, but I don't think anyone bought costumes in those days. We certainly didn't. And it was always fun to be disguised and see other peoples' getups—then guess who was inside them.

Even before the war, candy and other treats were hard to come by for a lot of people. I remember one year we went to a house that had run out of candy and were offered big wedges of chocolate cake instead—a rare and wonderful treat! However, many people simply couldn't afford to buy enough to satisfy the village children, so tricks became more evident and more damaging. In 1938, '39 and '40 the municipality came to the rescue with a brilliant idea, inviting everyone, parents and all, to a huge communal bonfire on what I think must have been an undeveloped part of Bullen Park. They made a wide track around the bonfire with basic fencing on either side. Families gathered around the outer fence, and children would be called inside in groups to parade around the track and show off our costumes for judging. As we trooped past a certain spot, each child was handed a bag of candy, some popcorn, a Torpedo or an all-day sucker, perhaps some peanuts or fruit or whatever else was going, and the winner of that particular category won a small prize. Meanwhile parents and onlookers were fenced off on the outside. In between those perambulations there'd be fireworks and singsongs. I thought it all thrilling.

One year our family decided to dress up as a horse and rider. Several of the older ones made up the horse part of the costume. Hilly led the horse. Michael was to be the rider, but he took so long getting into his costume and then down to the park that, when he got there, the horse had already processed around the bonfire with another rider on its back and had won first prize. I can't remember what I wore that year, but, feeling rather a fraud, I was that fill-in rider.

It was the adventure of being disguised and unrecognizable, being out well after bedtime and having the chance to sashay through the gardens of strangers that made it all so special. No one can remember if those bonfires were continued during the war, but with all the concern about blackouts and air raids, and the fear of bombardment, it would make no sense at all to light a fire—even for a night. And while the bonfires weren't quite as exciting for us children as trick-or-treating, parents considered them a great success for they meant fewer *treats* and far less *tricking*.

92. WAR

November seems the saddest month: leaves fall and so does rain. Our world looks drab. But there are, as always, miracles. Yesterday, November 9, 2006, we *had* to go to town—120 kilometres by small boat with storm warnings and hurricanes forecast. I went unwillingly, but it was one of those golden days: frosty with soft mists rising from calm water, and hillsides still studded with the last maples gleaming soft yellow in amongst the blue/green/mauve of conifers. Later I sat in the sun waiting for Dane, reading *The Royal Oak Disaster* by Gerald S. Snyder. When we returned at dusk, the sea was barely rippled. The wind struck once we were snug in bed. Tomorrow is the eleventh. Once again we are forced to think of courage, absurdity and the abominable waste of war.

Esquimalt was full of such reminders. So it wasn't surprising that as kids we gathered quantities of bracken arrows and built forts in what we considered strategic places—in the broom bushes up on the rocks near the golf links or in the clefts and ridges of the high rocks right across from them. Deep in our own blackberry jungle in the middle of Dad's Riding Ring was a stash of tongue-and-groove lumber about ten feet long. We built a log cabin-cum-fort with these planks way over our heads in height, so used stumps as mounting blocks to enter and exit. We spent a lot of time there, but I don't remember much in the way of battles. It was the building of forts, the planning of campaigns and the provisioning that was fun—that and waiting for an enemy who never appeared. But *they,* the potential enemy, kept changing. As soon as we got to know them, whoever they were, they joined us. Then fort became house—needing furniture and food—and those arrows were used for contests, to see who could launch them farthest.

At school, especially at Royal Roads, we memorized the kings and queens of England and all their battles royal. At play we crawled over gun emplacements built on rocks along the shore and were very much aware of the army barracks with its prison nearby on Peters Street, the naval base at Naden, the Dockyard and so forth. St. Paul's was a Naval and Garrison Church, after all. On Armistice Day, what we now call Remembrance Day, we went in a body to the Cenotaph, no shirkers allowed, and stood with the veterans of Dad's war and the Boer War: all those beautiful ancient faces—once young and eager to fight *for king and country*—now maimed and broken, remembering horrors, tears in their eyes. We did our best to stand still and think of *them,* through that eternity of silence, without straying to lunch, the book being read to us, or what we'd do later. Then we sang sad hymns. Nothing was explained. Sometimes we went to military tattoos. But the most poignant and curious reminders were right there among us: like the poor broken man who tried so hard to befriend us, the children of Lampson Street, by offering candies. We knew not to accept anything from strangers—but his strangeness wasn't unfamiliarity, just the crumpled way he moved, his strangled speech, how his hand shuddered constantly at his crotch. I didn't realize this was the result of shellshock or that shellshock also explained Dad's sudden outbursts of anger.

Dad was the top cadet at the Royal Military College in Kingston when he graduated in 1900, just as the Boer War was ending. He was demoted to second place because of what was considered a rather giddy social life, but he could still choose which regiment to join. Canada had next to no army at that time so he chose the Royal Horse Artillery—considered a crack British regiment. One had to be rich to pay for that honour: the uniforms, horses, mess bills, travel, etc. Before leaving home, he promised that he would return to look after his two eldest spinster sisters when their father died—thinking this would occur many years in the future—and off he went to England. In 1901 as a young subaltern, enjoying his new life enormously, he was part of the honour guard that lined the streets for Queen Victoria's funeral.

Dad chose the Royal Horse Artillery for his regiment. One had to be rich to pay for that honour: the uniforms, horse, and so on.

Then in 1906, when only sixty-two, his father died. Dad kept his promise, resigned his commission and returned to Canada, black-listed.

When war broke out in 1914 he tried to join the Canadian Army. It was so disorganized he went back to Britain to his old regiment. But they would not have him. He ended up in "B" Battery, 99th Brigade, 22nd Division of the Royal Field Artillery and was sent to Salonika in northern Greece, where he spent the entire war. Officers and men came equipped for winter in the mountains. When they arrived the coast was very hot. Though warned not to, his men traded their greatcoats for oranges. Later they froze.

The only good thing about that war, Dad said later, was that the Imperial Army suddenly realized why so many officers were being killed. In Dad's regiment, staff officers (those who worked with the generals) wore highly visible red uniforms. All other officers wore khaki (pronounced *car key*), which faded into the background, but with insignia that could be distinguished easily from a distance. A few simple adjustments saved a great many lives.

Dad didn't talk much about the ghastly things he saw (what Sandra Gwyn, in her extraordinary book *Tapestry of War: A Private View of Canadians in the Great War*, calls the "unmitigated military madness") but was appalled by how poorly his campaign was conducted, with both Allied and British troops ordered to fire over and at their own men. One day his best friend was blown to smithereens by friendly fire—while fighting right beside him. Dad suggested changes to his senior officers. The generals considered this *colossal colonial cheek* and saw to it that he was not promoted nor given all the medals he won. (We understand that after the war at least two of those generals were certified insane.)

Not long ago I met a woman in Paris whose father was an officer with the French army and also in Salonika, fighting alongside the British, as were the Greeks. Annie showed me a collection of water-colour postcards painted on the spot by a French artist in her father's regiment. On the strength of this connection she gave me her duplicates. Then I learned that the father of my Greek friend Rena, who was at l'École Supérieure des Beaux-Arts with me in Paris in the 1960s and is still one of my dearest friends, had been the French

Dad (front row, third from left) and fellow officers of the Royal Field Artillery in England, preparing for Salonika, 1915. His message on the back: "Dear Mums: Why I look fat in this picture is because I have particularly thin men all round me. Can't explain why I look dirty!"

consul in Crete and, on the strength of that, was sent to Salonika at the same time to translate for the French. And now I know that Miss Morrison, the nurse at Lampson Street School, was there too, as a nursing sister. Did any of them meet?

Dad would have appreciated Miss Morrison's efforts but I am not sure about the others. In their combined efforts against the Germans, the Russians, the Bulgarians and the Turks there was a lot of blundering at cross-purposes and a terrible waste of human life. This haunted Dad. He was utterly revolted, traumatized by what he experienced. So when the war ended he didn't wait to be demobilized. Instead he picked up Mum and his two small boys in the south of France and took them to London.

Mum found him almost unrecognizable. Always generous and gentle, delighting in conversation, in laughter, now he was full of rage—rage at what he'd witnessed; rage at what he'd been made to do; rage at what he could not stop. For a long time he could scarcely speak. Then, if he couldn't explain himself fast enough, he'd burst forth in fury.

While waiting for passage to Canada they stayed with old friends, Sir John and Lady Lees, who nursed them through the Spanish flu. Using their last remaining bits of coal, they kept the family warm and saved their lives.

When Dad went off to war, his mum and two eldest sisters followed him across the Atlantic and stayed in London till it was over. They wanted to be near him—in Greece. It was back in Québec City in 1919 that Granny caught the Spanish flu and died.

After the Great War there was much talk of shellshock and its effect on the human mind and body. Dad pooh-poohed this—considered it *piffle*. "How could anyone not there know how it was?" he would say. But Mum knew perfectly well that those twenty-four-hour barrages of constant gunfire, roaring and thundering in both directions, had had a devastating effect on him. "We must bear with him," she'd say.

Some men "find" themselves in war. One was Sir Arthur Currie, a realtor from Victoria who had joined the militia as a way to meet clients. In France he developed into a military genius whose motto was *Neglect nothing*. Thanks to his extraordinary planning, the training of his troops, his use of aerial photography to map Vimy Ridge, and the building of tunnels to bring his men closer to the German lines, his Canadian troops succeeded as no other army had in those fruitless years of fighting on that same spot (see again *The Tapestry of War* by Sandra Gwyn).

It was called the War to end all Wars, but in no time Hitler was rattling sabres and invading neighbours, and everything began again—and on and on and on to this very day.

There is always, I suppose, some exhilaration with war in the air. Everyone gets involved in the excitement. Propaganda soars. After ten years of the Great Depression it seemed a godsend. At last men had a purpose, a paycheque. They were fed, shod, clothed and housed and got useful training. Children were thrilled by the appearance of new regiments marching up our streets—always uphill, never down. Whenever we heard a band, especially a pipe band, we'd drop everything and race down the drive to stand on the high wooden sidewalk

and wave and cheer. And we were delighted when young naval officers moved into the empty house next door.

Suddenly the air felt brisk and full of promise. There was bustle
and excitement—Esquimalt village came alive. So did Victoria, both
alive and crowded. Even our favourite treat, the all-day sucker, was
upstaged by a new one, the Torpedo—torpedo-shaped but dipped in
"chocolate" and wrapped in brightly coloured paper with its sly
promise: *Buy one and get another free.* Perhaps.

Then posters appeared all over the village and in town: *LOOSE
LIPS SINK SHIPS!* Another was of a handsome airman, rather
like Jamie. I can't remember his message. It was his face that
haunted me.

By mid-1940, we had to have blackout curtains covering all our
windows. Members of the Air Raid Patrol and air raid wardens—
men like Dad, too old or unfit to fight—skulked about with gas-mask
bags over their shoulders, searching for cracks of light that might
put us at risk. That sounds ridiculous now—but then it seemed a
real and ready hazard. Our house had a great many windows, yet
Mum made special curtains for all of them with layers of heavy cloth,
black on the outside and white in, using her super electric sewing
machine, a Singer that you engaged by pressing a lever with your
knee. At dusk we took turns checking that all those curtains were
pulled snug.

Even the headlights on cars were blacked out, with only a slit of
light allowed to steer by. Cyclists had to travel blind. Sylvia found
biking to Yarrows shipyard on the night or graveyard shift pretty
tricky—it was so dark.

Throughout the war, listening to the news became a ritual in our
house. After the five o'clock broadcast the news was repeated at dic-
tation speed so it could be written down and shared with those without radios. My parents always listened after supper, so instead of
going to the drawing room as they used to, Mum and Dad stayed on
in the dining room—sitting on those comfortable leather chairs between the fireplace and the French doors. With the blackout curtains
pulled and a crackling fire in the grate, one felt snug and safe. While
they read the paper, I lay at their feet doing homework or reading.
I'm not sure where the others were—probably upstairs in their

rooms. At eight o'clock the radio was switched on and we listened to Matthew Halton or Peter Stursberg of the CBC telling what they'd seen that day. By then I was sitting at Mum's feet. She'd undo my pigtails and brush and brush and brush my hair till the newscast was over. I think this repeated motion and the sense of doing something useful while the world was crumbling soothed her. The news was told with compassion, though the stories were horrific, terrible. It wasn't easy to sleep after hearing those ghastly details, yet our clever correspondents managed to add a little hope, a touch of human kindness in their reporting. I can hear their voices still: *This is Matthew Halton, reporting from somewhere in Italy.* Or *Goodnight, from Peter Stursberg.* They seemed like relations.

Rationing of food began in January 1942: sugar, butter, cheese, cooking oil, jams, jellies, and finally meat were allotted in small amounts. When you stayed with friends you took your ration book with you. It wasn't as desperate for us as it was in Europe, but it forced people to be creative when cooking. In April 1942, gas was rationed. Many cars that guzzled gas, like our Packard, were mothballed.

Nevertheless, throughout the war and on into the fifties, when rationing was still severe in England, we received regular shipments of large tin boxes containing different sorts of biscuits from Peek Frean and Co. Ltd. in London, ordered by Dad's two eldest sisters in Montreal. Were all those ships that crossed the Atlantic to England with munitions filled with *bikkies* on their return voyage? The biscuits arrived in perfect condition, protected by two layers of metal. But how bizarre. Both metal *and* food were scarce in England!

After World War II some veterans claimed those were the best years of their lives. Perhaps in contrast to the Depression that is understandable, yet once back on what they called "Civvy Street," fewer seemed as enthused. And curious things happened. While most veterans received handsome land grants, sums of money and/ or free university educations, the men of the Merchant Navy—who ferried endless convoys of troops, munitions and food to our desperate Allies at great personal risk and in terrible conditions—and the men of Ferry Command—who flew thousands of new bombers made in Canada or the US through the ghastly weather of the North Atlantic, sometimes without radio contact or navigators—those brave men who helped turn the tide of the war got neither recognition nor compensation. Nor did the survivors among the Canadian soldiers sent to save Hong Kong in 1940, who spent all but a few weeks of the war in Japanese prison camps. They too were ignored, as were some Aboriginal veterans. Why?

Dad suffered agonies in Salonika between 1914 and 1918 yet had some rudiments of comfort with him—things he took as a matter of course when on manoeuvres. I have a shelf made from one tier of his three-tiered collapsible washstand of solid mahogany and brass rods. His horsehair mattress is here too and has waited all these years for gypsies to come in June to open the ticking and pluck it soft again. It isn't a favourite of visitors. When I went home, after graduating from UBC in 1952, to pack for a summer-long archaeological dig in central BC, Dad said, "By Jove, Ba, I have just the thing for you!" And he produced a vast mosquito-net tent he'd used in Salonika. We strung it up under trees wherever we went, and the female members of our expedition blessed him as we squatted under it in those bug-infested woods. Had that net been standard gear for British officers—or was it a present from his clever mum?

In Dad's day, there were no treats at all for returning veterans. One did one's duty. Kept what had gone to war with you. And your memories, whether you wanted them or not.

Once the war started, "for the duration" was repeated—a phrase with shape and therefore an end. At first we said this with pride. We could manage *without* for weeks, months even. It made us feel strong, important—even groovy. *Carry on, Canada!* a rallying cry. But as the years dragged on it got irksome, downright aggravating. Yet it wasn't something one could complain about without seeming unpatriotic. So the *duration* went on and on for over six years.

93. THE TELEPHONE

The telephone was our lifeline. It sat on a little oak table in the front hall—at the bottom of the stairs, tucked against the wall, near the door that led to the back hall and through it to the breakfast room or the kitchen. Sitting there you had a certain amount of privacy. We had only one phone for the whole house, with an extension upstairs in Mum's bedroom. For intimate calls, you did your phoning there.

When the phone rang we would run from all directions to be the one to answer it. There were two exchanges in Victoria: Garden and Empire. Our number was *Empire 3440*. Auntie Bella's was *Colquitz 32*. It was probably the number most used in our house, as the twins, though at loggerheads about many things, had a visceral need to communicate daily. *Oh! I must phone Ara!* was a constant refrain.

The downstairs phone was rather beautiful. It had a round brass base that curved up slightly to support a narrow brass cylinder about a foot in height. A black Bakelite mouthpiece sprouted from its top at angles that always made me think of a daffodil. On the left-hand side of the cylinder, near the top, was a hook that held the earphone, also daffodil-shaped. That left you free to write messages with your right hand. The dial was on the base and the phone book was tucked in on a shelf below the base. A pad and pencil were at the ready when needed.

The upstairs phone was much more modern and quite like some phones today—Bakelite with both mouthpiece and earphone together on either end of the handle, and the dial fixed on its squat stand.

Sylvia remembers how things were in the twenties, when they had to turn a little handle and, then wait for an operator to give the number wanted. But in my "modern times" we actually dialled. The Colquitz exchange was a little more primitive. There, one still had to ring for the operator. And unless you were lucky, you were on a party line. So you could listen in on the neighbours' calls, if you had a mind to, but you had to hear their different rings all day long. There was an urban myth that someone who had a summer job as the Colquitz operator fainted dead away from the strain of running that exchange single-handed. And for several hours the whole system collapsed.

So much business was done on our phone—we would have been stymied without it. Dad ordered hardware and feed or consulted his broker. People called him to arrange polo matches, to confirm or cancel riding lessons, or to announce lectures or meetings or special shipments up for auction. Mum phoned her friends or placed orders with Mr. Scott, the grocer, David Spencer's department store, Fulmer's

Drugstore, Durrant's Bakery or one or other of the village butchers. Shopping would have been far more complex without a phone. As for the rest of us, we used it often and somehow managed well with only one phone between so many.

The workings of telephones had been explained to me. It was the particles of carbon in the earpiece that made it possible for voices to be carried great distances—spoken voices, too low to be heard across a large room, much less from the upstairs of our house to the down-stairs, unless one shouted at the top of the stairs. I found it hard to accept this information. The whole process puzzled and bothered me. How could anything in the phone suck my voice down a tube and carry it far away? That idea seemed incredible and made me uncomfortable, so I had a tendency to hold the earphone slightly away from my ear.

Long-distance calls were rare, and I found them daunting as usually they were harder than ever to hear. And if someone made me nervous, I was apt to mumble. Once when I answered it was Jamie, calling from Québec or Ontario. I was in awe of him and found his voice really difficult to hear at the best of times. Thinking it my fault and feeling embarrassed, I kept apologizing, "Excuse me! Excuse me!" Seeing his change bleed away, Jamie yelled down the phone, "Ba, you little idjit! Get someone else!" He didn't mean to be cruel—but shy, like me, he was inclined to be hopeless with children.

But most calls, thanks to those wiggling particles, were a piece of cake!

94. FAT, FOIL, FRUIT and BOXES

During the war, all of us are urged to *do our bit*. Join up. Buy Victory Bonds. Build battleships—things like that. There isn't a great deal children can do—at least those like us, who don't get an allowance. We wave at and cheer soldiers who march up Lampson Street—especially the three dazzling regiments from Ontario, the Lincoln and Welland, the Dufferin and Haldimand and, my favourites, the Argyll and Sutherland Highlanders, kilted and glorious, accompanied by their pipe bands. Then we hear that Ontario's children are trumping us, gathering masses of milkweed seed to stuff life jackets—but milkweed doesn't grow in Esquimalt. We feel useless again, until we hear that fat and silver paper are in great demand. So Mike dusts off his wagon and off we go.

It is one of the best jobs I've ever had. We can go to any house we choose—large, small, wooden, stucco, flat-roofed, elegant, grand or dingy. I don't remember ever being refused. Some would say, "Come back in a week." Others have a supply on hand. People are pleasant and enthusiastic and we catch glimpses of the way they live—their dressing gowns, the insides of their houses and the way they smell. In my memory it is always early morning—fine, with a slight mist and foghorns groaning. So I suppose we did this before school and on weekends.

Mike and I go to hundreds of houses, yet those that stick in my memory are in a row near Saxe Point Park, their gardens stretching down to the rocks at the edge of the sea. I can picture the faces of those people, hear the timbre of their voices and catch the scent of their houses when they open their doors.

We gather vast quantities of fat and foil yet somehow we never bump into other children doing this. And what becomes of this loot? Did they really make bombs with the fat? Dazzle enemy planes with the silver paper?

After school we have another job. We pick Dad's raspberries and loganberries in season, filling hallets (the split wood folding boxes that hold a pint) or tin tops (the fixed wooden boxes edged with tin that hold a generous quart) until Mike's wagon is full. Then, taking a different route, we peddle them door-to-door. For some reason we never go to our fat customers with fruit—probably because they are slightly more affluent, with time and land enough to grow their own.

In retrospect our war effort seems puny, hardly worth mentioning, but it is our first real initiative—something Mike and I do on our own, without anyone else's urging. And it's a success in that it goes on for months, for years. Our earnings buy several hundred-dollar War Savings Bonds. But I prefer our fat and foil collections, where no money changes hands. On the strength of them I give up my dream of being a surgeon to join the Fuller Brush Company. What more satisfying job can there be than one that allows you to see how other people live?

When Jamie dies we are completely dispirited. Mike, in high school now, is Dad's chief helper in the stables. He spends all his spare time there. I knit mufflers. Concentrate on filling boxes for prisoners of war. Spare cash buys toothpaste, toothbrushes, face cloths, safety pins, needles, candies, five-cent chocolate bars—things they might appreciate. Mothers do this too. And Mum seems to forget the Peace River people in her fervour to send parcels to strangers in distress, off into the unknown from the village post office to that ominous place called *OVERSEAS*.

95. ROSEMEAD

Rosemead, the house next door, was designed by Samuel Maclure and built in 1909 for Mr. T.H. Slater, a realtor in Victoria. Maclure often worked with his patrons, and in this case both Mr. and Mrs. Slater were very much involved in the design and details of their house and garden. They apparently achieved their every wish, but the result seems a jumble of gables jutting in all directions, too many styles of half-timbering on the exterior, a *porte cochère* too large for the house, and rooms that are rather small and of awkward shapes. Perhaps it was a question of too many cooks.

Like Wychbury, Rosemead was built with dark brown shingle below and dark brown half-timbering on cream above. The two houses looked somewhat similar. In fact, the day Dad drove Mum to view their new house, it was raining so hard she could see very little. Then a break in the storm allowed her to catch a glimpse of Rosemead as they came up the drive, and she thought *it* was the house he was buying.

Rosemead was smaller, though from the street it seemed to sit a little higher than Wychbury—but not as comfortably on the land. From a child's point of view it was a more exciting-looking house, and I loved it. But Mum, who came to know it well, claimed our house was far superior architecturally. I can't dispute this as I was only inside Rosemead twice—quite recently. The first time it was in transition—between owners—and seemed both rundown and unloved. But I was delighted to see that the little wooden gate, built in

1909 to give access from one house to the other, was still there and still green, but covered with wood mould and moss.

Though Mr. and Mrs. Slater achieved their *dream house*, tragedy struck soon after they moved in. First their daughter died, then Mrs. Slater fell ill so they only actually lived in Rosemead for ten months.

After that it seems to have been rented to a succession of people for short periods. No one remembers who lived there when Dad bought Wychbury in late 1924, but while the Griggs were there, Peter, Sylvia and Joan played with their two girls. Then the Murrays lived there for a while, and two of my older sisters had glorious fun playing with their daughters, Rona and Dawn. Joanie remembers lots of nooks and crannies inside and other wonderful places to hide in their woods.

Next came Dr. and Mrs. Rickard, Americans, I think. He was a scientist and we didn't see much of him, but she spent a lot of time in the garden. And she sang, so we often heard her lovely operatic voice drifting from open windows as she practised for concerts. Sometimes we heard her scolding her cook or instructing her gardener—telling him exactly what to do and when—in a rather loud voice. Her special love was roses and she spent hours fluttering over them. Once, for her birthday, Dad appeared with a wheelbarrow full of ripened horse manure—a treat for her roses. She was delighted and gushed about this *chaaarrrming present* for ages.

Whenever she caught glimpses of me peeking through the fence that edged our two properties she would call out in a loud theatrical voice, "Is that you, my daaarling Ba?" And it was, for she intrigued me. She was utterly unlike all the other women I knew. Even when gardening she wore flowing full-length dresses of bright blues or gauzy pinks with wide-brimmed hats or parasols to match, looking as if about to rush off to some grand performance. And perhaps she was, for her white hair was always beautifully set and marcelled, her face powdered, her lips a brilliant red—ready to step onstage in a second. Though she claimed I was her *special* friend, she never ever asked me in. And how I longed to see the innards of that house. I might have asked, but she was rather a daunting character—both frosty and friendly at once. So the closest I came to it was attending their Garden Fêtes. They, at least, gave me the right to be in their garden. Otherwise it was a quick hop over the fence to snitch a neglected apple lying on the ground (theirs were intriguing varieties, unlike ours) if their Chinese cook and gardener weren't around. When they caught us in the act—they'd roar! How I wish now I'd found the courage to ask Mrs. Rickard if I could see her house. She might have enjoyed showing it to me. But in my day, children were seen—not heard.

When the war began, Dr. and Mrs. Rickard moved to Oak Bay. Perhaps they felt safer there, or had Rosemead grown too large for them?

Then a group of young naval officers moved in and called it Stag Home. From then on, respectable young women were not seen there. Nor were prepubescent girls, so my chances of an architectural tour were slimmer than ever. But the inmates were a friendly bunch, coming and going at all hours. We could hear their chat and laughter when they sat out on the roof of the *porte cochère*—mid-height between our first and second floors—but we couldn't see much because of the laurel hedge that edged our land. Sometimes we'd catch snatches of conversation as they went out to the garden or stepped into cars at the front door. Some would offer me lifts to school—eager to find which of my brothers' wives I preferred, silly questions like that. Or they came across to our place through that little green gate to talk, play tennis, have a meal or court Sylvia. Joanie was in residence, training to be a nurse and much too busy to be bothered with these neighbours. And Mary, who by then called herself Frances, had her own pursuits. But those most adoring of Sylvia were always turning up at our front door—or standing perfectly still in the garden, gazing up at the drawing room windows, hoping to be noticed and asked in.

There were a lot of attractive young men stationed in Esquimalt in those days, and more at Hatley Park who were in the Royal Canadian Naval Volunteer Reserve or Wavy Navy. It was my job to entertain those who came to take Sylvia out while she got ready. Sometimes I felt I knew them better than she did because it took her such hours to primp and attain what she considered perfection. Once I misunderstood her signals and made a terrible mistake. I told her favourite, a man I liked very much, that she preferred someone else.

I had no idea that he'd proposed to her and she considered accepting. But I remember his face—the slow way he turned, the stiffness of his back as he stalked off. In that same sad, concentrated manner I've seen African men in full tribal dress standing, as if frozen, on Boulevard Saint-Michel, the whole of Paris swarming around them, their bodies taut, leaning uphill, heads raised, eyes closed—trying in desperation to recapture something lost—or sniffing the air for scents of home.

Sylvia didn't seem to mind too much. She was miffed that I had dispatched her nice young man, but not devastated. While she danced the night away in her elegant evening gowns with all those gallant young men (not, of course, at Stag Home), she spent her days in goggles and coveralls at Yarrows shipyard (in both #1 and #2 yard), burning huge sheets of steel—the steel that other women, and men too, riveted together to make the hulls and superstructures of the ships those young naval officers sailed away in. For this she got seventy-five cents an hour at first, and then one dollar. That was excellent pay in those days—far more than for any other job she'd had. Then most of it was taxed away.

One Hallowe'en during that era of Stag Home, Mike and I dressed up, and for some reason Mum said not to go far. So we slipped through the little green gate to trick-or-treat the neighbours. Their housekeeper opened the door and shrieked at us, "Go away! This is no place for children!"

Rosemead ceased to exist as the private family house it was designed to be when an English couple, Sam and Rosina Lane, bought it in 1946. Businessmen—with the blessing of endless Chambers of Commerce—have often tried to sell Victoria as a cute little outpost of Empire, to the dismay and disgust of the citizenry, and the Lanes, inspired, perhaps, by the local beer parlour—The Tudor House—transformed both house and garden at Rosemead into a pseudo-Shakespearean village-cum-theme park they called the Olde England Inn. By degrees they absorbed more of our land and built what they called Anne Hathaway's Cottage smack in the middle of Dad's Riding Ring, then added more buildings to complete their "village." Luckily Samuel Maclure didn't see what became of his quintessentially Canadian house designed for a specific family on a specific piece of land in Esquimalt. Nor did we, the Piddington family. By that time he was dead and we were well away.

New owners took the "e" from "olde" and added it to Rosemead. I went there with my friend Cicely, hoping to have lunch in their restaurant. We were too early in the season but had a glimpse of the interior. Snazzy crystal chandeliers and a plate glass front door don't seem at ease in that setting, but the house looks cared for. Outside, the Shakespearean village has grown. A row of new *olde* buildings has been added, and a rather featureless rectangular house, built in the forties, which her family once lived in has been fancied-up with gables and renamed the House of Verona in an attempt to make it more Shakespearean. The little wooden gate we treasured has been torn down and bits of it flung across into what was once our property.

But the garden, long neglected, is spectacular. A great deal of care and money has made it a place of beauty. According to the young man we spoke to, another million is to be spent on it soon. I couldn't help thinking how pleased Mrs. Rickard would be to see her garden in its new glory. She might complain about a lack of roses but would, I'm sure, burst forth into song in her delight.

I doubt she would approve of the changes in the house, though. Nor would the Slaters, who took such pains to design the beautiful Arts and Crafts house of their dreams. While Mr. Slater might demand: *What on earth is a million-dollar business doing in my house?* Samuel Maclure might bellow, if he were a bellower: *A little half-timbering doth not a Tudor house make!*

All of them might be tempted to haunt Rosemeade, the English Inn and Resort, as the house is now known. But based on the description of Rosemead's ghosts in Robert Belyk's *Ghosts: True Tales of Eerie Encounters*, many of those haunting the place may be ancient English ghosts—imported along with the armour and furniture the Lanes brought from England to decorate the house in the forties and fifties.

Could it be that Mrs. Rickard is one of them? Belyk describes an extraordinary female voice that can be heard, on occasion, singing arias. Perhaps it is her lusty voice that scares the other local ghosts away. But then why isn't Dad, who loved her singing, his house and

Mr. and Mrs. Slater were very much involved in the design and details of Rosemead, but the result was too many styles, and rooms that were rather small and of awkward shapes. (This recent photo also shows later modifications.)

land even more, haunting the place too? He might well be marching through or around Anne Hathaway's Cottage, built on his beloved Riding Ring. With his exuberance and enthusiasm, why hasn't *he* made an appearance? He might, at least, be stomping along the property line between Wychbury and Rosemead in his old riding coat and breeches, pushing a manure-filled wheelbarrow and shouting out in a loud voice: *Preposterous! Preposterous! This is utterly preposterous! What's going on here, I'd like to know?*

96. THE CAT MAN

Both Sylvia and Fran were employed as burners in Yarrows shipyard during the war. Along with a great many women and a few men, they cut up heavy sheets of steel to be welded together to make warships. Their shifts were sometimes at night, which meant they would come home in the early hours of the morning, either in Fran's red roadster with the rumble seat or on their bikes. If we woke up really early, we might hear them putting their gear away, having a snack or taking a bath. Stoko was occasionally on night shift too. So we were accustomed to hearing footsteps coming up the front or the back stairs, and in Stoko's case going on up to his room above. He slept in the billiard room then.

During that period, Hilly slept in the pink and green bedroom between the front and back stairs, once Tom's room, then used by others in turn. It was a bright room with an eastern and southern exposure and its own fireplace—perfect for someone convalescing, as Hilly often was after a bout with a sore eye.

One night she woke to the sound of footsteps shuffling past her door, then shuffling back again—back and forth. Then the meowing began. She knew perfectly well it wasn't Pooh, our cat, and she was pretty sure it wasn't a family member. The shuffling and the meowing continued. She sat up without turning on the light—feeling more and more disconcerted. Who was it?

After what seemed to her a very long time she found the courage to ask, "Who is it?" From the hallway a strange voice answered: *It's your daddy!* Terrified now, she wondered what to do. To reach any-

Sylvia and Fran worked night shifts as burners in Yarrows shipyard during the war, and would come home in the early hours in Fran's red roadster with the rumble seat.

one she'd have to go along the hall *he* was using. So she stayed put—sitting bolt upright and perfectly still. Waiting.

Eventually Sylvia and Fran came home. No, they hadn't been in earlier and they certainly hadn't been creeping about meowing!

Mum phoned the police. All they could say was: *That fellow was probably harmless—but please be aware, Mrs. Piddington, there are some very strange people in the village these days. We don't know everyone as we used to. So be sure to lock your doors from now on.*

What made the Cat Man choose our house? How many other houses did he visit, and where had he come from? That mystery was never solved.

97. THE COOK'S ROOM

The cook's room was in the basement. It was a fair-sized room with its own separate bathroom and a sink and hot plate in the corner. On the walls were Egyptian appliqués in stitched cloth. I thought the choice of decor odd as most of our cooks were Chinese, but Mum liked the appliqués and felt they added needed colour. The windows gave a glimpse of the garden, trees, garage and road. As far as I know only one cook disliked this room—the one who complained about everything.

Later on, during the war, when there were no more cooks, the room was rented to servicemen as temporary quarters. Once we had a young couple from Ontario with a brand new baby. They loved it and were perfect tenants but found a bigger place. Others with small children were considerate and so quiet we scarcely noticed them.

But there was one family of horrors. They had two children, Ernie and Elsie. Mum had told them the room was too small for four, but they were desperate and insisted on renting it.

That was a big mistake. If the children weren't squalling and screaming at each other, the parents were yelling—both inside their quarters and in the garden. They were obviously unhappy so Mum suggested they leave. They wouldn't go.

Mum went before the Wartime Housing Appeal Board in an attempt to evict them. She succeeded after a great struggle, but the *Daily Colonist* told the story from the tenants' side, under the headline "Heart Hardens," and depicted Mum as an ogress who had taken in two darling children—then turned against them.

Eventually they left. But the whole episode upset Mum so much she refused to rent that room to anyone else.

98. ANDRÉ

There was a lad in Esquimalt whose face haunts me. He was dark, handsome, sympathetic and smiling. My hero. His name was André Gagnon.

He was a year older than I, but when I returned to Lampson Street School in the fall of 1941, we were in the same grade. Large classes like ours would be split sometimes, but he was in my room for at least two years. Anyway, everyone met on the playground. And there he was, with his special air about him: sympathetic, diplomatic and wise. André could smooth problems and stop fights yet was a pleasure to be near, whoever you were. To me he was beautiful. I longed to be his friend, and he would smile at me as if he were.

Then, on the terrible morning of June 8, 1944, he and a friend, Robin Sim, were waiting at the corner of Lyall and Lampson for a third boy who hadn't quite finished his breakfast. They would bike up Lampson Street hill together, as they always did, to school. André had pulled his brand new bike well off the road and onto the wooden sidewalk. Robin was there with him.

As their friend appeared at his gate, pushing his bike, so did an Army truck travelling extremely fast. Perhaps the driver was trying to thrill the fourteen CWACs (Canadian Woman's Army Corps members) on board—driving without hands or showing off. Just as it reached the boys, the truck went out of control. It swerved onto the boulevard and struck André and Robin and their bikes. Then it veered off onto the next-door lawn, where it stuck fast, up to its axles in earth. The driver and his passengers were treated for shock.

André died that afternoon, of a fractured skull. But as he fought for his life, each time he regained consciousness he called: *Look out! Look out!* As if trying to save Robin, who died soon after him.

All but one of the newspaper reports of that time imply it was the boys' fault. It was unpatriotic to complain about servicemen and women, so at the inquest their parents actually apologized—as if somehow the boys had enticed the truck twelve feet off the road so it would crash into their bodies. No one blamed the driver. Only Olwen Rodstrom, the mother of André's best friend, questioned the speed, the careless, reckless driving. "From every side come expressions of protest against army driving," she wrote. And about the accident and the attitude of many at that time she said: "Everyone seems mad!"

I didn't know Robin Sim. He was a year younger than André and in a different class. He lived with his parents on Joffre Street and was, I am sure, mourned by all who knew and loved him. Just as those of us who knew André were devastated. Crushed. I have grieved for him all my life. The Gagnon family, who lived on Fraser Street, had lost their only other son earlier. He went down with his ship, HMCS *Fraser*, in June 1940.

Recently I mentioned André to my brother Michael. He is a retired Anglican parson and knows a lot about grief. His reaction wasn't what I expected. "You grieve for him, too?" he cried. "But he was my friend!" And he told me how he and a group of his pals, all of them three years ahead of me and already at Esquimalt High, had tried to go to André's funeral in Victoria only to find the church jammed full. They couldn't get near it. So as they were in town with permission to be away from school, they went to a movie. This troubles Mike still.

Then, when I mentioned André to Hilly, who was a year ahead of Mike, she thought of him as *her* friend!

What a marvellous tribute to a lad of fourteen, that he should be revered by so many of such a wide age group—and be loved and re-membered for well over sixty years. It seems bizarre that we didn't or couldn't share our mutual grief at the time. I considered André's death as my personal tragedy. So, apparently, did my two siblings. And how many others?

Could André, had he lived, have helped somehow to heal the fes-tering wound that afflicts so many—those who aren't or don't wish to be bilingual? His mother was Scottish; his father French. And ac-cording to Olwen Rodstrom, André was intelligent. Perhaps he could have helped obliterate the division—imagined, if not encouraged and imposed—between French and English speakers in Canada. I like to think so. His first fourteen years were extraordinary—think what he might have accomplished had he lived!

99. HINDSIGHT

Hindsight is so clear and convenient. One sees immediately what *should* have been done—and where to place whatever blame seems due. But there are so many sides to every situation, and sometimes one must choose the "best" solution quickly for whatever the problem is.

In wartime, harsh and terrible decisions are made that would not be allowed in times of peace. During the 1939–45 war, the "Second War" as we called it, everyone was agitated and fearful. People were losing husbands, fathers, brothers, sisters or children with terrifying frequency. Ships were sinking, planes crashing, bombs falling. Servicemen and civilians of all ages were being killed or taken prisoner. We were told to keep calm, keep quiet. And keep a sharp eye out! So people did.

The Minister of Justice could intern anyone he deemed "in any manner prejudicial to public safety or the safety of the state." Both enemy nationals and Canadian citizens were interned right from the beginning of the war—some merely for being trade union leaders, fascists or communists. Immediately after the Japanese attack on American ships in Pearl Harbor—on December 7, 1941—thirty-eight Japanese Canadian men were interned.

Everyone was nervous. Some had glimpsed conning towers from submarines skirting the BC coast. But Canada didn't have any subs! A lumber-carrier was torpedoed off Cape Flattery the same day Pearl Harbor was bombed. Some claimed to have seen a Japanese admiral in full dress uniform in Steveston. Then *fogos* were dropped on South Pacific islands—carved figures of soldiers hanging from parachutes—terrifying, as their size and scale were impossible to gauge as they drifted downward. We were warned to watch for these and also for parachutes carrying *butterfly bombs* that would set BC's forests aflame. Luckily the only damage was to a wooden fence in Saskatchewan in 1944. Those were anxious times.

Throngs of strangers milled about in towns and villages. Esquimalt, with its army barracks, naval barracks and drydock, seemed almost under siege. For the first time ever, people were urged to lock their doors. There was talk of a fifth column. Our Japanese fishermen were, and still are, superb navigators who knew every nook and cranny of this coast—and the thinking was that if Canadians of British heritage didn't hesitate to fight for England's cause, might not Canadians of Japanese ancestry feel more loyalty to Japan than to our European allies? Those were the seeds of fear that grew—especially after the shelling of Estevan lighthouse on the west coast of Vancouver Island on June 20, 1942. By then the decision had been made to move all Japanese Canadians inland for the duration. Their land and possessions were to be held in trust till the war was over.

At that time, with so many ghastly things happening around the world, this move seemed a small price to pay. But it didn't take into account the feelings of those uprooted. No one ever imagined what a deep and pervasive wound this "sensible precaution" might cause. Or that, through graft and greed, others would abscond with the land and belongings of the Japanese Canadians who were interned.

One day my stoical brother came home from school crying. His friend Seiji Takata was leaving. Mike couldn't understand why.

When the war ended he went to the RCMP in Victoria and asked where Seiji was. They said they had no idea. But when Mike found him finally, in Toronto, Seiji told him the RCMP knew exactly where each interned person was, at all times. Mike and Seiji met regularly after that, and about ten years ago they walked through Victoria's Kinsmen Gorge Park—where once Seiji's father and uncle had run the famous Takata Gardens.

Not long ago, at an Esquimalt High School reunion, Sylvia met her old classmate Toyo Takata, Seiji's older brother. With utmost graciousness, he asked her to join him and his wife at the head table. He had been sent to Toronto and wanted her to know he felt no bitterness about it. Being sent east was a blessing, he said. His whole outlook broadened and his life changed for the better. Both Takatas are dead now—but not forgotten.

When I returned to Vancouver in 1957, I shared a house with friends near the UBC Gates. Next door was a houseful of students. One of them was Japanese. When he studied on the adjoining lawn we often talked, and one day I apologized for all he and his people had suffered during the war. His reply surprised me. The gist was this: His family came from Steveston. They were fishermen. In those days, tradition would have demanded that he be a fisherman too. But when he was interned he met educated Japanese—people he would never have met otherwise. From them he realized that he could do whatever he wanted with his life. "I'm going to be a lawyer!" he said proudly. "But for the war I would never have *considered* such a thing. So I, for one, am grateful for what happened to us."

100. THE UNCLES CHARLIE

We had two Uncle Charlies. Mum's brother Charlie lived in Québec and had a full life, but for me he existed only in photographs: as a child, fair with round cheeks; as a middle-sized boy; and as an officer in the Canadian Army. He probably wrote to Mum occasionally or perhaps sent cards. Otherwise he ignored us. Like most of our eastern relations, he thought we should go to see them. As if we'd step on a streetcar, slip across the country for an hour or two, at their pleasure, and then go home. What intrigued me was his wife. She had a beautiful name: Marguerite de Lotbinière-Harwood. Surely she must be a princess! Then at the end of her name came Uncle Charlie's Scottish one: Porteous. So hers was a métis family—blended, like ours.

Our other Uncle Charlie was much closer—tangible, a treat for all the senses. Someone we could rely on to visit us several times a summer, just as we could visit him. He had had an exotic wife too. She was Dame Nellie Melba—the Australian singer for whom Peach Melba and Melba toast were invented.

This Uncle Charlie was a great-uncle of our Nixon cousins, Eckersal, Pat and George, and enjoyed seeing those three boys while they were at Shawnigan Lake School. When it could be arranged for them to get away for an hour or two, he'd suggest they pull the bucket from his well. In it might be a batch of his homebrew, nicely chilled, or some other treat. So he wasn't really *our* uncle at all, but our *chosen* uncle—someone we loved and admired. Toward the end of his life he saw much more of us than he did of them. And he asked us to call him "Uncle"—so we felt he really was!

He and Dad met soon after our family moved to BC in 1924, just after his nephew Edward A.E. Nixon died. Whenever Dad drove Tom and Jamie up to Shawnigan Lake School, he'd drop in on Charlie Armstrong and chat. They hit it off immediately and became great friends. And after we bought Savira in 1926, he was our neighbour all summer long—living just five miles up the lake.

Born to a titled family in Ireland, Charlie Armstrong was a superb horseman and, as a younger son, went to Australia for adventure.

One day in a small outback church he noticed a beautiful young woman in the choir. Her name was Helen Mitchell and her voice was glorious. They met, fell in love and married. He paid for singing lessons and in no time she was giving concerts and calling herself Nellie Melba after her birthplace, Melbourne. Then he took her to Ireland to meet his family, and they travelled together in Europe. In 1888 she sang at London's Covent Garden—becoming world famous almost overnight. Uncle Charlie was delighted by her success but it isn't easy living with a *prima donna*, and he loathed being called Mr. Melba!

Around the turn of the century they separated. She and their son stayed in Europe while he moved to Canada and bought fertile waterfront land on the west shore of Shawnigan Lake, near the north end. His nephew, Neville Armstrong, joined him on his return from the gold rush and bought property nearby. It seems rather a remote spot for either of them to choose, but there were already a number of families, couples and single men of similar background living there year-round, all well-educated and interesting, who chose the area for its mild climate and its beauty. I am not sure how social Charlie and his nephew were, but they could have been had they wished. Neville didn't stay long, but Uncle Charlie lived there for some fifty years, quite content in his small shack between the woods and the water, tending his garden.

In 1918 Nellie Melba was appointed Dame Commander of the British Empire. She died, internationally famous, in 1931. Meanwhile Uncle Charlie lived on in solitude with his cat—perfectly self-sufficient, reading, discussing world affairs, growing superb fruit and vegetables and rowing across to the village for whatever else he needed. When the lake froze he would walk across, carrying a long pole on his shoulders so if he went through the ice he could haul himself out again. Eventually a road was built along the west shore in 1928. From time to time his son would visit him. So did friends from Victoria.

As far back as I can remember, and well before that, Uncle Charlie would sail down the lake to Savira with the afternoon wind, bringing a basket of whatever was in season—often his succulent homegrown peaches—arriving in jig time for afternoon tea. He knew he had an open invitation so he came when it suited him. He would talk and have tea. When the wind switched, he'd sail home again. He was always immaculately dressed in white flannels or white ducks, his leather shoes whitened to perfection, with a white shirt and blazer and a broad-brimmed Panama hat. I don't believe he had help from anyone, so his clothes would have been washed by hand or in a washing machine of his own creation, then ironed with a sad iron. He was a crusty no-nonsense sort of a person, gruff but gentle with twinkling blue eyes. Even in his eighties he was strong and agile. And how he loved to talk!

Later on he bought a boat with an inboard engine. That meant he could stay for supper and well on into the night. Many is the time I fell asleep on the verandah listening to Dad and Uncle Charlie swapping their marvellous tales! Talk flowed from them. Ideas bounced back and forth. Their voices might have been instruments—a cello, perhaps, and an oboe. One would spark a response in the other, setting them off on a new tangent—while we, the audience, listened entranced. It wasn't just speech—it was magical, musical—almost a performance with history, geography, politics, humour all mixed up together. Talking for the joy of it—as only the Irish can!

As Uncle Charlie grew older, Dad and I would paddle up to check on him. If it were morning he'd insist we stay to lunch, and if he were low on homemade bread, he'd whip up a batch of delicious bannock— teaching me the method he'd learnt in Australia. And he'd tell me once again: "If you want to impress a man, always use two cans of soup to one of water!" His little house wasn't fancy but it was clean and neat and functional, and he was always glad you'd come.

Dear Charlie Armstrong—you were one of the dearest men I've ever known and certainly my favourite of all our uncles!

101. MICHAEL

After a string of four girls in a row, there was rejoicing at Michael's birth. Perhaps this time Dad would get his Olympic figure skater, his champion! Mum wanted an architect, so added "Christopher Wren" to his name. He was a beautiful baby and an adorable child

*Even as a child, Michael was careful, deliberate, and conscientious—
his nannies could sit him down on a rug and know he'd
be there whenever they came back.*

with his thick mop of golden curls, but he had weak ankles and no interest at all in architecture. He was his own man: careful, deliberate, taking his own good time, making his own decisions.

He and I were chalk and cheese. Companions, yet utterly unalike. Mum and his nannies called him "the perfect child" as they could sit him down on a rug and know he'd be there whenever they came back. Even as an infant he thought things out, considered them—the sort of person who reads instructions, is dependable, conscientious. It took him a year to read a book, though—not just hours. But then he would know it almost by heart. He is the one who remembered our Esquimalt phone number instantly—sixty-two years later.

As the last two kids, we were bundled together, sent off on errands, shared chores, even shared bedrooms for quite a long time—together with Hilly in a huge room when small—then just the two of us in Peter's room. At first we were side by side, with a bedside table between us—then Mike in the centre of the room and me by the window. When we couldn't sleep we'd exhaust ourselves debating. The only topic I can remember was whether it should be my choice, *Pink Bluebells* and *White Bluebells*, or his, *Pink Bells* and *White Bells*—a matter never entirely resolved.

This was when I began placing brand new shoes on either side of my pillow so I could dream of them and breathe in their fresh leather smell as I slept. Mike thought this outrageous. Then, one Easter, I begged off going to church—claiming a pain in my pinny—but really because I wanted to finish *The Hunchback of Notre Dame* and a large chocolate rabbit. He would never have done either.

Mike had already started hiding the five-pound boxes of chocolates the Aunts sent him each Christmas and Easter—given to him *because he was a boy*! And he would only allow Hilly and me one a day.

Sometimes Mike's slow reactions really upset me. How could I speed him up? Make him react? Twice, when very young, I took a nip of his leg—actually bit him—but that didn't work. We played a lot of croquet in those days. It was supposed to improve hand-eye co-ordination, so the hoops would be set out in spring and left during fine weather so we could play at any time. Our mallets were adult-sized—large and heavy—and we took shots from the side to get optimum force. Once, when Mike's slowness had driven me to distraction, I gave him a little tap on the head with a mallet to speed him up. That didn't work either.

Curiously, he doesn't remember these incidents at all, and what he does remember, I didn't—until he mentioned it. The rage, at that time, was to use empty five-pound Rogers' Golden Syrup tins as stilts. We either put strings through them so we could lift them by hand with each step, or we threaded wires through that fitted over our shoes. In any case, he claims that on one occasion when we were racing across the lawn on those tin stilts and *he was winning*—I threw a tin at him. It didn't hurt, but it did hit him, and he was quite surprised. It is marvellous what one remembers and why.

Whatever I tried, he refused to change to suit me. And I'm glad of that, because I am very fond of him as he was—and is! If Mike seemed to lack fire sometimes, he was a serious steady lad. He helped inside and out, however he could, was a good student and a good horseman and did more than his share of work in the stables and helping to exercise the horses. And at a very young age he would ride a horse, with another on a lead, to gymkhanas and polo matches, even up over the Malahat to Duncan. He was dependable and kind. Our right-hand man. And my brother, my playmate and my friend!

But oh—if Mum could have had another *boy—I would have loved another brother!*

102. NYLON STOCKINGS

In the thirties, women wore silk stockings for best, wool when it was cold, or lisle if they had hard work to do. Silk stockings felt and looked far more elegant, but they were costly and fragile. The slightest contact with anything rough would cause a *ladder* or a *run*. There were women who could mend these for a hefty price, but those stockings never looked the same. Some would touch the end of a run with a damp bar of soap, hoping that might stop it in its tracks. Others would dab it with nail polish. That worked well but left you with a spotted stocking—unwearable, except at home.

Then nylon stockings appeared. They were much stronger than silk and seemed the answer to a maiden's prayer. Like silk stockings, they had a seam up the back, so women got good exercise twisting their torsos and peering around and down to make sure their seams were where they should be: straight up the back of their legs. Twisted seams showed a sloppy woman—so unacceptable!

When war was declared, both silk and nylon were commandeered, made into parachutes and sent overseas. Women were left with lisle stockings. Many didn't mind a bit—but the fashion-conscious refused. They went bare-legged. That was okay in summertime, but in winter chill red, pink or, worse still, *white* legs looked hideous. So some bright entrepreneur solved the problem by making special leg paint. Women rushed to this, and we became accustomed to seeing legs of lurid yellowy brown. Then, of course, seams had to be drawn down each painted leg with an eyebrow pencil. This was tricky to do yourself and required more twisting and turning to etch each seam. Then this wretched stuff would come off in the rain and would have to be washed off each night or your sheets would be ruined and your seams smudged. How women suffered!

I remember my sisters applying this leg paint. It came in bottles with little sponges on wire sticks attached to the stopper. It took ages for them to get each leg painted exactly the same colour and tone—without streaks, spots or blotches. And then both seams had to be drawn on just so. Meanwhile their lads waited downstairs—often entertained by me because Hilly was too shy. She remembers the process of leg-painting well, though. And the application of seams. The wonderful thing is that our sisters, who used the stuff, don't remember doing it at all.

103. TOYS and GAMES

When I think back, our house seemed full of toys—masses of them. But they weren't all mine. Many were the castoffs of my siblings, stretching back twenty years to the childhood of our brother Tom— for that life-sized dog on wheels had been his. By the time I rode about the house on him, his iron backbone was poking through his plush coat so we had to be careful where we sat. Tom's, too, were the articulated wooden animals made in Montreal ca. 1911. The dog, I remember, was intriguing—beautifully designed and built, but all it would do was sit on its haunches or lie down: an adult's idea of a toy. No wonder it survives—almost untouched, in perfect shape.

Each child in our family had one special doll and, later, a bear. My Edward was given to me when I was seven, so he has lasted well. Mum made him a navy blue greatcoat with black buttons and red buttonholes. She also dressed my baby dolly in a blue woollen outfit decorated with white French dots. Around about that time my god-mother gave me a boy doll dressed in mustard yellow *suitings* she'd knitted herself. I found both doll and garments hideous, and she re-alized that, poor woman. It was the first and last thing she gave me. My other godmother, Aunt Vivian, in Montreal, had wanted Joanie as godchild and ignored me utterly—until we met, when I was adult.

There were boxes of Meccano and round wooden disks with pegs that fitted together to make things, jigsaw puzzles and wooden blocks, decks of cards, kites, long wooden stilts, tops and two spotted wooden pigs of unknown vintage that wobbled down slopes, but not up. Once, when I was sick in bed, someone gave me a fur beaver who zigzagged around the floor when his key was turned—until he got tired of moving. Grey Owl was in vogue at the time. So was Shirley Temple. But I loathed my Shirley doll and popped it, brand new, into the Peace River Box without a whimper.

My own special treasures fit into a covered toys box Mum made from a small wooden butter box she covered with padding and pretty coloured cloth showing characters from Mother Goose. It was both seat and treasure chest and it was *mine*! I sat on it while operating on my dolls or reading books—probably upside down. Mum used butter boxes to paint on, so her friend "dear Mr. Scott, the grocer," saved them for her. Always in a hurry, she could do a ten-minute palette knife sketch directly on their waxy surface. We have one she did of me standing on Fleming's Beach.

While the others were in school I tagged along with Mum and did what she did. For instance, when she made dresses for Hilly and me, I made dresses for my dolls. She didn't need patterns—I did, and could never get the stiff arms of my dollies into the narrow sleeves of my creations, but in the process I learned to sew on buttons, make buttonholes and sew seams and hems. Lying on the nursery floor I spent hours reading (i.e., imagining stories from pictures), playing with Mum's vast button collection, painting, colouring, cutting pictures from old magazines and gumming them—or those glorious shiny brightly coloured Victorian printed stencils I was given—into scrapbooks. Once I had a book of blank church windows plus sheets of coloured glassine so I could make my own stained glass. If really lucky, I played with cutout dolls. Sometimes Hilly let me try her special fuzzy-surfaced doll whose clothes stuck on with no need of those pesky shoulder tabs.

I almost forgot the dolls' house! It was quite grand, with two chimneys, two bedrooms and a bathroom upstairs, and a drawing room, dining room, kitchen and garage downstairs with snazzy Edwardian furniture throughout. What impressed me most were the mauve bathroom fixtures and the wallpaper with its tiny William Morris designs—torn out, unfortunately, by a sister-in-law who found them too *gloomy* for her children. Still, there are lattice windows and a front door that opens. The roof, chimneys and front steps are removable, and the front walls can be unhooked and folded back. Years ago, Peter installed electric lights but they work no longer. The walls need repapering and the lead furniture, kept out of harm's way in the attic, has been replaced by an odd collection of bits and pieces. But the dolls' house, a little ragtag and down-at-heel, continues to fascinate children, and when they come to visit it is hauled down from a high shelf.

We played all manner of games like chequers, Chinese chequers, Fish, Snakes and Ladders, Monopoly, pick-up sticks, tiddlywinks and marbles. But of all our games my favourite things went on outside: playing in the garden, climbing trees, exploring the rocks, the sea edge or the woods.

104. HARES and RABBITS

As a family we still say *Hares and Rabbits* to ensure a good month: *Hares* being the last word said aloud as you fall asleep at the end of each month, without uttering another word until waking—when your first word must be *Rabbits!* This sounds a cinch, but it isn't—especially if you share a room and are inclined to be chatty. Or if you share with a trickster. But if you miss either word, no matter—another month comes along in jig time. Where does this custom come from? I've never been able to find out. Some of my siblings claim they've never done it. Others always say just *Hares*. But my eldest sister and the last three say both words at each month's turn.

Another custom when drinking tea, especially China tea: if a leaf floats on the surface we pick it out carefully and place it on that flat bit near the knuckle on the top of our clenched fist. Then we tap that hand with the other fist. If the leaf falls off we are out of luck, but if it clings to our fist it means a letter, parcel or visitor—depending on the size of the leaf—will arrive soon, the date depending on the number of thumps needed to lift it.

This is May Day! The air is rich with the scent of fresh leaves, wild flowers and grape hyacinths. The wind blows inland and makes me want to breathe and breathe until my lungs are full to bursting and I feel capable of anything. This is the day for lovers—*Hey Nonny Nonny*—even the wind feels lusty. Who cares if there's no sun. I want to prance and dance about barefoot! I said *Hares and Rabbits* and washed my face in dew. It should be a good month. This is my favourite of our ceremonies—washing the face with dew on May Day morning, to be beautiful for the rest of the year. Nothing makes skin as fresh and tingly!

On long-ago May Day afternoons we had a holiday to watch the crowning of the village May Queen and her Princesses—enormously exciting for those chosen, but sometimes disheartening for others as, more often than not, choices were made to solve some civic problem rather than reward the intrinsic goodness or beauty of a girl. This celebration took time, with speeches to aid the metamorphosis from ordinary schoolgirl to Queen or Princess—but dancing around the Maypole was fun, even if we got tangled up in ribbons, and who doesn't love a parade—especially if your friend is Queen of the May! Queen for the Day! Or even a Princess!

Another small tradition happened each summer as we approached Shawnigan Lake. After struggling up the Malahat, then down the long twisting Cut-off, we'd make our dusty way along Shawnigan

West Road, all of us on the *qui vive*—for the first to see water through the trees would shout *BEAVER!* As we got near our place, Dad would honk several times: two longs, two shorts, which stood for *P*. Once I asked, "Why are you honking, Daddy, when the house is empty?" "Ah," he said, "you can never be sure. If someone's there who shouldn't be—he'll have a chance to vamoose!" Whenever he went back down to Esquimalt to check on the horses, the house and garden, he would honk the same signal as he drove away. And we'd call "Goodbye! Goodbye" and wave—whether he could hear and see us or not. When he came back, perhaps that same evening or a day or so later, he would signal his approach again—so we could rush to the bottom of the drive, as he bumped down the hill, and help ferry in fresh raspberries, milk, cream and groceries. Luckily there weren't as many people around then, to endure our noise.

Departures and arrivals of family members were always special occasions, with send-off and reception parties in attendance. Some Canadian Pacific boats left Victoria at night, so when I was small I missed those dockside send-offs. But I was there for the others—or on the front steps waiting for the Packard's sweep up the front drive

We are saying goodbye to Jamie, who has been home on leave from the R.A.F in the spring of 1939. We all try to look happy as he takes our picture in front of the CPR express and ticket office.

in fair weather, on the porch if it were raining, or peering out the library window if it were cold. Then I'd give the signal and everyone else would muster and there'd be hugs all round. It was usually brothers going and coming, but both Joanie and Sylvia went to Québec, and so did Mum. Plus there were the arrivals of Granny and Aunt Fran—all the more exciting if they were staying with us. When you arrived you were swept back into the fold again, with the local news: *There were only five eggs this morning! We had a wonderful crop of loganberries! Blanco is lame! Syl is playing polo now! Hilly is riding well! Ba can walk! Michael can swim! Joanie fell off her bike!* But in all the excitement, rarely did anyone ask about the traveller's experiences. They'd eke out later on.

For all those years that I lived in Esquimalt, I had my own particular ceremony each fall. As soon as we got back down to Wychbury after a summer at the Lake, I'd rush to the orchard and pick my first tart apple—then rub its bitten flesh with a blackberry. What a treat for the senses: the sound, the taste, the smell and especially the sight of that incredible glistening purple.

105. SUITORS

All my sisters were attractive in their own way, and young men kept coming to court them. Some were spurned. Once when Mary was sick in bed, her "follower," as Mum called them, brought her a bouquet of yellow roses. *Anyone who likes me should know I loathe yellow roses!* He wasn't seen again.

The most ardent of those followers courted us all. Knowing he was no one's darling, he'd arrive with his family in tow. It was hard to tell four people: *I am so sorry—no one is home.* Especially hard as his aunt and father were our friends. They'd be asked to stay for lunch or tea or both. So scouts were posted on weekends, and sometimes we took turns watching the driveway from the drawing room. Whenever we saw their pale grey touring car pull up we'd call *Jiggers!* so the others could hide. Once we were all stuck behind the sofa for ages, but someone giggled and gave the show away. After that he checked there first, as soon as he arrived.

He was incredibly persistent but had nothing interesting to say, poor fellow, and besides that he had a speech impediment. Our names came out as *Syria, Roan, Phrys* and *Heron. Mary* was his one success but she scorned him most of all. Nevertheless his family came often, in town and to the Lake, where they'd stay all day. Luckily his aunt and father were charming. The mother and son were the problem.

We weren't the only ones he courted. In fact there was scarcely an unmarried girl *of good breeding* (she had to be special for him) in Victoria who wasn't hiding when he showed up. We were never allowed to forget that his mother was an aristocrat and, what's more, had had the *best seat in England*—that is, she rode well, once upon a time. One girl leapt into a china barrel, another out through a bathroom window at his approach.

Eventually he married a woman who saw money-making potential in his family's house. I hope he realized wedded bliss.

106. THE CELLAR

The cellar at Wychbury was not a place to linger. It was more like a cave than a room: dim, full of cobwebs, with dark, earthy-smelling corners. There, before your eyes, was the great mound of rock the house was built on. Whatever space was left was taken up by the furnace, the laundry room, the cook's quarters, and a long and solid workbench under the windows, which looked out over the back entrance yard, the garages and the road. Dad loved puttering there. His bench held a multitude of tools, a wood-vice and chunks of wax for polo sticks, with more tools, supplies and pots of paint stowed on shelves below. Across from the cellar door was a gap between the foundation rock and the ceiling, and stuffed in were things that had come west by accident—including two wonderful old wooden beds from The Pines, Mr. Abbott's old house in Abbotsford, P.Q. where our family lived briefly, after the fire.

Mum knew these beds were treasures, but she never had time to do anything about them. Then, to her astonishment and without consulting her, Dad gave one to Lolo just before we moved away in the summer of 1945. I was passing through the cellar and saw it—a dark red frame with four tall knobby bedposts.

The other, Mr. Abbott's own bed, was older. It was a deep rusty red colour with four corner posts—a series of elegant turned rounds. Years later, when Mum wanted something from our storage unit in Victoria, I saw this second bed and was thrilled by it, so she gave it to me. It was obvious no one had used it for eons as it was strung with rope and expecting a *paillasse* or straw-filled pallet for a mattress. And Mr. Abbott must have been short. His bed was only five feet long. Luckily I was able to find someone to lengthen it with the appropriate hardwood. Then I painted the planks almost the same colour, using an old recipe for milk paint. So Mr. Abbott's bed became mine.

When I was an art student in Paris I met the Québec artist Jean Palardy at a party in honour of his new book, *The Early Furniture of French Canada*. I told him about this bed. He was easy to talk to so I found myself telling him I'd taught spinning and weaving in Ungava and was now studying lithography and *vitrail* or stained glass. Not long after, he phoned to say he was invited to spend the weekend in the country with some old friends—all of them weavers but one, who made stained glass. Would I like to come and meet them?

On a Saturday morning we took an early train and travelled south. M. Palardy's friends were delightful people. I was taken to local churches to see the son's stained glass and then shown all the different sorts of weaving done by the rest of family. They lived in a large farmhouse with a loom in every room. *On tissé tous!* they told me. I love that phrase—it sounds so much like weaving. The time flew: in talk, delectable food and wine. Then more talk. The next day I got a lift back to Paris with one of the daughters. She was pregnant, and when her baby was born I was invited to see her, a darling dark-eyed child. *Elle est curieuse comme une pie!* her mother said. I regret not keeping in touch with that family—they were so warm and charming.

And Mr. Abbott's bed is still in use.

107. DAD'S FADS

A man of enormous enthusiasms, Dad's life took quirky turns. He intended to be a career soldier in England's Royal Horse Artillery. But keeping a promise to his father he returned to Québec City in 1906, six years after arriving in England, to look after his elder sisters, thus infuriating his commanding officers *and* his sisters, who felt they had no need of him. The positive thing was his chance encounter with Helen Mary de Tessier Porteous—who became his wife and our mother.

Dad kept reinventing himself. Between 1906 and 1914 he was an astute businessman increasing his holdings. Then, after the Great War, like so many men returning from battle, he was determined to do something useful, healthy, productive. So he studied horticulture at Macdonald College, bought land in the Eastern Townships and ran a successful apple orchard for six years. The move to the west coast was not his idea. It was the last thing he wanted. He came because his mother-in-law insisted someone be near her widowed daughter, Mum's twin. He and Mum seemed the obvious choice.

When they arrived in the late fall of 1924, he was a wealthy man. But it didn't take long for the "sharks" to smell blood and nibble away at his resources. In the crash of 1929 he lost heavily. The rest slipped away during the Great Depression. So Dad was on his uppers—working the soil once more, growing food to feed his family. From then on, brokers, bankers, lawyers, businessmen and especially politicians seemed *black devils* to him. And he'd share this idea with whoever would listen. These tirades bothered Mum. Her father had been a manager of the Bank of Montreal, and she had the blood of two founding fathers of that bank in her veins. She thought of bankers as careful, honest men.

Perhaps they were, but Dad would come upon something—a theory, a political party, a leader or a person—and be engulfed by it. His waking hours would swirl around this new focus, and he'd discuss his ideas with anyone who'd listen—often to our extreme embarrassment. Then he'd read all the articles, newspapers and books he could find—and worry it all out in conversation. Or he wrote letters, masses of them, to complain—or to people he admired. For instance, in the mid-thirties, intrigued by the new but ancient concept of organic gardening, something he had been doing on his own for years, he started a correspondence with Lady Eve Balfour, who encouraged it in Britain. Through her, he imported special tools, her plans for moveable chicken houses, a humane killer for dispatching hens, potions to speed up compost heaps, a revolting drink called Cloudy Charcoal to cleanse the body, and a mysterious black salve called Exogen to heal through the skin. Sometimes, as quickly as he'd become intrigued, he would drop an idea. But organic gardening was a constant in his life—that and his horses.

When Hilly and I were in London in the early fifties we were poor as church mice, cold and always hungry. You had to keep putting coins in heaters in your *digs* in those days, and even if you stuffed the wretched things, the change in temperature was minimal. Both of us were studying and doing odd jobs to keep fed. In December we received a heavy parcel from home—a Christmas package! On the way back from the post office, we imagined all manner of delicious treats inside it. But no, it contained two quart bottles of Cloudy Charcoal, two jars of Exogen and a note saying: *I know you could never afford this so am sending some! Love Dad.* The wretched stuff had travelled from England to Canada and back again—at considerable expense. We used the Exogen but the Cloudy Charcoal sat in the bathroom we shared with five others in our "fashionable" Queensgate basement flat. Eventually it was poured down the drain.

Dad had a sweet tooth and loved rich food. One day he announced that no white sugar was to be consumed in our house—in fact, nothing but natural sugar was to pass our lips, and as for candy, only barley sugar would do. Next he decreed we'd eat no white flour. Luckily his theories didn't hold much sway in the kitchen—Mum made cakes as usual and Dad continued to lap them up, as well as the delicious bread from the village bakery. At the dinner table he'd talk about natural food and the benefits thereof. Everyone groaned, but our diet, healthy anyway, was scarcely changed. Next came the ultimatum that each mouthful be chewed forty times, slowly. We tried that and decided thirty was more appropriate and twenty quite adequate.

Good health meant good posture. We must, all of us, sit up like the Queen. Never slouch. Walk with heads held high, shoulders back and breastbones to the world. Then it was deep breathing that was essential—but only at the Lake. Perhaps we were not as easy to muster in town, but at Savira, first thing each morning, even before our early morning dip, he lined us up to breathe in unison. In—out. In—out. In—out. Till we thought our lungs would burst. Then that phase was over too, and we could slip into the lake again—warm from our beds.

Then, to Mum's horror, Dad became fascinated by Stalin's "Utopia" and what he considered his splendid successes and clever reforms. In the mid-thirties he was on the point of moving us all to Russia. Then, as suddenly, he became disenchanted. Or had communism been replaced by Bible Bill Aberhart's idea of printing money? He could do with some free money, goodness knows. So could his sister-in-law. Both fell for Social Credit, became members, attended rallies, subscribed to party rags. Dazzled by the promises of social credit, they bored everyone else to distraction. This was their common bond. They almost became friends.

Next came rants against the English economist John Maynard Keynes. Dad felt Keynesian economics were exacerbating the monetary and banking problems of the Depression—if not causing them. Keynes became a black devil, too. Mum claimed Dad was spending too much time reading his *rags*—but in this case it was Keynes' *General Theory of Employment, Interest and Money*. Imagine Dad's disgust when Keynes was given a peerage for his good work. For in 1942 *that terrible man* became the Baron of Tilton. Nowadays his ideas are questioned and some of the brightest minds agree with Dad.

All through those Depression years he found it hard to earn our keep. Though he grew much of our food and we had milk from our Holstein, Bunch, and eggs and meat from our chickens, more was needed. What could a retired officer of a British regiment do? He had no pension of any sort. We hadn't enough land for a commercial apple orchard. But he had a stable full of fine horses—why not teach riding? To his delight a lot of people wanted lessons. The trouble was only a few were able to pay. Those who could were apt to be friends, so he was embarrassed to ask for payment. Thus his days were filled with arduous and often unpaid work. His students, however, provided a sounding board, so he came home almost talked out and quite pleased with himself.

Dad wanted us to be strong and healthy. When he read about the importance of iodine, he had us add one or two drops in each glass of drinking water but put five to ten in his own, on the theory that if something is good, more is better. Soon after that, we were not to drink with meals at all. A little wine perhaps, on occasion—to toast the king—but certainly no water.

One of his delights was "*saving* food." Leftovers might languish in the cooler—a floor-to-ceiling cupboard of many shelves, screened to the outside air. It kept food well, and everything was put there or in the icebox on the back porch (we had no refrigeration until the 1950s). Sometimes a bowl of pudding, some soup or macaroni and cheese would reappear—a little long in the tooth. If he saw it, Dad would insist on eating it—to *save* it—rather than throwing it out.

When he heard that ultraviolet light was beneficial, Dad invested in a heat lamp and had us sit for a set time, bare-chested, wearing goggles, in a dark bathroom-cum-lab. Luckily for them, most of the older ones had left home by then. When that fad fizzled, Mum used the lamp's solid leather suitcase as a sewing kit.

We turned out to be a pretty healthy lot. But without the inoculations and vaccinations of today, most of us caught measles, mumps, chicken pox—whatever was going around—however carefully we were quarantined by Mum. Yet we sailed through them all pretty well unscathed. There was a theory then that bright light, sunlight especially, could damage the sight of those with measles and chicken-pox, so Mum made sure the curtains were drawn in the sickroom and kept us in bed for weeks. Normally we slept with both windows and curtains wide open. But whenever there was a full moon, Dad would creep into our rooms and close the curtains to save us from being moonstruck and our minds, even temporarily, addled. His mum was one-hundred-percent Irish and was very strict about such things. Mum, on the other hand, more French than Irish, would have had us sleep outside in the moonlight to absorb its powers. Sometimes their differences were intense, and if ever it came to shouts I would hide inside a cupboard full of greatcoats until they became friends again.

When Dad suffered from sciatica, he had Mum iron his back with sad irons heated on the wood stove. When his shoulders ached she rubbed them with horse liniment, Absorbine Senior. If he had bronchitis she made mustard plasters and, at his insistence, left them on all night. Somehow they never burnt him.

Both parents had afternoon naps. Dad's was short—a power nap. He'd lie on the sofa in the drawing room with his feet raised—his riding boots resting on an old newspaper—while Mum put the lunch things away and washed up. In those days it was *infra dig* to remove your shoes inside, whether at home or while visiting someone. Once when Granny was staying with us, she knitted him a special rug for those naps. She used large wooden knitting needles and wonderfully soft wool of gorgeous colours. It was long enough for Dad to roll it several times around his person, armpits to feet, and lie down, purring, wrapped in his very own *blankie*.

Dad wanted us to be what he called "natural beauties," especially Mum, so he insisted she wear no makeup nor have her hair permed, crimped or cut. Mum's hair was exceedingly fine and would rise like a halo about her head. The marcel, which was in vogue then, was the perfect solution for Mum's hair: a series of tight waves made by heated curling tongs—waves that never moved. But Dad loathed that look. So at home she pulled her hair back in a bun and if wisps rose, no matter. When she went out, in all seasons but summer, she wore a fine veil pulled back from her nose, across and around a tricorne hat, then tied at the nape of her neck. She looked marvellous— though somewhat eccentric. For dinner parties a hat was acceptable—but a hat and a veil would not do. So there she'd be, looking rather pale, with a mist of fine hair around her head. When they got home, Dad was apt to say: *"Helen, did you notice Mrs. So-and-so? She looked so fresh and pretty. And her hair was lovely! Why can't you look like that?"* And Mum would laugh and say: *"Of course! She has a perm and she's slathered in makeup. Shall I do that too?"* Dad thought she was jealous. He was even more insistent about nail polish. Mum didn't like nail polish either and, even if she had, was far too busy to fiddle with it. But I yearned for some and would pore over the ads in magazines—choosing my favourite colours. The Christmas I was twelve I got some as a present from my sister Sylvia. She was building battleships at Yarrows shipyard, was generous with her earnings and knew what I wanted. She gave me a red silk purse—super enough in itself—but inside was a set of Chen Yu nail polish, including some remover and several colours—one of them called Dragon's Blood! Delighted, I painted my nails and brought the little red purse along with me to the breakfast table. When Dad came up from the stables, there I was, *all tarted up* and feeling beautiful. He roared at me, "Take that stuff off your hands at once! I won't have fingers dipped in blood!" He didn't even know about the dragons! I realized he had probably seen a great many *painted women* and also fingers dripping their own blood during *his* war. And with another one raging, that outburst sank in. I kept the purse for years but didn't wear nail polish again in his presence and gradually came to loathe the stuff too. For Mum, the annoying part was hearing Dad admire his five daughters when we curled our hair, had perms or wore makeup.

One of his sisters was dark and looked Italian, and when Hilly and I hitchhiked through Italy, people claimed we'd stepped straight out of Botticelli's paintings. So perhaps we have some Italian blood way back. Certainly Dad loved any project involving stone. When he and Mum were living at the Lake year-round, he decided one summer that the lower part of the driveway needed help. So he removed the topsoil and paved the entire area—some one thousand square metres. Luckily there were a number of very large boulders nearby—all he had to do was move them, split them and lay the rock in place. He did this alone and enjoyed himself hugely. Then, of course, he had to replace the topsoil. That winter when the lake rose, as it always did to varying degrees, it covered Dad's parking area. Trucks from Scott and Peden and the Island Freight Company, which brought up all our supplies from Victoria, refused to deliver if their trucks had to park in water. Undaunted, Dad repeated the whole project until the surface was high enough to stay dry.

From time to time Savira needed painting. The house was large and built on legs like stilts to avoid winter flooding, so it was more like a two-storey building. Dad always tried to do his own maintenance so

Dad always tried to do his own maintenance at Savira.
Here he is sawing firewood. H.V.P photo (1941)

used his longest extension ladder, balancing it on the uneven ground. To appease Mum, he laid a mattress beside it in case he fell. The last time he did this he was over eighty.

I always felt our parents were lovers rather than friends, as they squabbled and fought so often—especially when money was short and more gear was needed for polo or the horses, or when another *certain winner* stock had been suggested. But after their years alone at Savira, living right at the edge of Shawnigan Lake without electricity or running water, they seemed to mellow and become good pals rather than antagonists. They enjoyed living simply and being together, even in considerable discomfort. They called that time their "second honeymoon."

Just once was Dad "undone." While at university, I would end up eating two Horlick's Malted Milk tablets, those small round pills in their own tiny blue metal box, for lunch—so convenient for a student in a hurry. I had two jobs on the go to pay for food, as well as my studies, and was always rushing. When I needed a health certificate for a scholarship, the doctor classed me as *under-nourished.* Poor

*During their years alone at Savira, Mum and Dad became
good pals rather than antagonists.* H.V.P photo (1945)

Dad. I thought he'd be amused because I had always been so healthy,
but he took it as a personal affront. He felt a failure. I wish I hadn't
told him.

When I think back now, much of our conversation at table came
from Dad telling his stories, his opinions, his slant on the news, his
new theories—the rest of us hardly got a word in edgewise. The consequence of this "deprivation" is a generation of people who cannot
stop talking. We delight in it. So much so that now we must be
stopped—or stop each other.

One remarkable thing about Dad was his belief that females were
as capable as males and could do whatever they wished—if suffi-
ciently determined and hardworking. And he was right, of course.

Yet even today my contemporaries and much younger people say: *Of course women couldn't be explorers, engineers, doctors or lawyers, pilots, bankers, CEOs or even artists way back in the '40s, '50s or '60s*—or whatever seems *long ago* to them. But that is absolute rot, as Dad would say, and I bless him for it. Imagine allowing a fourteen-year-old girl to play polo!

I almost forgot his cleverest trick of all: painting the handles of his tools canary yellow so that "the Outside Man," as he called himself, wouldn't lose them in the garden. It wasn't foolproof, but it certainly helped.

In the spring of 1959 both he and Mum had a series of small strokes. Their doctor ordered absolute quiet—no visitors—not even family. I was commandeered to stay with them and keep everyone else away. It was just the three of us—a lovely, peaceful summer. I did a lot of painting, a lot of cooking, and they got stronger. On my birthday, Dad's *good-for* was inscribed *For my one and only Ba!* He had terms for all of us.

Dad seemed foolish sometimes, gullible or embarrassing—but more and more I see how sensible he was and ahead of his time—way ahead. And oh how I wish I could hear him say, as he did so often, "When my ship comes in"—a wide grin spreading over his face. "*When my ship comes in I'll...*" setting off on another tangent, another dream.

108. THE LIBRARY

Sometimes in the middle of the night I walk through Wychbury in my mind's eye. I saunter up the front drive, keeping to the left-hand side, well away from that thicket of native rhododendron that stretches for about ten metres downhill from the huge arbutus our drive curves around. I skip up the front steps, cross the porch and go in the front door—without knocking or ringing the bell. I am not expected so can wander at will.

To the left of me is the wooden armchair whose seat contains the family's collection of figure skates. Straight ahead is a mahogany sideboard and on it a silver tray waiting to receive my calling card.

To one side is a small cabinet filled with carved wooden animals and other relics. We aren't supposed to touch them and nobody ever explains why. There are brass hooks for coats along the walls, and a brass pot that holds umbrellas. A door leads into the lavatory where there is a roller towel for family use and several folded linen guest towels on racks. Another door leads into the toilet. This is the only washroom on the ground floor and the one Lucky used when he was stuck in the house overnight.

I go through a wooden door to the left—the top half is of stained glass in simple Arts and Crafts style—and I'm in the front hall. To my left is the brick fireplace fronted by its long wrought iron bench stuffed with horsehair. Straight ahead, light floods the hall from the windows above the stairs—they too are of partly coloured glass.

The library is through the first door on my left. Dad's desk is just inside the door to the right. It is a huge flap-down desk with many cubbyholes and shelves. This is where he does his accounts and his planning and where he writes letters. For most people, long-distance phone calls are out of the question—the expense prohibitive. But telegrams or *wires* are quick and cheap, and Dad enjoys sending them. They are used for all occasions: sad and happy. Even on our wedding day in 1972 we received telegrams. They are private and you can keep them. Cousin Patrick sent a poem!

The library is not a room I'm fond of—but it always intrigued me. For though our parents' favourite editions of the classics and other books are kept in the glass-fronted bookshelves on either side of the fireplace, it seems to me there are fewer books here than in some of the other rooms. A round mahogany table sits in the far left corner of the room surrounded by chairs. When not in the hall, two huge stuffed leather chairs sit in front of the fire. French doors give out onto the terrace, and in warm weather they are kept open so the room is full of woodsy smells and the scent of flowers.

Often the Ping-Pong table takes centre stage, and when it does the round table is tilted up like a screen. It is here that Dad coaches his polo team, practising manoeuvres. Otherwise the rest of us play Ping-Pong often and hold wild tournaments. There is space enough to race around the table and we get quite good. But this is also where you come to be quiet, to read a book or back issues of *Blackwood's*,

Maclean's or *The Beaver* that stuff those shelves. There is no lack of interesting reading material in our house. Or you can do your homework. When it is pouring rain outside, this is a splendid place to be. The lighting is good and the pipes keep the room warm and cosy, whether or not there is a fire in the grate.

For the last two years of the war we were asked if we would house a WRCN (a member of the Women's Royal Canadian Naval Service) of high rank who worked at Naden. She was fed there and could have baths and showers. What she needed was a comfortable bed and lavatory. All our bedrooms were full, so the Ping-Pong table and Dad's desk were removed from the library, and a bed was put in the corner with a lamp, a bedside table, a clothes stand and a chest of drawers. The library became her room exclusively, to use as she pleased. I believe she had a driver pick her up each morning and bring her back at night, and somehow she slipped in and out of the library so quietly we were scarcely aware of her. Which only added to that room's air of mystery. But when she left—she said she had loved staying in our house.

It was lucky we didn't know we'd be moving away too, until the last gasp. Our hearts would have broken.

109. SISTERS

I couldn't manage life without my sisters. They were and are my friends, my mentors, my examples—both good and bad. When I was a toddler, they would carry me when my legs gave out on family walks. Later, some jeered at my fears: of rowing over rocks before I learned to swim—or of swimming in the sea where an octopus might lurk. They said I was a booby and should be fearless, like them. And then for years they claimed I was *too young* to join in whatever was happening. Now we are much of a muchness.

The beauty of it was each one was different. Sylvia was, and still is, the perfect eldest sister: kind, generous, compassionate, but also demanding—her standards high. She was a second mother to me—instructing me in the facts of life, only hinted at by Mum and Dad. I went to her for advice and comfort. When almost adult, she heard that she was, in fact, the second female child. Dad was so thrilled at her birth, he called her *Girlie,* which soon became *Ger* or *Ger Ger.* And somehow she survived his spoiling.

The middle two were casualties of the Depression, snatched too soon from the comforting arms of nannies. Only thirteen months between them, they were always together when young and seemed two against the world, their expressions surly. They felt they never got enough of anything—not even food. Yet there they were, amongst us, sharing our sumptuous meals. Curious though it seems, these two complained about their childhood. They felt deprived. They either did not know or refused to believe that Dad had lost almost all his wherewithal.

Hilly, on the other hand, much closer in age to them, was always lumped in with Mike and me: *the young ones.* She and I were treated alike, dressed alike, though there were four and a half years between us. This must have riled her but she didn't complain. We share delightful memories, and she, Sylvia and I agree our childhood was magical—wonderfully free—and that Esquimalt was the perfect place to grow up.

110. CUCKOO in the NEST

All of us siblings were different in character. We disagreed, argued, fought. Then got over it—made friends, were glad to be together. We enjoyed being a family—except for her. She wasn't interested in *the way we did things* or *family history* or even in books. Born cranky, discontented, she would gaze at us, eyes smouldering—*looking daggers*—hatred and loathing in her face. So disconcerting, we tried to ignore her.

Physically there were family likenesses: a way of moving, a cast of features, a timbre of voice that made people say: *Ah—you're a Piddington!* And we'd laugh and say, *Yes, I am! How did you guess?* She sounded like the rest of us but otherwise she was unalike in every possible way and proud of it. She could have been a foundling, adopted. Mum said she resembled distant cousins, people we'd never met.

At birthdays and Christmas we enjoyed giving presents. She didn't bother and was proud of that, too. Then disliked what she'd been given. Felt gypped. We thought her a greedy hog, but we were careful. She was extraordinarily strong and not beyond attack.

Sometimes she would appear with a big bag of candy—a treat in those days. When asked where it came from, she'd say she'd earned it but wouldn't say how. Then she'd sit in our midst and eat it all. She had always done this. When very young and given a box of chocolates, she hid behind a sofa and ate them all. Then was sick all over her favourite doll. I asked her once why she didn't share. *How was I to know you'd want one? You didn't ask!* So the next time I said: *Please may I have...?* Only to hear: *If you hadn't asked, I would have given you one!* And so it went, this odd behaviour in a family where treats were passed around as a matter of course.

When it came time to wash the dishes or tidy the house or be part of some joint venture to help Mum, she was apt to escape.

She was full of energy and eagerness and could be fun but you never knew how she'd react. Those who didn't know her found her beguiling. Those who did—kept out of her way.

When I went off to art school in England, Dad, in a fit of grandparental doting, packed up the lovely old wooden French Canadian bed, washstand and small chair—all homemade and fitted together with square hand-forged nails, that he'd painted blue and given me earlier as a special treat. All that furniture, together with my childhood books, were packed and taken to her, without asking whether she wanted them. Annoyed by this, she left them outside in all weathers, along with the red leather armchair from Wychbury she'd demanded—until everything was sodden and rotted and eventually turned back into soil. She was busy with several children by this time, but it seemed such a waste, such a pity, as the child my things were intended for would have loved them—especially the books.

It was hard to fathom a sister so careless. She seemed a thorn in the flesh, a renegade, a cuckoo in the nest. And I was convinced she loathed me—yet when her first child was born, only fourteen years between us, of all her friends and sisters she chose me as godmother.

111. OUR POLICEMAN

Our village policeman was our friend. And there he was—or always seemed to be—on the corner, standing outside Fulmer's Drugstore, grinning at the passersby—with no gun, not even a police dog. Just a smile or a greeting: *Good morning, Mrs. Piddington.* Or *Good afternoon to you.* Or *How are you then, my dear?* He was our very own cop—with few, if any, robbers. He knew about all of us, it was said, where we lived and all our names. But did he ever catch any baddies, I wonder? You'd think it would be boring, just standing there outside Fulmer's Drugstore, grinning. But with his ear to the ground, Dad said. A nice man, though—a gentle man and a comfort to us.

Later on, I was back there, in the village, with no policeman on the corner and a tickle in my throat, so I thought I'd pop into Fulmer's Drugstore for some Evans Throat Pastilles—those hard black cough drops in their rectangular tin box that Mum would pass to us in church if she saw a cough coming—or at least some Sucrets to soothe the throat. But Mr. Fulmer wasn't there anymore either. Nor was his drugstore—just a junk store in its place with a jumble of things. Hanging from the ceiling was a little chair with a carved back and curved short legs. They took it down for me to see. Its back felt marvellously smooth and I liked its shape—so I bought it, instead. Its paint was chipping and the seat, covered in something—not quite leather, not quite plastic—was coming apart. I eased it off and found in the stuffing a newspaper from the 1880s. And under all of it was the lovely smooth surface of the wood with holes drilled for caning.

Scraped, cleaned and re-caned, it is a darling little chair with a French air about it. A cottage chair, somebody's treasure—all its parts of different wood. I love it and use it often—for low jobs when I need to be near the floor. But where did it come from, I wonder? And who brought it to Esquimalt all those years ago? Did it come around the Horn by sailing ship or across the country by train?

There's a whole lot of history in that one small chair. Perhaps once upon a time it belonged to our policeman's great-granny. Who knows? That would give reason enough for smiling.

112. THE CHAPERONE

After my last uneasy year at Lampson Street School, the move to Esquimalt High seemed momentous. I was with my friend Cicely again, and we'd walk to and from school together and, more often than not, eat our lunches there. I don't think the teaching was nearly as good as at Lampson Street School. It certainly didn't engage me in the same way—except for art class.

For an art competition I painted a large rock—of the sort I knew from roaming around Macaulay Point. With the war on (the war was always described as being *on*—as if it all happened on a table), all that area was about to become what it always had been: military turf—soon to be behind high fences and off limits. My painting was a lament for what had been my playground, my delight. I wanted to catch something of the peacefulness of the past. So my rock sat on a grassy slope above the Strait of Juan de Fuca, a sentinel above the sea—but with no conning towers, no battleships—no *menace* showing—just moonlight and smooth water. I won the competition but

Helen Piddington and Marilyn Mckenzie can't stop dancing in this unposed photo taken by Cicely Rossiter outside Esquimalt High, 1945.

Mum made disparaging comments. She didn't believe in painting from memory, nor did she know or like that area as I did. We disagreed about quite a few things in those days.

One plus at high school was the organized sports with teams and games with other schools. As well, we became air cadets and marched about—saving Canada. But the best thing of all was the music: the dancing, the jazz! Every lunch hour and often after school the jazz band would practise, and we—the devotees—would dance. The school basement-cum-gym had a splendid dance floor, and we would jitterbug until exhausted—our heroes playing saxophones all around us. It was glorious!

When we got our report cards at Christmas, Cicely and I both got zero for a dull course called Citizenship. Eyebrows were raised in both houses—but little was said. The wheels were turning, however—the end approaching. But the dancing and that glorious sense of freedom—of everything being possible—the floating on air—eyes shining—cheeks glowing—on it went.

In June there was a dance to celebrate the end of term, and Cicely and I went together. I don't remember any of it—or the walk home afterward. Perhaps my heart was broken. I knew we were about to leave our beloved house and Esquimalt. I knew the house was to be cut up to make apartments for strangers. I knew I was to be sent to board at Strathcona Lodge School, and Cicely was to be a daygirl at St. Anne's Academy, but how could I have forgotten—because there he was—that lad I'd had a crush on all year long. Sure, I'd danced with him quite often, but he was older and never said a word he could avoid. But that time, Cicely tells me, he walked *me* home! Only she came too. And when we reached our front gate, for some reason she can't imagine now, she came up the long driveway with us. So there was no *fond farewell*—no *goodnight*—no *goodbye kiss*—no *hug*—nothing. And the two of them walked back down the drive in silence. And at the gate she went downhill to her house and he went up to his.

You hear of people who have suffered some terrible shock and are changed forever. That's not my case. All I know is that I have never felt able to dance with the joy and abandon I knew there—at Esquimalt High. I have tried often but seem stiff and awkward. Even when I've been with wonderful dancers I have not been able to re-lax—felt crimped and cramped, as if wounded—so begged off. It is only now, at my great age, when I am alone and hear Irish jigs or boogie-woogie, that I come alive. And I begin to dance—and dance and dance—all around the kitchen until the music ends!

113. VANCOUVER

There was a place I longed to see: *Vancouver!* My chance came when the last three of us were at Esquimalt High in 1944–45—Hilly in Grade Twelve, Mike in Grade Eleven with me in Grade Nine. Hilly and I belonged to a club called High Y. It was, I believe, a junior arm of the YWCA. Neither of us can remember much about it: where we met or what we did. What we do remember was a trip to Vancouver for some sort of conference with many other High Y members from Vancouver Island and Vancouver.

It was heady stuff to be going off on our own—to stay with strang-ers! Hilly had once visited family friends for a weekend, but this was my first trip off the Island—apart from those annual jaunts to the Beaumonts' on Discovery Island. I'd heard so much about the archi-tecture in Vancouver, the beautiful North Shore mountains, the vast trees in Stanley Park, and a dream place called Spanish Banks. Per-haps we'd be billeted there. Perhaps we'd see the Lions! And we would share a stateroom on the overnight boat to Vancouver. It was all very exciting.

Dad drove us to the Canadian Pacific wharf only to find there were no staterooms. All had been commandeered by the army. Okay, we'd sit up then. There were lots of us going from various high schools, and there'd be safety in numbers. We strode onto the boat—spirits high—chins in air. But almost all the chairs were full of sol-diers. So we shared the ones remaining or sat on the floor, playing games, chatting or trying to doze. There was noise and a fug of too many bodies. It was almost impossible to sleep.

We stepped off the boat into a downpour to find our billet wasn't exactly by Spanish Banks. Rather, it was in deepest Burnaby, al-most in New Westminster. It took hours to get there by trolley, and we were drenched walking the last part. The house was tiny. There'd be three at least in our bedroom. I think they gave us some food. We'd had neither breakfast nor lunch. Then we left our bags and, with our billet, trundled back into town to find the main proceedings were over.

Back we went to Burnaby, cold, wet and dispirited. Everything looked unbearably bleak. There were no distant views at all.

The next morning we returned to Vancouver, lugging our bags, and kept them in sight all day. More low cloud, fog and rain. The joyful city I'd imagined did not exist. There was no sign of lions, trees or mountains. It was hard to see anything through the rain. And the journey back, on the overnight boat to Victoria, was a repeat of the first.

Dad met us and drove us home. Oh how glad we were to see him—to be in Esquimalt again. After some food we revived and went off up the hill to school.

So much for foreign travel!

114. THE PIECE DRAWER

The *piece drawer* was Mum's one indulgence, her secret stash, the place where she kept her treasures: it held scraps of cloth and yardage that had caught her eye throughout her lifetime—fabric for things she hoped to make some day and pieces of what she had made—or had had made for her, dating back to the start of the twentieth century. Tucked in amongst them were scraps of veiling—from her wedding veil, perhaps. And tiny garments—probably Little Anna's—things she couldn't bear to be parted from. The problem was her accumulation kept growing, and there was never quite enough space for it all. So after a while it became her *piece chest of drawers* and then her *piece cupboards*. Yet it was always spoken of in the singular.

Whenever she needed cloth for some purpose she would look in her *piece drawer*, to see if it held something suitable, before stepping out to buy more. Sometimes we'd hear her exclaim: *Oh—how lovely! I'd forgotten all about that!* And she would mull over the circumstances surrounding her purchase of that particular piece of cloth and whether or not something had been made of it. So it wasn't a sad place at all—just a history lesson of sorts, but one I didn't learn well enough at the time as I long to know whether she wore some of the lovely garments tucked in amongst the cloth. They seem so old. Did they belong to her grandmother, Charlotte Augusta Hayne Drury, whose father, Colonel Richard Hayne of the Royal Staff Corps (later the Royal Engineers), built the Ottawa River section of the canal linking Montreal to Kingston via Ottawa? Charlotte Augusta was born in Carillon, Québec, in 1835— during the construction. In looks she was a double of Mum. Did she wear that silk shoulder cape from Paris—of deep peacock green with narrow black stripes? Or perhaps the black net evening dress with inset strips of satin was hers.

Tucked in there somewhere, but probably in a cupboard with the overflow cloth, was the dress Mum wore for the tercentenary of the founding of Québec City by Samuel de Champlain. It was a mammoth celebration organized in 1908 by an Englishman with a reputation for arranging historical re-enactments involving suitably costumed participants. As a member of the court of Louis XVI, Mum wore a pink silk dress with a vast hoop skirt. Her twin, Arabella, wore another of blue. Their younger sister Evelyn wore an orchid dress, cut down from one of Granny's ball gowns. Mum had on her dressing table a photo of the three of them, and I would stare at it in amazement—their skirts were so wide that even with arms outstretched they could scarcely touch each other's fingertips! Meanwhile their brother, our Uncle Charlie, danced a minuet in mauve and purple silk. Granny called it a week "of great goings-on," with balls and all manner of receptions and parties, plus re-enactments of important events in Québec's history back to its earliest days. At one point in the proceedings, men of the Royal Navy hauled a vast pale blue carpet covered in *fleurs-de-lis* up the cliff Wolfe and his men had climbed long before. Running across the Plains of Abraham, they placed it in front of Louis XVI and Marie Antoinette (both a trifle preoccupied, I'd guess, trying to instigate useful reforms in France, to worry much about what had once been Louis XIV's *royal province*—but by then was their *lost colony of Québec*).

Earl Grey was the Governor General then, and Mum's favourite memory of the tercentenary took place on the day it all began. It was pouring rain, and the Governor General's daughters were helping in the reception line. As one of them shook hands, she remarked to each guest in turn, in a very serious way, "Unconscionable weather—are we not having?" Mum said you could hear this being repeated on and on, all along the line, and it was terribly hard not to laugh.

Members of the family taking part in the tercentenary usually went across to Québec City from l'île d'Orléans each morning by boat, but sometimes they spent the night with friends in town. There were ships of the Royal Navy there (as there had been all through Mum's childhood—some of them anchored just below their house) and lots and lots of parties. Granny came home one night by boat, well after midnight, when the twins could not be found. They were grown-up women of twenty then and came back later, in style—each in a ship's boat, escorted by young officers of the Royal Navy.

In 2008 the quatercentenary of that same event was celebrated. As we drove the eighty kilometres over the mountains from Kelsey Bay, where we leave our boat, en route to Campbell River, we listened to a program on CBC Radio about the celebrations planned to commemorate this occasion. One woman interviewed was from an old English-speaking family in Québec City. I was stunned. The lilt of her voice, the words she used, were so familiar, she might have been one of my sisters!

115. SMELL

Smell is the most evocative of the senses. In an instant it can transport us enormous distances in time and space. So it was that sitting on a bus one day in Paris, passing under the arches of the Palais du Louvre and into the Place du Carrousel, I caught a whiff of freshly mown grass—and I was there on the lawn again, at Wychbury—a small child with her dog-nanny beside her, and all the others running circles around us. It almost made me cry.

In spring, when I drink in that marvellous clean scent of wild red currant, I'm transported straight back to Esquimalt. Or when the wind blows from the southeast—having swept over endless forest-covered ranges, then across almost three miles of seawater to Sidney Bay—I catch a hint of something dear and familiar…and I'm passing the Woods and approaching Fleming's Beach as it used to be: fresh and strong and sweet. And when the buds of the black cottonwood I planted some twenty years ago burst open, the air is rich and sharp and I am there again, on Kniver Street, passing under those same trees and almost at the beach.

Yes, it is the smells of Esquimalt that I miss so much: that rich and wonderful tang of salt and wild plants, of seawater crashing on rock and the dark rotted muck of the forest. How lovely it was!

Such scents may draw me backward—but they are part of me, with me, wherever I go—as is my birthplace.

116. MACAULAY POINT

We have just heard that the Macaulay Point woods will henceforth be *OUT of BOUNDS*. So Hilly, Mike and I are going for a last look. It's a Saturday morning in late May. Although it rained hard last night, the sun is shining and everything glistens. The lawns are a dazzling green but wet, so we take the Bluebell Path—resplendent now, in full bloom, edged with white candytuft. Then we leave through the small latch-gate in the holly hedge and go east, down to the end of Wychbury to the tangled island of hawthorn that blocks the road where the paving ends. It is full of birds' nests—for they can breed there in safety. Anything else that tries to enter gets ripped to shreds by hawthorn spines. But soon this too will go—will be cut down so army trucks can go straight ahead. Not around that fragrant island of birds.

From here we follow the same route we took to the Sismans' that snowy winter's night years ago, and we scurry along the unpaved track that curves up under the Garry oaks—up past our broom forts, now a mass of blazing yellow. Wherever grass is uncut there are carpets of purple-blue camas and other wild flowers of white and pink and yellow.

We reach the height of land and there down below us—spread right across our horizon—is a shimmering curtain of blue: the Olympics in their glory, with only the sea keeping us apart.

Now we veer off diagonally across to the Macaulay Point woods. Work is underway already. Fences are being built. The man in charge tells us we can go through the woods this one last time—but we must keep going and go quickly. And we cannot retrace our steps. Instead we must skirt the rocks along the sea edge and get home that way.

I hate to think what they will do here. Fall all the trees, most likely, dig up the wild flowers, lay concrete, and build barracks, lookouts, parade grounds. Change this place forever.

Grass grows thick under these lovely old trees, and there are carpets of lilies: white fawn lilies, trilliums, shooting stars and lady's slippers. We yearn to pick them but know we mustn't. They need every chance to survive.

Being here is rather like visiting someone sick and dying. You want to drink them all in, remember them in each and every detail—without staring. This was my favourite of all our woods. Here each Douglas fir is thick-trunked and separate, with space around it and strong spreading branches—many of them forced to lean inland from centuries of wind howling in off the Strait of Juan de Fuca. There are clumps of arbutus too, and each tree begs to be remembered. But how can we? The best we can do is take in the black or rusty red of their branches with snatches of brilliant blue sea and sunlight behind them, and all the silken greens of fresh leaves and the grass beneath them—and all the colours of the flowers. There is a special scent here too—unlike that of our other woods. Sweeter perhaps.

We keep going—longing to stay all day—climbing these trees or lying under them, staring up at their branches. But we cannot stop. We burst through into salt air and brilliant sunshine. A stiff breeze is tweaking the surface of the sea. And there are the Olympics again—only lower, paler and somewhat farther off, though we are actually a little closer. Now we slither down the grassy bank, past drifts of sea blush and chocolate lilies. Then lower, over thrift and saxifrage and all those flowers that can withstand wind and drought, and down again onto the moss-damp rocks. Then we go westward. I glance back up to those beloved trees. They seem quite different now—more like a dark Mongolian yurt curving up and over the land, protecting it.

We clamber on along the sea edge—up over all those high rocky hummocks and across small beaches. Then more rocky headlands and finally we crawl up onto the land again, not far from the Sismans' house. Then we go home up Lampson Street.

We arrive pink-cheeked from exertion, having travelled much faster than usual—that awful need to *keep going* spurring us on. Normally we'd spend all day exploring one headland: its smooth surfaces and all its cracks and crevices and the plants growing in them, its small pools and the beach below—if there was one—and all its special pebbles. Then we'd wade out as far as we dared in that icy swirling water. And if it didn't feel too cold that particular day, we'd swim!

Mum gives us a bang-up lunch and, sensing my sadness, quotes one of her childhood favourites, only I can't remember which. "It's always hard to say goodbye, you know, yet nothing stays *as it used to was*, much as we wish it would. There's a lot to be said for change, remember. Keep your chin up and your eyes open and you'll find wonders wherever you go." A bit of a conundrum and not very soothing—but something to mull over, certainly.

And she was absolutely right. Nothing stays *as it used to was*—except in the mind's eye.

117. "POP-OFF"

As long as I can remember, Dad talked about his imminent demise. "When I pop off," he'd say—then follow with a list of cajolements: "You'll all be able to do just what you like. Mum can paint all day. Everything will be easier. And there'll be no arguments!" When I was small, this seemed more like a threat than a joke. I didn't like it a bit. I didn't want him to leave us—or worse, die.

But "pop" was one of our favourite verbs: we popped upstairs, we popped down to the orchard, to the stables, to the village—even into town. We popped in all directions. There was no great threat in "popping," so I joined in.

Years later, when Mum and Dad decided to have our house cut up into apartments for servicemen and their families and move up to our summer cottage at the Lake, he wrote to tell his sisters, Aunts Flossie and Ethel. They lived in an apartment in Montreal and never went out. Nevertheless, they took a keen interest in what was going on in the outside world—especially his. They put on their thinking caps. What could they possibly do to help their baby brother adjust to such change?

Then one day, before anything was done about the house, Dad got a notice from the CPR express office. A parcel had arrived, rather a large one. We went to collect it at that Greek temple of a building (now the Wax Museum) down in the Inner Harbour, where the CPR boats left for Vancouver. It was, indeed, a vast parcel and had to be trucked home.

Inside was a motorboat, rather boxy in shape (but perfect for a lake, the Aunts assured him). She was canary yellow and came complete with an outboard engine. Now Dad was not afraid of much, but he loathed anything mechanical—to the extent that years before he had promised Mum he would keep her supplied with pails of water, carried up from the lake, rather than deal with a pump. And he did. But this boat. "She'll be the death of me!" he declared. And promptly christened her *Pop-Off*.

Eventually, during the summer of 1945, with the war all but over, the family (the last four of us at home) made the switch and moved up to the Lake. *Pop-Off* came with us. Gradually Dad became fond of the new boat and used her a lot. But when the engine stalled and refused to respond, he switched back to the rowing skiff and his beloved canoes. Mike and various brothers-in-law tinkered with *Pop-Off* and used her on occasion.

After Dad and those aunts died, *Pop-Off* spent most of the time in #2 bedroom, where the tools were kept, rising like a phoenix when the house and all its contents burnt to the ground. But bravo to Aunts Flossie and Ethel for attempting to modernize their brother!

My favourite memory of *Pop-Off* was on that first Christmas at the Lake in 1945, when Hilly, Michael and I were home for the holidays. The day dawned fair with no wind so we decided to go to church in Shawnigan village, five miles up the lake. We had no car in those days, and a taxi there and back would have been prohibitive, if one

"She'll be the death of me!" Dad declared, and promptly christened the boat Pop-Off. *(Our summer place, Savira, is in the background—1942.)*

were available—it was by boat or not at all. So wrapping up well we set off—all five of us squeezing into *Pop-Off* and puttering to the north end of the lake. Then we walked the half mile or so to the church.

It was a lovely service. Glad we'd made the effort, we headed home to stuff our turkey and put the Christmas pudding on to steam—both to be cooked on our faithful Great Majestic, the old wood stove that came with us from Esquimalt.

Not far from the village we noticed mist collecting along the shore, wrapping itself around tall trees, islands and points of land. Suddenly mist turned to fog and we could see nothing ahead or behind. We had two choices—keep going and hope for the best, or drift.

It was eerie moving through that blanket of fog. With Uncle Charlie in town for the winter and almost no one else living along Shawnigan West Road, there were no sounds of axes splitting wood, no barking dogs, no human noise at all: just silence and the slap of water against our hull. We sang carols—hoping our voices would bounce off the land, if we were too near it. Anyway, they cheered us, raised our spirits.

Usually the coming back is faster than the going but this time it seemed much longer as we puttered slowly under dead reckoning, with no way of knowing which way we were going—the air dank, cold and getting colder—all of us stiff and uncomfortable, longing to stretch our limbs.

Then, with no warning, the fog thinned to mist again and there we were—just about to bump into our very own Bunny Island. And to starboard, a stone's throw away, was Savira, our cottage—our home! *Pop-Off* had brought us back safely. There was rejoicing. We'd had our own Christmas miracle. And the Aunts, of course, were thrilled.

*

Dad popped off during afternoon tea, his favourite meal, on St. Patrick's Day in 1960. He was sitting on the verandah in a comfortable chair, facing a view he loved: our garden, its woods and meadows that stretched all the way down to the gate and Burnside Road, and southward across Portage Inlet—an extension of the Gorge. Mum had gone to the kitchen to get some hot water to extend the tea a little. When she came back he was perfectly still.

EPILOGUE

Throughout my early years, Mum was the centre of my world: my friend, my mentor. Dad seemed a sideshow—more often than not, an embarrassment. But with all his bluster and noise he taught us, by example, the importance of adaptability, the joy in hard physical work, the need to think beyond the crowd. He was our guiding force—yet tempered always by Mum's good sense.

ACKNOWLEDGMENTS

First, I want to thank the people of the village and municipality of Esquimalt as they were during the 1930s and '40s, making it the free, friendly, magical place it was. And, to all accounts, still is.

There are so many others to thank, especially Mavis Gallant, whose questions about my childhood lay dormant, unanswered—until comments by Doris Lessing jolted me back in time (see Chapter 1, "The Field in Snow"). I am enormously grateful to both of them. Then, my surviving siblings: Helen Mary Sylvia Nixon; Deborah Joan Cartwright; Phyllis Angela Norris; and Michael Christopher Wren Piddington, who were endlessly patient and helpful corroborating names, dates and situations and providing and identifying old photos, as were my cousins: Fran Humphrey (née Sise); Patrick and Gordon Nixon; my nieces Helen Muir Wood and Pam Clancy (both née Piddington), who sent me many of her father's photos that I'd never seen before because he'd had them with him in England during the Second War.

Susan Green, while archivist of the Esquimalt Municipal Archives, gave me copies of Samuel Maclure's elevations and plans of Wychbury that were given to Michael Hanna by Madge Wolfenden, when she was archivist of Victoria, and then donated by him to the Esquimalt Archives. His son, Christopher Hanna, having been born and brought up in Esquimalt, has been a tireless provider of data and a great help indeed, combing through the manuscript and checking historical facts. Thanks to Barry Mathews for details of Wychbury during its first 15 years when his father and grandfather lived there. I thank, as well, the staff and volunteers of the Esquimalt Municipal Archives, who were so welcoming, especially Gladys Durrant, wife of Ernest Durrant, who greeted me as an old friend when we met there for the first and only time.

For encouragement and help with details and dates I thank my old friends: David Barlow and his wife Mary (née Emmerton); Cicely Meek (née Rossiter); Nancy Braithwaite (née Grant); Lizzie Armour and Maggie Oliphant (née Molson); Jean Nicholson (née Tyson); and Dr. Margaret Prang, with her vast historical knowledge. And Marjorie

Hawker (née Coton) of Round the Corner, Ceanne Wong of Gloss on South Granville, and Thomas Homer-Dixon.

Sue Boedecker of Birnie, Montana helped with computer problems, as did Harbour Publishing's expert Richard Currie; my children, Arabella and Adam; my niece and nephew, Frances and Peter Cartwright; Sebastian Watt, a young Canadian who sailed here from Virginia and rescued me from complete standstill by pushing one button. Mary Donlan researched dates at the Vancouver Island Regional Library in Campbell River, as did John Donlan at the Vancouver Public Library.

And special thanks to Jan Gemall of Maxima Photos, in Campbell River, whose magic pulled clear images from dim snapshots—some dating from the nineteenth century—and to Charli Casorzo for suggesting her. My splendid editor, Audrey McClellan, who pulled it all together. And everyone else who helped in the production and/or urged me on, especially my husband, Dane.

BIBLIOGRAPHY

Armstrong, Christopher, and H.V. Nelles. *The Revenge of the Methodist Bicycle Company*. Toronto: Peter Martin, 1977.

Bosher, J.F. *The French Revolution: A New Interpretation*. London: Weidenfeld and Nicolson, 1989.

Brown, Craig, ed. *The Illustrated History of Canada*. Toronto: Lester and Orpen Dennys, 1987.

Duffus, Maureen, ed. *Beyond the Blue Bridge: Stories from Esquimalt*. Esquimalt, BC: Esquimalt Silver Threads Writers Group, 1994.

Esquimalt Silver Threads Writers Group. *Seafarers, Saints and Sinners: Tales of Esquimalt and Victoria West People*. Esquimalt, BC: Author, 1994.

Fischer, David Hackett. *Champlain's Dream*. Toronto: Knopf Canada, 2008.

Gwyn, Sandra. *Tapestry of War: A Private View of Canadians in the Great War*. Toronto: HarperCollins Canada, 1992.

Jacobs, Jane. *Dark Age Ahead*. Toronto: Random House Canada, 2004.

Jenkins, Kathleen. *Montreal: Island City of the St. Lawrence*. Garden City, NY: Doubleday, 1960.

Marsh, James H., ed. *The Canadian Encyclopedia*. 3 vols. Edmonton: Hurtig, 1985.

Martin, Paul-Louis, and Pierre Morisset. *Promenades dans les jardins anciens du Québec*. Montréal: Boréal, 1996.

"Regional Transit System: 1890–1990." Advertising feature. *Victoria Times Colonist*, February 22, 1990.

Robinson, Leigh Burpee. *Esquimalt: "Place of Shoaling Waters."* Victoria: Quality Press, 1948.

Schama, Simon. *Citizens: A Chronicle of the French Revolution*. Toronto: Vintage Books, 1989.

Segger, Martin. *The Buildings of Samuel Maclure*. Victoria: Sono Nis, 1986.

Snyder, Gerald S. *The Royal Oak Disaster*. London: William Kimber, 1976.

Wood, William, ed. *The Storied Province of Québec: Past and Present*. Vol. 3. Toronto: Dominion Publishing Co., 1931.